TRACK'S GREATEST WOMEN

by Jon Hendershott

Tafnews Press

Published in 1987 by Tafnews Press, Book Division
of Track & Field News, Box 296, Los Altos, CA 94023 U.S.A.

Standard Book Number 0-911521-22-4

Printed in the United States of America

Cover design by Teresa Lee

Contents

This book

is dedicated to

my daughter,

Megan

Introduction

A BIT OF HISTORY

Organized track and field competition for women probably dates back to 1895. In November of that year, New York's Vassar College held its first "field day." Various women's competitions also were staged in Australia, New Zealand and South Africa early in the 20th century.

Competition in Europe dates from 1917 and the founding of the *Federation Feminine Sportive de France.* In 1919, FFSF founder Alice Milliat requested the International Olympic Committee to add women's events to the program of the Olympic Games, but she was refused.

On October 31, 1921, Milliat founded the first international governing body for women's track and field, the *Federation Sportive Feminine Internationale.* The FSFI was established the day following the first match between teams from France and Great Britain.

The previous March, the first-ever multi-national women's meet was held in Monte Carlo. Several sports were contested, including 10 track and field events. The Monte Carlo Games also were staged in 1922 and '23.

Because the IOC had refused to include women's events in the 1924 Olympics, the FSFI staged its own version in 1922 in Paris. The Women's World Games were then held every four years: Goteborg 1926, Prague 1930, London 1934. The high number of 19 competing nations was reached in London.

In 1926, however, the IOC reconsidered the proposal to add women's events to the Olympics and this time agreed. Five events were added for the 1928 Amsterdam Olympics. The women's Olympic program continually expanded until it reached the 18 disciplines contested today.

The FSFI merged in 1936 with the men's governing

body, the International Amateur Athletic Federation, to give the sport a single governing organization.

A WORD ABOUT SEX TESTS

Sex testing first was conducted in 1966 at the British Commonwealth Games and European Championships. The basis for the test is a chromosome check, a normal woman having an XX chromosome pattern.

The 1967 season produced a *cause celebre* in Polish sprinter Ewa Klobukowska, who failed a chromosome test at a European Cup semi-final match, as well as a followup test. Klobukowska was ruled ineligible for women's competition and IAAF recognition was withdrawn of her 100-meter World Record, as well as a 4 x 100 relay WR of which Klobukowska was a part.

Before testing was introduced (it is now universal at all major regional and global championships), a number of leading women athletes had been considered questionable by knowledgable followers of the sport. Chief among them were USSR stars Tamara and Irina Press, Maria Itkina and Tatyana Shchelkanova (all of whom retired from international competition when the tests became mandatory), and from earlier eras, Soviet Aleksandra Chudina and Poland's Stella Walsh.

At least two World Records from earlier days which were claimed to have been set by women actually were set by men posing as women. Czech Zdenka Koubkova (800 in 1934) and Germany's Dora Ratjen (high jump in 1938) were revealed to be men. Ratjen, whose real first name was Hermann, claimed he had been forced into the charade of competing as a woman by officials of the Nazi regime, who were eager for international sporting successes.

ACKNOWLEDGMENTS

The idea for this book was born during the editing of *Track's Greatest Champions*, the milestone compilation of men's all-time stars authored by *Track & Field News* cofounder Cordner Nelson. Cordner generously allowed the author to adopt his format, especially the unique "honors line" feature. To Cordner, my thanks for his generosity.

Sincerest thanks to filmmaker/author Bud Greenspan,

who generously provided written and cinematic materials—which were kept far too long by the author.

Grateful acknowledgments must be made to three volumes from Britain's Guinness publishers, all masterfully edited by Peter Matthews: *Book of Athletics Facts and Feats, Book of Olympic Facts and Feats,* and *Track & Field Athletics, The Records.* Thanks, too, to Mel Watman and his *Encyclopedia of Track and Field Athletics.*

To my office mates, E. Garry Hill and Dave Johnson, thanks for their encouragement. Ed Fox's criticisms invariably were constructive—and correct.

A special word of appreciation must go to *T&FN* Women's Editor Howard Willman: without his help, this book still would be many scraps of paper, note cards and loose ends. My deepest thanks, Howie.

The continual support of my family and friends got this book written.

Finally, a word of personal thanks to the following, for many hours of solace and inspiration: Messrs. Mozart, Beethoven, Pachelbel, Vivaldi, Tchaikovsky and Satie. Also Messrs. Dylan, Petty, Floyd and most especially Springsteen.

JRH   Los Altos/June, 1987

BABE DIDRIKSON

As one of her competitors at the 1932 Olympic Games in Los Angeles mused, "Babe thinks she is the whole show, the star attraction—and, of course, she *is.* "

Mildred Didrikson was a slim, long-limbed 21-year-old when the Games began in the motion picture capital of America in the middle of a hot summer. It was the depths of the Great Depression, and with economic woes plaguing the world, people needed a diversion from their struggles just to endure. The lanky Texan, whose oversized ego and brash boastfulness almost matched her enormous athletic talents, filled the bill perfectly.

Nicknamed "Babe" (and there are even a couple of versions about that), Didrikson won two events in Los Angeles, setting a World Record in the 80-meter hurdles (11.7) and an American best in the javelin (143'4"/43.86), as she claimed her gold medals. She also placed second in the high jump to American teammate Jean Shiley as both cleared the World Record height of 5'5"/1.65.

True to form, Didrikson claimed the victories were a breeze—no matter if some observers felt then (and some historians feel now) she was at least tied, if not beaten, by teammate Evelyne Hall in the hurdles. And in the high jump, a potentially winning leap by The Babe was ruled invalid by Olympic officials, who claimed she used an illegal style to clear a record height.

It seemed that Didrikson never did anything quietly. That just wasn't her style. She was a great athlete and she knew it—and she never hesitated to inform anyone within earshot. Yet in a track career which lasted only three seasons, she proved to be a record-setting performer such as the world had rarely seen before.

And the Los Angeles Olympics were only one episode

1

in the colorful sporting life of Babe Didrikson. She later turned to golf and won three U.S. Women's Open titles, as well as the U.S. and British Women's Amateur titles. In an Associated Press poll at the end of 1950 to select the leading athletes of the first half of the 20th century, Didrikson was a landslide women's winner. Some observers contended at the time, and some still do today, that Didrikson was the greatest athlete *ever*, man or woman. Babe certainly would have agreed.

Didrikson was born Mildred Ella Didriksen on June 26, 1911, in Port Arthur, Texas, to a family of sturdy Norwegian stock. Both the spelling of her name and her birthdate have become intertwined in the voluminous tales of nearly legendary proportions which surrounded Babe when she lived, and which have survived since her death from cancer in 1956.

Her family name was spelled Didrik*sen*, but in filling out team information forms for the '32 U.S. Olympic squad, Babe wrote it as Didrik*son*. "I wouldn't want no one to think I was a Swede," drawled Babe and it stayed Didrikson thereafter. As well, on the same Olympic team form, she listed her birthyear as 1913. A Texas state historical marker near her gravesite says 1914. But the headstone above her grave, plus a baptismal certificate and a family Bible, gives the year as 1911. So Babe actually was 21 years old when she wowed the crowds in Los Angeles, not a teenager of 19. But such minor discrepencies never could dim any of her shining athletic achievements.

Young Mildred seemingly always had athletic ability, whether it was simply running fast playing tag as a little child or growing in the next few years into the tall, lanky girl who could hit a ball farther than anyone, throw anything the longest distance, or still outrun all comers. She was the first player chosen for any neighborhood or school teams. One story claims she was christened "Babe" by older children when sides were chosen for games—Mildred could outplay anyone of any age, so maybe it was just a way to try to bring her back down to mortal size. Other stories say she was tagged with the nickname after baseball immortal Babe

Ruth—after all, both of them could hit a baseball a country mile.

If anyone ever embodied the term "natural athlete," it was Didrikson. She got her first real coaching, in any sport, as a frosh at Beaumont High School from physical education instructor Beatrice Lytle. As Lytle told William Oscar Johnson and Nancy Williamson in *Sports Illustrated*, "Her muscles just flowed when she walked. She had a neuromuscular coordination that is very, very rare. Plus she was the most teachable person I have ever known. You could explain the rudiments and rules of a game to her and she could play it."

Lytle introduced Didrikson to golf, but it was in basketball that she first starred. Babe's Beaumont High team never was beaten while she played on it. In 1930, at a high school tournament in Houston, Didrikson was noticed by Col. Melvin Jackson McCombs, a retired military officer who headed the women's athletics teams for the Employers Casualty Insurance Company of Dallas. Those teams were a well-financed public relations arm of the company and McCombs offered Babe the then-extravagant sum of $75 a month to leave school and move to Dallas, work as a stenographer for the insurance company and play basketball for the company team. After much debate, Didrikson's parents agreed to let her to to Dallas—and a sports legend began to grow.

Only a month after she left Beaumont in February of 1930, Babe had been named an all-America guard for the Employers Casualty Golden Cyclones basketball team. The squad had finished second in the national AAU tournament and Babe had scored 210 points in five games. Several other companies—other insurance firms, an oil company—tried to entice Didrikson away from Employers Casualty with grand offers of increased salaries and bonuses for basketball victories. But she stayed with Employers, at least partly because after basketball season ended, she was allowed to pursue her new-found enthusiasm with track.

Employers also had a women's track team and Babe—are you surprised?—was the star. She entered her first meet ever in June and just one month later won two national titles at the national AAU meet. Held in Dallas on July 4, the AAU

The Babe at the Los Angeles Olympics, 1932.

saw Didrikson hurl the javelin 133'5"/40.68, then the longest throw in American history. She also won the baseball throw with 268'10"/81.94, another "American Record" in the now-discontinued discipline.

But Babe also got a taste of defeat when she placed second in the long jump to Stella Walsh, the multi-talented star who was born in Poland but reared in the United States. Stella spanned 18'9¼"/5.72 to just a bit beyond 17 feet for Babe. Yet even such a minor setback as a defeat never seemed to dim the boundless enthusiasm—and outspoken panache—of Didrikson. After the first meet of her life a month earlier, she had written a newspaperman friend at home and casually stated, "Heck, if I hadn't sat down on my last jump, I would have broken the World Record like taking candy from a baby."

In 1931, the Employers basketball team won the national AAU title and Babe was again selected All-American. Other teams still tried to woo her away, but a little raise—not to mention some golf lessons from the company president— kept her happy. At the national AAU track meet, Didrikson again was a one-woman team in scoring three victories and all with American Record performances: 80-meter hurdles in 12.0, long jump at 17'11½"/5.47 and baseball throw at 296'0"/90.22.

It was at the '31 AAU in Jersey City that Didrikson first heard about the Olympic Games coming up the next year out west in Los Angeles. J. Lyman Bingham, president of the AAU and a high-ranking official on the U.S. Olympic Committee, was suitably impressed with Didrikson's performances and told her so. Babe later wrote a friend back home, "He said I had a place all sewed up on the Olympic team without a doubt." Such was the way Babe looked at anything related to her athletic ability: never a question; just a fact.

But that compliment did spur Didrikson to train more diligently for a shot at the Olympic team. "Practice makes perfect," she wrote. The trait in Didrikson which hadn't quite been pinned down yet—but which played such a vital role in her successes—was simply that she *had* to be the best. An unquenchable fire roared within Babe and stoked that flint-hard will of hers that would only be satisifed by being the absolute best in everything she did.

At the 1932 national AAU track championships, staged in Evanston, Illinois on the track of Northwestern University's Dyche Stadium, the legend of Babe Didrikson really was born. Earlier in the year, Babe had again earned All-America status in basketball as the Employers Golden Cyclones finished second in the national AAU tournament.

But Babe had found her niche in track. For the AAU in Evanston, she entered eight events. The nationals also served as the trial meet for selecting the U.S. Olympic team—and Babe won four events outright: the 80-meter hurdles (12.1), shot put (39'6¼"/12.04), the javelin (an American Record 139'4"/42.46) and the baseball throw (272'2"/82.96). She tied for the high jump title with Jean Shiley, both clearing an AR setting of 5'3"/1.60. For good measure, Babe placed fourth in the discus. She didn't place in either the 100 or 200-meters—but she won the national team title for Employers Casualty all by herself. The nation's sporting press raved about her.

And Babe raved about herself, too. Hurdler Evelyne Hall told Johnson and Williamson, "I first met Babe in Dallas at the 1930 AAU, and she was a modest, likable girl. By the time of the '31 AAU, she had gotten pretty cocky. Everybody was doing everything for her; if she wanted a drink of water, someone got it for her. She didn't snub me, but she wasn't nearly as friendly.

"At Evanston, she was almost unbearable. She was a great athlete, but she bragged so much she made all the other girls mad." It was clear she was the best athlete, but Babe rubbed it in unceasingly. At least part of the reaction of the women on the Olympic team was to vote Jean Shiley in as team captain ahead of Didrikson.

Once the U.S. team got to Los Angeles, Didrikson really was in her heyday. News reporters sought her out constantly—and Didrikson gained no friends when she would interrupt interviews with other athletes and try to turn the attention to herself. Some felt she was just a raw, country girl who had tasted success very quickly, without learning how to both win and lose graciously.

Of course, her scintillating achievements in the competitive arena made it a little easier to accept her sometimes abrasive personality. She started her Olympic competition off in a big way, winning the javelin on July 31 with an Olympic Record throw of 143'4"/43.86, also an American Record. Babe outdistanced the 142'8"/43.48 heave by Germany's Ellen Braumuller and then commented with characteristic Didrikson pluck, "Aw, my hand slipped when it took off. My hand slid down about six inches and then I got a good grip on the thing and let it go. If I had kept my grip, I could have thrown it 155 feet easy." Braumuller had set a World Record earlier in the summer at 146'5"/44.64.

Next up for the Babe came the 80-meter hurdles on August 4. There were only nine hurdlers entered in the Olympic competition, but heats still were required to pare the field down to six. In her heat, Didrikson won in 11.8 seconds to tie the World Record. Hall won the other heat, so the Americans were poised for a decisive meeting in the final.

It couldn't have been much closer for the Olympic gold medal. Hall led early, but Didrikson caught up halfway through the eight-barrier race. They remained even on the run for the tape and threw themselves at the string simultaneously. It seemed impossible to determine a winner—but Babe was certain who had won as she threw up her arms and danced a victory jig. Hall just stayed quiet and waited for the judges to decide.

Hall related to Johnson and Williamson that Babe had once counseled her, "Judges are dumb. If you act like you think you won, they will think you did, too." Hall continued, "After we crossed the line, Babe turned to me and yelled, 'Well, I won again.' I looked at some teammates in the stands and they held up one finger to mean I had finished first. But I wasn't certain and held up two fingers. I learned later that just at that moment a couple of judges looked at me. They might have made a judgment based on my gesture of two fingers for second place. I really don't know; Babe had had so much publicity it was hard to rule against her. I do know, though, that I had a welt on my neck for a week from the finish string when I broke it."

Didrikson was declared the winner with Hall second, both being credited with the World Record time of 11.7.

Didrikson en route to her hurdles win in Los Angeles.

Three days later, Didrikson contested the high jump, but this time a judges' decision went against her.

In a hotly-contested competition, Didrikson's every clearance was matched by teammate Shiley, who had placed fourth in the 1928 Olympic event in Amsterdam. Finally, both Americans cleared a World Record 5'5"/1.60 and remained tied when they missed all three attempts at the next height of 5'6¼"/1.685. In a jump-off at 5'5¾", both Shiley and Babe cleared.

Then came a shocker from the judges: Didrikson's jump was declared illegal because she dove over the bar. According to the rules of the day, a jumper's head could not clear the bar before the rest of the body. So Shiley won the gold medal and Babe the silver, although both were credited with the World Record of 5'5." But Babe had achieved something no athlete has to this day: she won medals in the same Olympics in a running event, a jump and a throw.

Didrikson's track career was over, but her life as a celebrity was just beginning. While in Los Angeles after the Games, she met Hollywood stars like Clark Gable and traded homespun quips with Will Rogers. She played a round of golf with four of the deans of American sportswriting—Grantland Rice, Paul Gallico, Westbrook Pegler and Braven Dyer. She quelled any skepticism about her athletic talent which might have remained in the veteran wordsmiths by consistently outdriving all four off the tee.

Didrikson claimed that the match with the reporting quartet gave her the bug to take up golf seriously. But she wasn't able to do it for more than three years because of a rules snafu with the AAU. After she returned home to Texas from the Olympics, a Dallas auto dealer used her picture in an advertisement. It didn't matter that Babe had nothing to do with the ad, nor that she never gave her permission for her picture to be used in the ad. The AAU found out, declared her a professional and banned her from amateur sport. The American golfing establishment agreed and Babe wouldn't be considered an amateur in golf until 1943.

When Didrikson did take up golf seriously in 1935, she went at it in typical-Babe fashion: she practiced seven days a week, 12 hours a day. In the first official round of her life, Babe shot an 86. She played exhibition rounds and in 1938 entered a Los Angeles professional men's tourney. One member of her foursome was a huge professional wrestler named George Zaharias. He was smitten by Babe immediately and it didn't take her long to fall for him. They were married late in 1938.

Marriage, the hassles regaining her amateur status in golf and just the wide experiences of life rounded off many of Babe's rough edges by the time she was allowed to play golf against America's best. In one stretch during the late 1940s, she won 14 consecutive tournaments, including the U.S. and British Amateur titles. By the end of the '40s, Babe had helped establish the Ladies Professional Golf Association and had turned pro officially. She won the U.S. Women's Open in 1948, the first time she entered the tourney, and again in 1950. Babe won 13 of 23 events in the first two years of the LPGA.

The Zahariases lived in Tampa, Florida, during Babe's halcyon years in golf. She was regarded as one of the finest athletes in the world. But around 1952, it seemed that Babe suddenly couldn't put together three consistent rounds in the 54-hole LPGA competitions of the day. She had a hernia operation, then returned to the tour to win a few more tournaments. But she wasn't able to play consistently well.

George urged her to have a checkup, but Babe was determined to play in the Babe Zaharias Open in Beaumont. She won the event with a birdie on the last hole and then went immediately into the hospital. Cancer of the rectum was diagnosed; Didrikson had an emergency colostomy and spent 43 days in the hospital. The whole time, her golf clubs stood in a corner of her room.

She returned three months after her surgery and later was awarded the 1953 Ben Hogan Trophy for Comeback of the Year. The next year, she won her third U.S. Open title with perhaps her finest golfing performance ever: a victory margin of a record 12 strokes. "This will show people not to be afraid of cancer," she said and she vowed to play golf "for another 20 years."

Sadly, it wasn't to be. She kept on playing, and won a few more tournaments. But her health deteriorated and she returned to the hospital. She died on September 27, 1956, in Augusta, Georgia, at the age of 45.

FANNY BLANKERS-KOEN

It was the largest parade ever seen in Amsterdam. One Dutch journalist called that celebration, held in August of 1948, a more important gathering of Holland's people than the welcome given to Allied troops who liberated the land of windmills from German occupation during World War II.

The center of everyone's attention sat with her husband in an open coach drawn by four white horses. Her two children, plus her athletic masseuse, followed behind in a similar livery. Through it all—while a hailstorm of tickertape, as well as the love and admiration of her countrymen, rained down on her—sat a mildly bemused Fanny Blankers-Koen.

"I could not understand why everyone was so excited," she recalled years later in her genuine, unassuming manner. "All I did was win some foot races."

Ah, but Fanny, what races they were. Another Dutch reporter wrote after the 1948 London Olympic Games, "We have now won a total of four gold medals in track and field at the Olympics. And Fanny has won them all."

At the age of 30, Blankers-Koen became the first woman—and has remained the only one—to win four gold medals at a single Olympics. In London, Fanny won the 100 meters (11.9, to equal the Olympic Record), the 200 meters (24.4, one-tenth of a second off the Olympic Record of 24.3 she set in the semi-finals), the 80-meter hurdles (11.2, Olympic Record) and anchored Holland's 4 x 100-meter relay team to victory (47.5).

And she didn't even enter two events in which she claimed the World Record: the high jump (5'7¼"/1.71) and long jump (20'6¼"/6.25). Most of all, though, Fanny had to overcome the criticism of a reproachful world.

"You are too old to be running around a track, Fanny," countless people told Blankers-Koen long before the London

11

Blankers-Koen wins the '48 Olympic 200.

Olympics. "You should be at home looking after your children." But Fanny was the type that you never told she *couldn't* or *shouldn't* do something. That just made her all the more determined to do it.

Blankers-Koen was no Fanny-come-lately on the world track and field stage by the time of the 1948 Olympics. She had, in fact, competed in the Games last held before the intervention of World War II, the Berlin Games of 1936.

Born April 26, 1918, Fanny was a girl of 18 in Berlin, where she finished fifth in the high jump (5'1"/1.55) and ran on the fifth-place 4 x 100 squad. She had begun serious training and competing only three years before at age 15. Fanny was a young country girl then, but her father realized, "You are an athlete. You run and jump all the time."

Fanny's parents belonged to the Dutch Reformed Church and didn't want their only daughter competing on Sundays, the only day meets were held. But father knew best and relented. It didn't take long for Fanny to show her prowess, and three years later she was competing in the Olympic Games.

About that time, Fanny also met Jan Blankers. A former national triple jump champion, Blankers had had his career ended prematurely by a heel injury. So he turned to coaching and one of his first pupils was the brown-haired Francina Koen. "The thing I noticed about Fanny was her long legs," Jan Blankers would laugh many years later.

Fanny recalled, "He had a girlfriend at the time." But it didn't take long for the coach to be won over by Fanny. They were married in 1940, and two years later, Jan. Jr. was born. Life was not easy during wartime occupation, but Fanny felt the old urge to train only months after her son was born.

Ten months after the birth of Jan, Jr., Fanny broke the high jump World Record—her 5'7¼" mark would last for more than eight years. Shortly after, she broke the long jump record—that mark of 20'6¼" survived more than a decade.

The war cancelled the 1944 Olympics, when Fanny would have been 26 years old. And when her second child—a daughter named Fanny—was born in 1945, it seemed that her international career surely was over. But someone forgot to tell that to Fanny herself.

Just like during the war when she had only one child, Fanny turned training into a family affair. Children accompanied parents to the track or gymnasium, usually resting comfortably in a baby carriage. The children grew watching their mother respond to the training regimen conducted by their father. Running tracks became their playgrounds; long jump pits were natural sandboxes.

At the 1946 European Championships in Oslo, Fanny won the 80-meter hurdles and anchored the 4 x 100 team to victory. She also placed fourth in the high jump. Since she had placed third in both sprints at the 1938 Europeans, a keen observer of the sport might have noted the possibility for Fanny to at least take a shot at winning all three track races, plus the relay, in London two years hence.

But the naysayers persisted. Fanny set World Records right up to London, including one at 100 meters of 11.5. But the pundits said she still was too old. Fanny was most incensed by the published declaration from Jack Crump, then manager of the British track team. "Certainly Fanny was good," was the gist of Crump's article. "But 30 years old? Too old, Fanny."

Blankers-Koen later told American filmmaker Bud Greenspan, "I'm not sure why, but Jack's article made me so mad. I didn't even know him then, although he became a close friend. But I found him at the Olympics and I told him, 'I will show you!' "

As we said, don't ever tell Fanny Blankers-Koen she can't do something.

When she arrived at Empire Stadium, in the London suburb of Wembley, Fanny was asked for her autograph by some of the younger Olympic athletes. After all, she was a World Record holder, a European champion and she had competed at the last Olympics prior to the war. She was a "veteran." But the unassuming Fanny was puzzled why anyone would want *her* autograph.

Given her humble and self-deprecating outlook, Fanny might have turned right around and walked out of Wembley, had she somehow known in advance the efforts which lay ahead of her. She would run only the qualifying heat of the 100 on July 31, then not compete at all on August 1. But from August 2 through 7, she would compete every day and sometimes in two races on the same day.

In her first Olympic test, the 100, the prime competition was expected to come from Britain's Dorothy Manley and Australia's young Shirley Strickland (later de la Hunty). Each won her qualifying heat by wide margins: Fanny and Strickland each by five-tenths-of-a-second, and Manley by a huge nine-tenths.

After the day without competition, the sprinters returned on August 2 to a track made heavy and slow by constant rain. Runners left deep divots in the Wembley cinders, so moisture-laden was the running surface.

The first semi-final pitted Fanny against Strickland; Fanny won in 12.0 seconds, four-tenths ahead of the Australian. Manley won the second semi in 12.4, two-tenths faster than Canada's Patricia Jones. In the final several hours later, Fanny never gave anyone else a chance to win, surging to an early lead and romping to an 11.9 clocking to equal the Olympic Record. Manley edged Strickland for the silver medal as both clocked 12.2. One event down for Fanny, three to go.

Next came the 80-meter hurdles. Fanny had slashed a remarkable 0.3 off her own World Record with an 11.0 effort two months before the Games. And in the heats and semis on August 3, Fanny ran the fastest times, each by three-tenths. But the final of the barrier race turned out to be the toughest test of them all.

Fanny recalled, "I arrived at the stadium dressing room and Jan was waiting for me. He asked if I had slept well; I told the truth and said not very. He asked if I had eaten well; I told a fib and said yes. In reality, I had been so nervous I hadn't been able to eat anything.

"We went to the practice track and I was able to subdue my jangled nerves while I warmed up. Then Jan left, so he could get a place in the competitors' seating area. That is where he liked to watch the race. But before he left, he teased me by saying, 'You're too old, Fanny.' It was shrewd timing by Jan—it reminded me that many people had written me off as too old. I was determined to show them."

As luck would have it for the August 4 final, Fanny drew the lane next to her chief rival, young Briton Maureen Gardner. Also expected to be right in the thick of the fight was the multi-talented Australian Strickland. But as misfortune would have it, for one of the few times in her career, Fanny got a terrible start when the gun sounded to start the final.

"I expected there would be a recall gun," Fanny remembered. "But there wasn't, and the field was out a meter ahead of me. One meter out of 80 can mean the difference between winning and losing."

But if there is one thing in this world Fanny Blankers-Koen categorically despises, it is losing. She dug in and halfway through the eight-hurdle contest, she was even with Gardner. Then she clipped the fifth barrier and slipped behind again. She later admitted she doesn't know how she got over the final hurdles. "I felt like a staggering drunkard," she said.

With a tremendous burst of speed, however, Fanny pulled even with Gardner and they flashed across the finish line as one. Strickland also closed fast, although clearly in third place. "Maureen was certain she had won, and I just shook hands with her and congratulated her on a job well done," Fanny said. "I felt she had won, too."

The finish-line judges weren't nearly as certain. They huddled together for long minutes after the race. Fanny just went to Jan, who said only, "A fine race, Fanny. You weren't too old after all." Then the military band, which played the national anthem during the victory ceremony for each winner, struck up "God Save The King." Now Fanny was positive Gardner had won.

At the same time, however, the stadium scoreboard began to display the order of the finish: "1. Blankers-Koen. . .". Fanny was confused. Then she realized the British anthem had been signaling the arrival in the stadium of King George VI. An official soon confirmed what the scoreboard first hinted: Fanny had won. Both she and Gardner had run an Olympic Record time of 11.2 seconds, but Fanny had a winning edge of a couple of inches.

The 200-meters was up next on the schedule; the heats and semi-finals were set for August 5, with the final on the afternoon of August 6. The morning of the 6th also would see Fanny run on Holland's team in the heats of the 4 x 100-meter relay.

But Fanny could have cared less. "I was tired, I missed the children and I was upset," she recalled. "I cried and told Jan I didn't like the 200 and that I just wanted to go home. Jan just said, 'That's fine, but you may never get the chance again to try this. Just run easy in the qualifying and we will see what happens.' "

What happened was that the 200 turned out to be Fanny's easiest win of the Games. Again, she easily was the fastest in the heats and semis, and her 24.4 won the final by 0.7 from Britain's Audrey Williamson. That victory margin still is the largest in the history of the Olympic 200-meters. Even if she hated the distance, Fanny attacked the 200 with a vengeance. By the time the field rounded the curve and entered the homestretch, Fanny held a lead of some five meters. She powered away to a gap of more than 15 when she broke the finish tape. It was crystal clear who was the best—and the little English girl who presented a bouquet of flowers to each winner could clearly see it was Fanny.

Finally, there was just the 4 x 100-meter relay final left, on August 7. Rather than nervousness, Fanny felt a pleasing sense of calm. "I wasn't nervous because the other girls were there and I wasn't alone," Fanny said. And Fanny made all the difference for the Dutch team. Taking the baton for the final leg some five meters behind the leader, Fanny quickly made up the difference and bolted into the lead. Holland had its fourth gold medal of the London Games—all thanks to Fanny.

By now, the whole world knew about "Flying Fanny." For the trip home to that glorious reception in Amsterdam, Dutch officials offered to fly Fanny and Jan. She declined, preferring to take the ferry trip across the English Channel with the rest of the team.

"I had bought a raincoat and some towels in London, so I was concerned about customs," Fanny recalled. "But all the officer wrote that I had to declare was, 'Some gold medals'."

Fanny's running career was far from over. At the 1950 European Championships, she duplicated her Olympic victories in the 100, 200 and hurdles, and also anchored Holland to second in the relay. No woman won more European gold medals than Fanny's five until 1986, although the great Pole Irena Szewinska matched her total with five career golds. But in '86 at Stuttgart, the marvelous Marita Koch of East Germany won her third consecutive double over 400-meters and in the 4 x 400 relay to bring her total to six gold medals.

At the 1952 Helsinki Olympics, Fanny was 34 years old, but by now everyone knew better than to discount her because of age. Shortly before the Games, however, she developed painful boils and her physician put her on medication and insisted that she cut back on training. She went to Helsinki anyway, "to show I wasn't too old or afraid."

The medication made her dizzy and Fanny hit two hurdles in the 80-meter barrier final and dropped out. She earlier had failed to qualify in the 100. The relay team finished sixth, and last, in the 4 x 100.

Fanny retired for good in 1955, at the age of 37. She tried coaching, but found she didn't have the patience. She served as a manager of the Dutch team at the 1968 Mexico Olympics. During her illustrious career, Fanny set 13 World Records in seven individual events and two relay distances. That was in addition to her medal hauls in the Olympics and European Championships. Plus she won 58 Dutch titles between 1936 and 1955 in events ranging from the sprints, hurdles and jumps, to the shot put and pentathlon. No woman in track history, from any other nation, has won as many national titles.

Fanny was the first woman track and field athlete in history ever to have a statue erected to memorialize her achievements. It stands in Amsterdam, but even if many of today's Dutch youths don't know of her accomplishments, history will hold secure Fanny's place among the elite of the all-time greats.

In reflecting on her historic career, Fanny said, "To be champion. . . all my life, I just wanted to win. I wanted to do

18

everything the best. To become the best in any sport, you must have that will to win.

"Was I too old? Well, I *was* old," she laughed. "But did I *feel* old? No, never."

Fanny's narrowest victory came in the hurdles.

Strickland competing one month before the 1956 Olympics.

SHIRLEY STRICKLAND de la HUNTY

Financial times were tight in the Australia of 1948. World War II was hardly two years over and life had barely settled back into the harmony of peacetime. In athletics, the big event of 1948 was the London Olympic Games, but that too presented problems. The staging of the Games halfway around the world meant heavy expenses to transport an Australian team to England.

But officials of the Australian Olympic Committee were determined to send a team—at least partly because Australia was one of only four nations which had competed at every Summer Olympics since the modern Games were revived in 1896 (the others being Greece, Great Britain and the United States).

So AOC officials took the lists of athletes nominated for the '48 Olympic team in the various sports and ranked them in order of merit. In track and field, the first name to head the entire list was that of Shirley Strickland.

Shirley had barely turned 23 years old by the time of the London Olympics, but she had been surrounded by track and field virtually all her life. Born in Guildford, Western Australia, on July 18, 1925, Shirley spent her childhood on her parents' farm. Her early education came via correspondence courses.

Strickland's father had been a good professional sprinter as a youth, and her brothers were runners, too (one finished fourth in the 220-yard low hurdles at the 1953 Australian championships). But it was blue-eyed Shirley who developed into the star of the family.

In high school, Strickland won 47 of the 49 races she contested in the sprints and hurdles. She moved on to the

University of Western Australia, where she starred not only on the track and the field hockey pitch, but also in the classroom. She graduated with honors in science and then moved to Perth, on Australia's southwestern coast, to lecture in mathematics and physics at Perth Technical College.

All the while, she had been establishing and then enhancing her reputation as one of Australia's brightest young track and field prospects. Her performances at the London Games more than justified her place at the head of the list for the Olympic track team.

Like the great Fanny Blankers-Koen of Holland, Strickland was entered in four events for London: the 100-meters, 200-meters, 80-meter hurdles and 4 x 100-meter relay. So Shirley's time schedule duplicated that of Blankers-Koen: heats in the 100 on July 31; a day off on August 1; 100 semifinals and final on August 2; heats and semis in the hurdles on August 3; hurdles final on the 4th; 200 heats and semis on the 5th; the 200 final, plus heats in the 4 x 100 relay on August 6; concluding with the relay final on August 7.

In the 100, the only sprinters who ran faster than Strickland in the qualifying rounds were the brilliant Blankers-Koen and Britain's Dorothy Manley. In the final, Flying Fanny swept to the first of her four victories, while Manley and Strickland finished so close together, they had to be sorted out by the photofinish camera. Both clocked 12.2 seconds, Manley just edging Shirley for the silver medal.

Over the hurdles, Shirley ran the race of her life—at the same time that Blankers-Koen and Britain's Maureen Gardner were waging the race of the Olympics in women's track. Fanny recovered from a dismal start, and put on a stunning burst of speed after the final barrier to cross the finish line virtually even with Gardner. Long deliberations by the finish judges finally awarded to win to Fanny, second place to Gardner and third to the fast-closing Strickland.

Shirley was credited with a time of 11.4 seconds, 0.2 behind the times for Blankers-Koen and Gardner. The British timers were off, however, as films and photo-finish pictures clearly show Strickland no more than a half-meter behind at the finish. It is generally accepted that athletes at full speed cover about one meter in one-tenth-of-a-second, so Shirley should have been credited with the same 11.2 clocking to equal the Olympic Record.

In the 200, everyone was outclassed by Blankers-Koen, who won by a huge margin of 0.7. Strickland finished fourth, an eyelash behind Audrey Patterson of the United States. Ironically, more than 35 years later, the photofinish pictures from the London Games were discovered by British statisticians. Close examination of the picture of the 200 finish showed that Strickland actually finished third. No official action ever has been taken to alter the results, however, presumably because the photofinish device was used only experimentally at the '48 Games while the judgment of the human officials of the day was considered official.

After claiming her pair of bronze medals in the 100 and hurdles, Strickland had one last chance for a gold in the 4 x 100 relay. For three stages of the race, Australia led Holland after Shirley had started off the Aussie team. But Blankers-Koen was anchoring the Dutch; Joyce King held Australia's lead as long as she could but she couldn't stop Flying Fanny forever and Holland edged ahead to win in 47.5 seconds, with Australia one-tenth back.

So Shirley more than proved she belonged at the top of Australia's list of women's track stars. Two years later at the Commonwealth (then British Empire) Games, held in Auckland, New Zealand in 1950, Shirley showed that she had not slipped one inch from her lofty place.

In Auckland, Strickland captured the gold medal in the 80-meter hurdles and claimed an additional pair on two winning Aussie relay teams. Plus, she finished second in both the 100-yards and 220-yards to teammate Marjorie Jackson.

So it was no surprise in another two years that Strickland (now Mrs. de la Hunty) was among the highest-regarded athletes on Australia's team for the 1952 Helsinki Olympics. Another long journey to Europe for the Games wouldn't keep Shirley away.

Strickland passed up the 200 in the Finnish capital. But in contesting the 100 and hurdles she would compete on four consecutive days, July 21-24 and then have a break of two days before the heats and final of the 4 x 100 relay on July

27. There was no question Shirley was up to it.

Shirley again raced to third place in the 100, but Australia still claimed the gold medal thanks to the 11.5-second dash by Marjorie Jackson to tie the World Record. Jackson won easily from South Africa's Daphne Hasenjager, whose time of 11.8 edged Strickland by 0.1.

In the hurdles, though, no other performer's star shone as brightly as Shirley's. Defending champion Blankers-Koen was back, of course, but she was far from her form in London due to an attack of boils plus the effects of medication. Even at her very best, however, Fanny would have had a tough time with Strickland.

In her heat, Shirley merely equalled the World Record of 11.0 run four years earlier by Blankers-Koen. Times of 11.1 by Maria Golubnichaya of the USSR and 11.2 by Fanny herself let Strickland know she could take nothing for granted.

Her semi-final was aided by an illegal wind, but Strickland blazed 10.8 to show who would be the favorite in the final. And when the gold medal was on the line in the championship race, Shirley showed her stuff, setting a World Record 10.9 to finally claim an Olympic gold medallion. She finished well clear of Golubnichaya and West Germany's Maria Sander (both 11.1), as Blankers-Koen hit several hurdles and failed to finish.

In the relay, Strickland again started off Australia's team. Hopes for a win were high with Jackson on the anchor leg; Marjorie had also added the 200-meter title to her earlier victory in the 100. And a World Record clocking of 46.1 seconds in the heats by the Aussie team showed they could run.

For three-quarters of the final, Australia was right in the thick of the battle with the surprising U.S. and West German teams. But suddenly, Australia's third runner Winsome Cripps and Jackson fumbled the final baton exchange; precious fractions of a second were lost and the Aussies ended up in fifth place as the Americans lowered the World Record to 45.9 seconds.

After as successful an Olympic season as Strickland's in

1952, plus the memory of her five-medal performance at Auckland in 1950, it might have seemed like an automatic pick for Australian selectors to name Strickland to the team for the 1954 Commonwealth Games, scheduled for Vancouver. But she was shockingly omitted.

The team was named in March, 1954, following the Australian Championships. Shirley's son Phillip had been born the previous September and she had been able to resume training only late in December of 1953. Then, just a month before the championships, she was hit by a case of the flu so serious she was in bed for three weeks, and her doctor administered penicillin and advised her not to compete any further that season.

Strickland never was the type to give up, though. She sought permission from Games officials to be able to defend her title at her own expense. Commonwealth officials referred her request back to officials of the Australian Women's Amateur Athletic Union. Despite support for her request from the Men's Union, officials of the Women's Union turned her down.

Shirley then tried to earn her place on the team by running in the championships, but she was short on conditioning and eventually stopped in the hurdles final and failed to finish. Critics assailed her, saying she deliberately stopped rather than be defeated. But as one Australian track writer observed, "This is the small-minded cynicism that champions have to put up with, which they can neither ignore (because it is personal) nor answer."

Again in 1955, Strickland found roadblocks in her path—and not just the metal and wood variety on the track. Shirley was invited to a major international competition in Warsaw, Poland. But Aussie officials decreed she had to be accompanied by a chaperone—little did it matter that she was 30 years old, a mother and had competed in two Olympic Games, plus numerous meets in Europe.

Shirley won out, however, and exacted what certainly must have been considerable satisfaction in Warsaw. She competed in the 100-meters and merely set a new World Record, 11.3 seconds to trim 0.1 from the mark set in October, 1952, by Marjorie Jackson. Shirley's mark would not be tied for

25

another three years and would not be bettered until 1961.

Still, the critics wouldn't let up. The record just gave publicity to the meet, said the naysayers. But rather than buckle under the small-minded vindictiveness of a jealous few, Shirley buckled down to show them in the best way she knew—on the track at the 1956 Olympic Games, scheduled for Australia's largest city of Melbourne.

Strickland trained five days a week, regardless of the weather, on a sandy and poorly-lit grass track in Perth. She suffered a leg tendon injury in January, 1956, and in the spring was investigated by the Women's AAU when her photograph appeared on a cigarette carton label. But those were minor glitches which were soon resolved and Strickland continued her single-minded quest.

She was so eager in her training, in fact, she was the first Australian athlete to move into the Olympic Village in Melbourne when it opened in October of 1956. She wouldn't run the sprints this time; the relay, yes, but all her individual efforts would go toward the hurdles.

Even as her competitive focus zeroed in tightly on the hurdles, Strickland was her usual warm, helpful self off the track. Betty Cuthbert would emerge as the women's star of the '56 Games with three gold medals. In her biography *Golden Girl*, Cuthbert wrote, "Everyone was so nice and friendly, but Shirley was especially a great help to all of us and guided us along with the experience she had gained at the past two Olympics." Another athlete said of Strickland, "She is so sweet and charming. It seems she knows more about the sport than most men."

When the chips were down on the track, though, Strickland was all business. In the heats, West Germany's Zenta Gastl (World Record holder at 10.6 seconds) matched Shirley's Olympic Record of 10.9 in the first heat. In the very next race, Shirley sped 10.8 for a new Olympic best. Teammate Norma Thrower clocked 10.8 in heat four. In the first semi-final, Shirley beat East Germany's Gisela Birkemeyer, as both again matched the 10.8 Olympic Record.

In the final, however, Shirley didn't give anyone else a chance. She rocketed off her starting blocks and pulled away throughout the race to win in 10.7, another Olympic Record, from Birkemeyer (10.9) and Thrower (11.0). Her victory made Shirley Strickland the first woman ever to successfully defend an Olympic title up to then—and she remains today as the only woman ever to win successive titles in the hurdles.

If Australian prospects in the 1952 4 x 100 relay were good with Strickland leading off and double sprint winner Jackson anchoring, the outlook was just as bright in Melbourne. Shirley started for the third consecutive Olympics and new double sprint champion Cuthbert finished. The Aussies set a World Record 44.9 in the heats, beating the 44.9 of Germany. In the final, Cuthbert outran Britain's Heather Armitage in another global record of 44.5. Strickland finally had her relay gold.

Those Melbourne medals brought Strickland's Olympic tally to seven: three golds, one silver and three bronzes. Poland's great Irena Szewinska later won seven medals from 1964 through 1976 (three golds, two silvers, two bronzes), although Strickland could be considered the most prolific woman medalist in Olympic history if that disputed placing in the 1948 200 meters is considered. Even ignoring that, no woman has yet won more Olympic medals than Shirley.

Shortly after the Melbourne Olympics, Strickland announced her retirement. During her Olympic appearances, Shirley set 9 Olympic Records (6 in the hurdles, 3 in the 4 x 100 relay), more than any other man or woman in Olympic track and field history.

In 1960, at the age of 35, Shirley still was fit—and fast—enough to dash 100 yards in 10.9 seconds. She remains active in the sport today as a club and regional coach in Western Australia.

In her biography, Betty Cuthbert commented on what makes a champion athlete. She wrote, "[Some] are natural-born athletes who need only some coaching and training to be successful. Shirley was one of those." Just as important, though, is "the dedication of some athletes. They have a fierce will to win, and their dedication borders on fanaticism." Chief among such athletes named by Cuthbert was Shirley Strickland.

Cuthbert speeds to the '56 Olympic 100 title.

BETTY CUTHBERT

As Shirley Strickland steadfastly prepared during 1951 for the Helsinki Olympics the following year, June Ferguson, a teammate of Strickland's at the '48 London Games, had made a discovery. Ferguson was a physical education teacher at Parramatta Home Science High School in the Sydney suburb of Merrylands and at the school's athletic carnival, she had watched a gangly 13-year-old win the 75- and 100-yard dashes for her age group.

The girl's name was Betty Cuthbert. Something inside Ferguson told her this wasn't just another tomboy who sprinted in bare feet and who could outrun all the boys as well as every girl. After the school carnival, Ferguson approached Cuthbert and asked if she would like to train regularly with the club she coached in the evenings. Betty was enthusiastic and her parents finally agreed.

So began a coach-athlete collaboration which would raise Betty Cuthbert to new heights in world sprinting: four career gold medals in the Olympic Games, three as an 18-year-old sprint sensation in Melbourne in 1956 and the fourth eight years later at 400-meters in Tokyo; a total of 15 World Records, 11 of them in individual dashes. Just five years after June Ferguson first spotted her raw talent, Betty Cuthbert was on her way toward becoming one of the greatest sprinters in track and field history.

Betty Cuthbert was born on April 20, 1938, the first of twin girls; her sister Marie (later nicknamed "Midge" by Betty) arrived 20 minutes later. "Mum said I was a skinny little thing with long arms and legs," Cuthbert wrote in her 1966 autobiography, *Golden Girl.*

Her first footrace came at another school sports day, this one as an eight-year-old elementary schooler. Betty won the 50- and 75-yard dashes, which she claimed shouldn't have been a surprise to anyone, since she hardly ever was still as a child. She loved to run everywhere.

It didn't take Cuthbert long to make a name for herself, once she teamed up with June Ferguson as her coach. She represented her home state of New South Wales in the Australian Schools Championships when she still was 13 years old. By the time she was 15, she had pared down her best 100-yard time to 10.8 seconds. That was during the 1953-54 season and it was during the next year that she first tried the 220-yard distance at Ferguson's suggestion.

"As June said, I seemed to take to [the half-lap distance] like a duck to water," Cuthbert recalled. "I much preferred the longer distance too, and always seemed to do better over it than the shorter 100."

If Ferguson was a good judge of talent, she also knew when to leave things well enough alone. Such as Cuthbert's style: while technically sound in terms of arm action and leg motion, Betty's style was characterized by her running with her mouth open, as though she were in deepest pain, or gasping for air—or both. But, oh was Betty fast, and it didn't matter how she looked. She could run like the wind.

As the Olympic season of 1956 dawned, Cuthbert was poised to burst upon the national scene in Australia. In the New South Wales championships, Betty clocked times of 10.6 for 100 yards, 11.5 for 100 meters and 24.2 for 220 yards. She was second in all three races to better-known Marlene Mathews, however, so Cuthbert would have to perform extraordinarily well at the Australian national title meet in order to gain a place on the Olympic training squad.

The nationals were run in Brisbane just three weeks before Betty turned 18. Being in the southern Hemisphere, Australia's seasons are reversed from the northern half of the globe; for track and field, that means the spring and summer season runs from roughly October through early April.

Cuthbert didn't qualify for the 100-yard final, but two days later she won the 220. Her time of 25-seconds flat certainly was nothing for anyone to get excited about—except that the grass track was ankle deep in mud. Despite the cow-paddock conditions, Cuthbert outran

Mathews, eventual relay gold medalist Norma Croker, the super-veteran Strickland and '52 Olympian Winsome Cripps. Suddenly, all of Australia knew about the quiet teenager named Cuthbert.

Betty was named to the training squad and worked hard through a terrible winter of rain and cold. With the Games scheduled for late in November, the Aussie team assembled in September for training and several tuneup meets. On September 16, 1956, Betty Cuthbert came of age internationally.

She had run well in earlier meets, and won the 100-meters in 11.8 that September day, despite feeling the onset of a cold. Then in the 200, Cuthbert had to contend only with the diminutive Fleur Mellor. Betty's prime rival, Mathews, was sitting out the meet with a sore leg. Cuthbert and Mellor ran the curve strongly and hit the homestretch virtually even.

Cuthbert recalled, "I could feel Fleur going for her life just a stride behind me. It sent a bolt of fear through me and I shot off as though a firecracker had been dropped under me." Cuthbert rocketed down the homestretch and was traveling so fast as she sped across the line that she ran into a retaining fence 20 yards farther down the straightaway and nearly tumbled over it.

Then her time was announced: a World Record 23.2. "Me, a World Record holder! I couldn't believe it," Cuthbert remembered. "I was staggered to think I had sliced seventh-tenths-of-a-second off my best time and two-tenths off the record Marjorie Jackson had set up at the 1952 Helsinki Olympics. My time was flashed around the world."

So by the time of the start of the Olympics in November, Cuthbert definitely had a reputation preceding her into Melbourne. But Betty still was the shy, quiet girl of 18, thrust headlong into the worldwide circus which is the Olympics. She kept trying to keep herself calm, especially as she readied for her qualifying heat of the 100 on Saturday, November 24.

In the race just before Betty's, Mathews had clocked

11.5 for a new Olympic Record. Cuthbert also expected the short American Isabelle Daniels to be a factor, as well as Christa Stubnick, the police typist from East Germany. So what did Betty do? In her first Olympic appearance ever, she dashed 11.4 in her heat for another Olympic Record.

Later that day, Cuthbert was edged in her semi-final by Stubnick, 11.9 to 12.0. Betty realized she had let up mentally after 75 meters and Stubnick had kept bearing down to beat her. "Usually, I would always aim for a meter or two beyond the finish line before I would slow," Cuthbert revealed. "So when I crossed the line itself, I still was in full flight. I always ran races of 101 or 201 meters."

In the final, Cuthbert remembered her lesson well. First out of the blocks, she opened a gap of almost a meter on American Daniels by the 30-meter mark. Stubnick was another two feet back, with the slow-starting Mathews just beginning to accelerate. Past the halfway point, Cuthbert's margin was better than two meters. Stubnick and Mathews closed fast, catching Daniels and pushing her back to fourth. But nobody caught the flying Cuthbert and she crossed the line in 11.5.

"Towards the end, my mouth was open so wide, it began to hurt," Cuthbert wrote. "But I thought, 'You can't stop to shut it now.' So it stayed open till I thought my jaws were going to split. I'd done it. I'd won the highest prize in amateur sport—an Olympic gold medal."

As she walked back down the track after the race, Betty found her mother in the stands among her rejoicing countrymen, weeping with joy. Then Betty herself broke down, and again on the victory stand she cried tears of joy when she heard her national anthem.

Her confidence was buoyed tremendously by the 100 victory, and Betty naturally became the heavy favorite to take the 200 and duplicate the double sprint wins of Fanny Blankers-Koen in London and Aussie Marjorie Jackson in Helsinki. Her 23.4 gave her victory by nearly four meters and a share of Jackson's Olympic Record, which had been a World Record in 1952 and the global mark Betty had broken back in September.

It was after scoring her second triumph that Cuthbert

was christened with the nickname which remained with her the rest of her career. A Melbourne newspaper ran a full-page picture of Betty with the headline "Betty Cuthbert—Golden Girl." That she had won two gold medals coupled nicely with the fact that her hair was a golden blonde. Naturally, the name stuck.

Cuthbert's Melbourne mission wasn't quite finished. There still was the 4 x 100-meter relay to run. Australia's team would be led off by hurdles champion Strickland, who had announced she would retire after the Games. Norma Croker, fourth in the 200, would run the second leg, and Fleur Mellor the third. Mellor's place on the team had stirred some controversy, as some observers felt Marlene Mathews was the better pick.

Of course, Cuthbert would anchor the home squad. During the summer, the USSR had cut the World Record from 45.6 down to 45.2, a mark that both Germany and Great Britain later tied. Then in late September, Germany sped 45.1. Both Australia and Germany drew heat one of the relay qualifying and the presence of each had an obvious effect on the other. Australia clicked to a win in 44.9 for a new World Record, as Germany finished in the same time to equal the record.

In the final, though, Germany botched the exchanges right from the start and was hopelessly out of the race. Great Britain turned out to be the prime threat to Australia. Anne Pashley passed off slightly ahead of Strickland after the opening segment. Norma Croker and Jean Scrivens kept their teams even down the backstretch. Around the turn on the third leg, Mellor vindicated her choice for the team as she pulled fractionally ahead of June Paul. Cuthbert and British anchor Heather Armitage got their batons almost in unison and traded strides all the way down the homestretch. Armitage could get only as far as Betty's elbow, but never farther. Cuthbert brought Australia home in a World Record 44.5, as Armitage finished Britain's silver winning 44.7. The winning foursome danced a jig of joy when the record time was announced.

After the Games, Cuthbert was the toast of the world—something for which Betty was totally unprepared.

She just wanted to go back home and get back to her job at her father's nursery. She wasn't used to all the publicity and commotion which surrounded her. She even was self-conscious when well-wishing motorists would recognize her and call out from their cars or trucks, "Good on ya, Bet." Betty had always been the quiet one while her twin sister Midge was effervescent and outgoing.

She wrote in her autobiography, "I slowly realized that my identity was disappearing and I was no longer a plain, ordinary girl, but something different and unusual. I was no longer Betty Cuthbert, the girl, but Betty Cuthbert, the athlete. My life wasn't my own anymore."

Cuthbert struggled to cope with her fame, even if teammate Mathews ranked as the world's leading sprinter in 1957. The '58 season featured the Commonwealth Games in Cardiff, Wales in late July and as a kind of training-cum-fund raiser for the Australian team, some leading athletes would compete in exhibition races at the halftime of rugby matches. It wasn't the kind of preparation Betty liked; she preferred several months of top-level racing and contesting both sprints and the short relay in each meet. In that way, she could develop and hone both her speed and conditioning.

She was not thrilled with her form by the time of the Commonwealth festival. She ended up placing fourth in the 100 yards, which was won by Marlene Mathews. Cuthbert was determined to win the 220 and led Mathews into the final straight. But Mathews was to be the double gold medalist this time as she beat Betty by two-tenths in 23.6. And in the 4 x 110-yard relay, England exacted some degree of revenge for the Olympic defeat, beating the Cuthbert-anchored Aussies easily, 45.3 to 46.1.

Following the Commonwealth Games, Cuthbert and several teammates traveled around the British Isles and Scandinavia, seeing the sights and generally relaxing. They also trained some and competed in a few meets. In a meet in Goteborg, Sweden, on August 28, Cuthbert gave her first try to the 400-meters. She won the race in 54.4, which ended up being the fastest time in the world that year. "Since I hadn't trained at all for the distance, I expected to be carried off the track in exhaustion," Cuthbert recalled. "Nobody was more surprised than me at my time." Little did Cuthbert, or anyone, know, but she had run the race which would give her Olympic immortality.

Betty returned from Cardiff to her home suburb of Ermington to find the city council had named a street after her. And the domestic track season was well underway, so she decided to run some 440-yard races to score as many points as possible for her club. In her fourth race at the distance, early in 1959, she equalled the 55.6 World Record and two months later, she hacked her time down to 54.3 for another record.

The Olympic season of 1960 arrived quickly and Betty started it off on a record note, zipping the then-record distance of 60-meters in 7.2 seconds. She still had plenty of speed. At the Australian Championships in March, Cuthbert was beaten in the 100-yards, but sped the 220 in 23.2 to clip two-tenths from Mathews's World Record and also tie Betty's own standard at the slightly-shorter 200-meters. She felt her prospects for the Rome Olympics were looking good.

Betty was named to the Australian team in both sprints, plus the relay, and also was given the great honor of being elected captain of the women's team. As the early-September Olympics drew closer, a series of races were arranged, again much like those before the '58 Commonwealth Games. That meant racing at the half of rugby matches on Saturday afternoons during the Australian winter.

In early July, during a 100-yard handicap race with men, Betty suffered a hamstring muscle injury in her right leg. It was wretched timing for her to suffer the first injury of her entire career. She responded well to therapy, however, and quickly regained strength. Once she arrived in Rome with the Aussie team, she trained on the hard cinder tracks, very different from the softer grass ovals back home.

The leg muscle gradually became more and more sore. Betty couldn't practice with the relay team during its final two training sessions. She was naturally concerned about the fitness of her leg, not only just so she could compete at her best, but also because this time around all eyes were on her. She was defending double champion and had set World Records the previous year and leading up to the Games.

Once in competition, though, it was obvious that the leg

was far from healthy. Cuthbert finished second in her qualifying heat in 12.1 seconds, a slow time she hadn't run in years. In her quarter-final race, Cuthbert improved only to 12.0, but she finished fourth and did not advance. Her leg hurt too much anyway—Betty Cuthbert's Olympics were over. She withdrew from the 200-meters and the relay team. The Cuthbert-less relay squad was subsequently disqualified in the heats.

After returning home, Betty announced her retirement from running—but it wasn't for the reasons everyone supposed. "It wasn't, as so many people imagined, because of my hamstring injury, or because of the failure and disappointment it caused. I hated being a public figure to be looked at, talked about and pointed out every time I stepped outside my own front door. I'd been secretly nursing that hate for four long years, ever since my wins in Melbourne. Finally, it became unbearable.

Cuthbert realized her whole life had revolved around running. She desperately wanted to be like Midge, as she put it, "a normal 22-year-old girl." So for 18 months, she didn't run a step. She worked and sewed and went to parties and vacationed and led the "normal" life she wanted.

Gradually, however, as 1961 moved toward 1962—and the Commonwealth Games, which were scheduled for Betty's home nation, in Perth, Australia—she began entertaining thoughts of returning to running. At first, she fought with her inner feelings, trying to suppress her growing desire to come back. Finally, she faced herself: running *was* her life and she wanted to return to it.

She resumed training in January of 1962; the Commonwealth Games were set for November. Betty made the Aussie team in her usual two sprints and one relay, but displayed indifferent form at Perth and didn't make the final of either dash. But she anchored the Aussie 4 x 110-yard relay unit to the gold medal.

As the '62 season melded into early 1963, Betty regained some of her stature, but this time over the full-lap distance. In one 440-yard race, she passed the 400-meter point in a World Record 53.1 and continued on to 53.5 for the yard distance, also a global best. In her next race, she

clocked 53.3 for the 440—three World Records in two successive races. Cuthbert still had the magic.

The track seasons had moved almost as fast as Cuthbert
and 1964 brought the Tokyo Olympic Games. Cuthbert and
Ferguson made the decision that Betty would shoot only
for the 400-meters—actually, Cuthbert later admitted Ferguson told her pointblank that the 400 would be her race and
Betty just agreed.

Her preparation suffered minor setbacks here and there,
but generally progressed well. Once she arrived in Tokyo with
the Aussie team, Cuthbert pondered what she would do after
the Games. She decided then and there that—win or lose—the
Tokyo 400 would be her last race. She would retire for good
after the final on October 17.

She never considered what she might do if she didn't
win the race. Betty simply knew that winning the inaugural
Olympic 400 for women would be a perfect cap to her
career. "Inwardly, I was confident of my chances but I knew
it was going to be the toughest race of my life," she wrote. "I
was going to make it the toughest [because] I had to win. . .
I had to win then or never."

Cuthbert's training was indifferent in the last days
before the Games. But she wasn't worried; she had run well
all season and was confident the final would bring out her
best. She wasn't considered one of the favorites; the Soviet
Maria Itkina—who had run 53.0 early in the fall for the
second-fastest time in history behind the recently-ratified
World Record of 51.9 by North Korea's Sim Kin Dan—and
Britain's Ann Packer were the odds-on favorites. Dan's nation
did not compete in the Games.

Packer solidified her status with an Olympic Record
53.1 in her heat. Betty had finished third in her heat, but had
glided through race after only about 150-meters and was
excited that everything felt so easy. Betty and Packer met the
next day in the first semi-final, and the Briton powered to
another Olympic Record, 52.7. It was more than a second
faster than Cuthbert—but after the race, Cuthbert's spirits
were tremendously roused by none other than Packer herself.

"Putting on her tracksuit after the race, Ann casually

Cuthbert watches Packer receive the Tokyo 400 silver medal.

said, 'I can't help wanting to win every race,' " Cuthbert related. "That was enough for me. I knew she must have been close to her top." Betty knew she could lower her time by several tenths and her confidence blossomed anew.

The incident revealed one of the strengths in Betty Cuthbert which helped carry her to the top, and keep her there. Her sharp, probing mind always looked for signs of weakness in her foes, especially immediately after the finish of a race: "Those few brief seconds were terribly valuable. That was the time when a rival was completely unmasked and I could sum them up." Invariably, she concluded she could beat a competitor and her confidence would soar.

As she headed out for the 400-meter final on October 17, though, Cuthbert wasn't sure of anything. She remembers shutting the door of her room in the Olympic Village and wondering if the next time she opened it she would be the Olympic champion or a dejected also-ran.

During her warmup, her legs felt like jelly and her stomach turned flip-flops. She lay down briefly in a dressing room before the race and closed her eyes, trying not to think of the race because that made her heart pound all the more.

But when she rose to go out for the race, her insides were quiet and calm, her legs felt strong. Cuthbert had drawn lane two for the final, with teammate Judy Amoore in the next lane. Packer would run in the sixth corridor. As the eight finalists approached their marks, Betty cautioned Judy about the wind, which blew with the runners down the backstretch but which would hit them in the face when they rounded the second turn and headed for home down the last 100 meters of the red cinder track.

Then the gun barked and the runners were away. Cuthbert ran hard over the first 100, gaining on Amoore one lane outside her. They flowed down the backstretch and into the second turn, Cuthbert catching her teammate with about 180-meters to run. Betty saw Packer at about the same time. "I thought, 'Now's the time. Let it go.' I mustered every drop of speed I had in me and turned it loose," she recalled.

Cuthbert led Packer into the homestretch, where they were hit square in the face by the strong wind. But Betty kept her head down, kept driving forward, kept Packer at bay all the way down the long straight. Cuthbert crossed the finish in an Olympic Record 52.0, just one-tenth shy of the World Record, as Packer clocked 52.2 and Amoore was a solitary third place in 53.4. Itkina never figured in the chase and placed a far-back 5th in 54.6.

Betty had done it. Eight years after her first Olympic victories, she still was the Golden Girl. An ecstatic Cuthbert received her fourth gold medal—and wonderful-feeling goose-bumps as the Aussie flag was rung up the flagpole. "Nothing ever touched me as much as that medal ceremony," she wrote. "In Melbourne, I had been too young to realize what I had accomplished. But there in Tokyo I had at last achieved something I had wanted for so long, sacrificed so much for and worked so hard to get. My insides bubbled with happiness."

True to her word, Cuthbert retired after Tokyo. She went out on the high note she wanted. "I wanted people to remember me by that run, which I consider the only perfect race I ever ran," she recalled. "I always wanted to leave the sport when I was right at the top, and I did.

"If I had my life to live over again, I hope it would follow exactly the same course. . . with perhaps a few changes here and there. But I would like to be an athlete again because I truly loved the sport."

IOLANDA BALAS

The longest string of consecutive victories in any event in track and field belongs to a woman. Romanian high jumper Iolanda Balas won an astonishing 140 straight competitions between 1957 and 1966.

That fact alone would make historic the career of the long-legged Balas. But she hardly stopped there. Among that string of 140 victories were 13 World Record leaps, plus another jump to match the global best. Those 14 entries into the record book are the most for any woman in the history of the sport—and equal to the most records produced by a man (held by Finnish distance hero Paavo Nurmi).

As well, Balas's streak includes two Olympic titles, at Rome in 1960 and Tokyo in 1964, plus European Championships victories in 1958 and 1962. For longevity, honors won and a decade-long domination of her foes from every corner of the globe, Iolanda Balas is often considered the finest high jumper in women's track history.

Born in 1936, Yoli (as she was nicknamed) began competing in 1951. Right away, she showed she was something exceptional by winning the Romanian national title—at age 14. It was the first of her 16 successive national wins.

Three years later, Balas got her first taste of championship level competition when she ventured to Bern for the 1954 European Championships. Despite being several months shy of her 18th birthday, Yoli cleared 5'5"/1.65 to place second and win the silver medal. Her career at the world-class level was off and running.

Balas set her first World Record in the summer of 1956 when she cleared 5'8¾"/1.75 to put her name among the favorites for the upcoming Olympic Games, to be held at the end of November in Melbourne, Australia.

However, the prospect of facing Balas The World Record Holder didn't daunt the young American, Mildred McDaniel. "Babe," as she was called, one-upped Balas—and everyone else—by scaling a record 5'9¼"/1.76 to take the gold medal. And Yoli? She could manage only 5'5¾"/1.67 and she placed fifth. Throughout her long career, she never again would place that low in a major championship competition.

The Melbourne contest was notable for another reason: it was the last time Iolanda Balas lost until June 11, 1967. The string had begun.

During 1957, Balas regained at least partial claim to the World Record when she matched the 5'9¼" of McDaniel. The next season, though, Balas settled in for her long reign over the event. She upped the global record five times in 1958, the greatest number of elevations in one year in the event's history. Her fifth also brought down one of the event's "magic" barriers: on October 10, she cleared 6'0"/1.83, becoming the first woman to surpass that English-measurement milestone. She also earned her initial first-place in the authoritative World Rankings compiled by the great Czech statistician Jan Popper. No other jumper but Balas would rank first for the next eight seasons.

Balas didn't neglect honors, either. She won the '58 European title with 5'9¾"/1.77, shy of her own World Record but plenty good for a gold medal. The big one came two years later, however, when Balas went to Rome determined to make amends for her Olympic failure in 1956.

In the Italian capital, Balas was untouchable. Fifteen finalists met on the apron of *Stadio Olimpico;* after the height of 5'5"/1.65, there were only five left. Balas, though, had cleared every height on her first attempt and was firmly in command. When no one else could jump higher than 5'7¼"/1.77, the gold medal went to Yoli. But she did not finish her day's work until she had cleared her own height, the Olympic Record ceiling of 6'¾"/1.85.

Afterward, Yoli said, "Some people think my jumping style is passe. But I wanted to show everyone that it is the best technique for me." Balas's style was a modification of

Iolanda Balas

Balas signs autographs after her 1960 victory in Rome.

the scissors-kick: she ran straight at the bar, kicked her straight right leg up and over first and brought her trailing left leg over immediately thereafter with a quick, scissors-like motion. At the same time, she turned slightly so that when she landed in the sawdust landing pits of the day, she was looking back in the direction she had come. Most other jumpers used the popular straddle style, in which the jumper follows her lead leg over the bar by wrapping her body around it in a smooth rolling motion. But Balas had her own way of doing things—and it was unbeatable.

In the years between the Rome and Tokyo Olympics, Balas merely continued to build her dynasty. She set four World Records in 1961, her highest mark—and the final effort in her remarkable 14-record string—coming on July 16 in Sofia, Bulgaria, with a clearance of 6'3¼"/1.91. At that time, the next-best height in history was 5'10"/1.78 jumped by Taisiya Chenchik of the USSR, back in 1958.

Balas defended her European crown in 1962 by clearing 6'0" in Belgrade. It was no surprise, of course, that Balas went to the '64 Tokyo Olympics as one of the heaviest favorites—in any sport.

And Yoli merely continued to dominate her rivals. She needed only eight jumps to secure her second gold medal, and she cleared every height on her first try. That included an Olympic Record 6'2¾"/1.90. The best of the rest, Michelle Brown of Australia, went out after making 5'10¾"/1.80.

It was dark in Tokyo's Olympic Sadium when Yoli slashed over 6'2¾", but the stadium lights reflected off her white jersey and blonde hair as she landed in the pit and immediately threw up her arms in glee and triumph.

After consulting with long-time coach Ion Soter, Balas turned to the Japanese officials and help up two fingers. She wanted the bar raised to 6'3½"/1.92, ¼" above her own World Record. The crowded stadium held its collective breath as Balas took three game attempts at the record, but she missed all of them. It really didn't matter, though; Yoli had become the only woman ever to win consecutive high jump titles in the Olympic Games.

Considering her record, it was natural to expect Balas to be the overwhelming favorite to make it three European titles in a row at the 1966 championships in Budapest. But persistent leg injuries kept Balas on the sidelines, and although no one knew it then, an era in high jumping was ending. Some skeptics ventured the unfounded opinion that Balas was afraid to submit to the mandatory sex tests which had been instituted that year by the International Amateur Athletic Federation. But Balas had passed other sex tests in past years.

One test that became harder and harder to pass, though, was jumping itself. Almost two decades of it had taken its toll on Balas's legs. She was able to return briefly to competition in 1967—and East Germany's Dagmar Melzer became a footnote in the history of the event with her victory over Balas that June. Melzer cleared 5'7¼"/1.71 with Balas managing merely 5'6"/1.68.

Balas retired shortly after that and married her long-time coach Soter (himself a former world-class high jumper). Yoli once admitted, "Sometimes it was hard to compete; there was no opposition for me. But then I would tell myself inside that I had to try to do my best always, so I would." For more than a decade, the best of Iolanda Balas was second to none.

Rudolph flashes to her first gold medal, in the Rome 100.

WILMA RUDOLPH

She laughed when she told the story, but Wilma Rudolph swears it is true. "Ed Temple, who was my college coach at Tennessee State and also a strong guiding influence in my life, told me a number of years after the 1960 Olympics that before we left for Rome he had a dream one night," Rudolph told filmmaker/author Bud Greenspan.

"Coach Temple said he dreamed that I won both sprints at the Olympics and then anchored the 4 x 100-meter relay team to the gold medal. With my three gold medals, I was the star of the Games," Wilma smiled. "I asked him why he waited so long to tell me about his dream. He looked a little sheepish and said, 'I knew you would think I was crazy.' "

But real life sometimes can make even the craziest dreams come true. At the '60 Games, Rudolph *did* win both the 100 and 200 sprint gold medals, and then anchored the United States to victory in the 4 x 100 relay. What's more, she matched the 100 World Record of 11.3 in her semi-final and won the final in 11-seconds flat. That would have slashed the global best, but for a following wind barely over the allowable limit of two-meters-per-second. She won the 100 by the wide margin of three-tenths of a second.

In the 200, Rudolph's margin of victory was even wider. Her 24.0 took the gold medal by 0.4 from Germany's Jutta Heine. In her heat, Rudolph sped 23.2 to trim the Olympic Record by 0.2. In the sprint relay, the U.S. was heavily favored with Wilma covering the closing anchor leg. In their heat, the Americans lowered the World Record to 44.4 seconds; in the final, the U.S. foursome clocked 44.5 to beat runner-up Germany by 0.3. At the time, Wilma was barely 20 years old.

Thus Rudolph became the only American woman up to then to win three gold medals in one Olympics. It wouldn't happen again until 1984 when Valerie Brisco-Hooks won the 200, 400 and ran on the winning 4 x 400-meter relay team in Los Angeles. For nearly a quarter-of-a-century, Rudolph remained the only American woman triple gold medalist in Olympic track & field.

That Rudolph won her three gold medals is a notable enough achievement in itself. By those victories, moreover, track fans around the world learned about the early life of the lanky American who was tabbed *la gazelle noire*—the black gazelle—by one European reporter after her golden triple in Rome. That early life made Rudolph's triumphs truly remarkable.

She was born June 23, 1940, in Clarksville, Tennessee, the 20th of 22 children born into the family of an impoverished handyman. Life always was a struggle, but also filled with love and warmth in the crowded Rudolph house. When she was four years old, little Wilma had an attack of scarlet fever, plus a bout of double pneumonia. She suffered paralysis in her left leg as a result of the serious illnesses. There were fears she might never walk again—and running was out of the question.

Wilma was fitted with a leg brace, which she had to wear until she was 10 years old. In her autobiography *Wilma*, Rudolph revealed, "For a long time, I didn't see any improvement; the leg was still crooked and I wore the brace. I knew very little of what was happening, but I never let anyone else know that. What I finally did was learn to fake a no-limp walk. Just like when someone fakes walking with a limp so other people will think something is wrong, I learned how to fake a normal walk so people would think there wasn't anything wrong with me."

As well, Rudolph's mother had her brothers and sisters massage her leg every day. Eventually, the leg gained strength and by the time she was 10, Wilma walked normally. She first tried competitive sprinting at age 12 and by the time she entered Burt High School in Clarksville, she was winning every race she ran between 50 and 220 yards.

Rudolph made her international debut in 1956 on the biggest stage of all—the Olympic Games, held in Melbourne, Australia. She had competed in the U.S. national championships in both 1955 and '56 while representing the Tennessee State Track Club. The club, nicknamed the Tigerbelles, was organized and coached by Ed Temple, who worked at the state college in Nashville and who felt women should have the opportunity for coaching and competition in track and field. For many years, Tennessee State offered the strongest collegiate program for women track athletes.

Wilma was only two months past her 16th birthday when she competed in the U.S. Olympic team tryouts in Washington, D.C., on August 25, 1956. She finished second in the 200-meters to Mae Faggs, another Tennessee State Tigerbelle and a veteran of the 1952 Games in Helsinki (where she won a gold medal in the 4 x 100 relay).

At Melbourne, young Wilma experienced the eye-opening world of the Olympic Games. Half-a-world away from home, she was exposed for the first time to people, customs and ideas from ways of life very different from her own. And she learned about competition at the very highest world level.

Wilma drew the second heat of the 200 meters; in the race just before hers, Rudolph saw 100-meter winner Betty Cuthbert of Australia speed 23.5 seconds, just one-tenth behind the Olympic Record. Mae Faggs was a far-back second at 24.9. Wilma faced in her race two experienced Europeans, Maria Itkina of the USSR and Gisela Kohler of Germany. They finished in that order with respective times of 24.1 and 24.4. Wilma placed third in an American Record 24.6, but only the top two placers advanced to the semi-finals so Rudolph was eliminated.

Rudolph saw Cuthbert claim her second gold medal of the '56 Games with her victory in the 200. Wilma was back on the track for the heats in the 4 x 100 relay a few days later. She handled the third leg of the race around the second curve of the 400-meter track; the relay squad was an all-Tennessee State foursome of Isabelle Daniels, Faggs, Wilma and Margaret Matthews. They finished second in their heat in an American Record 45.4, one-tenth behind the winners from Great Britain. In the first heat, Australia won in 44.9 with Germany second in the same time as both matched the World Record.

For the final, however, the U.S. coaches shuffled the

order of the team—all except Wilma. Faggs was moved to the lead-off slot, Matthews to second, Wilma stayed in the third position and Daniels switched over to anchor. In the race for the medals, Faggs and Matthews got the baton to Wilma with the U.S. running third behind the Aussies and Britons. Germany was hopelessly out of it after fumbling the early exchanges.

Down the stretch on the final leg, Australia's Cuthbert held at bay British anchor Heather Armitage, while Daniels was a solitary third as the U.S. claimed the bronze medal. The Tigerbelle foursome cut its American Record to 44.9 seconds, which would have equaled the World Record had not Australia run 44.5 to win, with Britain at 44.7 in second.

So young, 16-year-old Wilma Rudolph took home an Olympic bronze medal. But she also carried back with her a driving motivation: "When I saw Betty Cuthbert win her three gold medals, I vowed to myself that at the next Olympics in Rome, I would win at least one or two of those medals for myself and my country."

Rudolph returned home to Clarksville after the Melbourne Olympics to complete her final year of high school. During the 1957 season, she won national Junior outdoor titles over 75-yards and 100-yards. Wilma missed the '58 season after the birth of her first child, daughter Yolanda. She returned in 1959 with a victory in the national AAU (the forerunner to The Athletics Congress) 100-meters, plus she ran third in the 200. Rudolph passed up competing in the dual meet against the USSR, staged in Philadelphia, but she did race in the Pan-American Games in Chicago and finished second in the 100 plus running on the winning 4 x 100 relay.

Then suddenly it was 1960, an Olympic year with the Games scheduled for Rome at the beginning of September. The month of July turned out to be pivotal for Rudolph. At the national AAU meet, held on July 9 in Corpus Christi, Texas, Wilma initially won the 100-meter title with an 11.5-second dash to match the American Record first set the year before by another Tennessee State Tigerbelle, Barbara Jones. Then in the 200, Wilma rocketed around the bend and held her speed down the homestretch to come home in a World

Record 22.9, becoming the first woman ever to cover the half-lap under 23 seconds. One week later at the women's Olympic Trials, held in Abilene, Texas, Rudolph won both sprints. She equaled her fresh American Record effort of 11.5 in the 100 and clocked 23.9 in the 200. She was off to Rome to make good on that promise to win some gold medals.

Rudolph was scheduled to compete in the qualifying heats of the 100-meters on September 1; one day before, however, she wondered whether or not she could even stand up, let alone sprint. While training on August 31, Rudolph had stepped in a hole on a practice field and severely twisted an ankle.

"I cried and carried on because the ankle hurt badly and I thought it was broken and everything was down the drain," she wrote in her autobiography. "But one of the U.S. team trainers immediately put the ankle in ice and later bound it tightly and I kept it elevated the rest of the day and all night. When I got up the next morning, I put weight on it and it held. I thought, 'Thank goodness it's only a sprain. I can handle that because I don't have to run any turns.' "

Wilma easily won both her heat and quarter-final races the next day, clocking 11.5 in each contest. She won her heat by 0.3 and her quarter-final by half-a-second, clearly stamping herself as the sprinter to beat. Also, defending champion Betty Cuthbert was eliminated in the second round; she had been bothered by a leg muscle injury and was only a shadow of the dominant sprinter from four years earlier.

The semi-finals and final of the 100 were set for September 2, and after warming up for her semi, Rudolph succumbed to her nervous tension. She fell asleep under a tree. "It was a nervous reaction and not because I was relaxed," she wrote. "I told several teammates to wake me up in time for my race and to stay with me until I ran. Most often, an athlete doesn't want anyone around before a big race, but I wanted as many people around me as possible, to keep my mind off the race ahead of me."

Rudolph showed in her semi that she was ready: she zipped to an 11.3 effort to tie the World Record. She outran Italy's Giuseppina Leone by 0.3, while Great Britain's Dorothy Hyman won the second semi in 11.5 from the 11.7

of the USSR's Maria Itkina.

The final was anticlimactic in a way, as Wilma rocketed off her starting blocks and got her long legs unwound early. She pulled away from Hyman after only 20 meters and never was threatened. Wilma's 11.0 clocking was aided by a wind of 2.8-meters-per-second, over the allowable. But that hardly mattered because she was the Olympic champion. Hyman beat Leone for the silver medal as both clocked 11.3.

Wilma then got her first taste of worldwide fame: she was mobbed by reporters and wellwishers on the way to the winner's press conference. Then at the conference itself, she faced a forest of microphones and a shouting gaggle of news-papermen. "I didn't know how I could face all of that," she remembered. "I just burst into tears." After a brief period of answering questions, U.S. officials hustled away the shy, bewildered Rudolph. "One of them said to me, 'Your life will never be the same,' " she recalled. "How right he was."

The very next day, September 3, Rudolph was back on the track, contesting the qualifying heats of the 200-meters. Wilma ran in the last of the six heats and had seen Leone in heat one and Hyman in heat five clock the fastest time of 23.7. So in her heat, Rudolph churned around the curve to record 23.2, a new Olympic Record. The half-lap contestants had the next day off, but returned on September 5 for the semi-finals and final.

Rudolph again was fastest in the semis, her 23.7 out-distancing the long-limbed German Jutta Heine. Leone (24.5) won the other semi from Hyman and Itkina (both 24.6). The final was another anticlimax, almost as if the other sprinters were content to race for the silver and bronze medals after conceding the gold to Wilma. She won easily in 24.0, while Heine collared Hyman in the final 30 meters to take the silver in 24.4.

Two down, one to go. And could there be any doubt whatsoever that the United States was the heavy favorite in the 4 x 100 relay after Wilma's glorious golden double? Hardly, and the American foursome only underscored its position in the heats on September 6. The all-Tennessee State quartet of Martha Hudson, Barbara Jones, Lucinda Williams and Rudolph dashed and passed to a 44.4 clocking to lower both the World Record and the Olympic best of 44.5 run four years earlier by the Cuthbert-anchored Australian team. The Americans were only one-tenth-of-a-second slower in the final, their 44.5 taking the gold medal comfortably from Germany (44.8).

So the dream of Ed Temple had come true. Rudolph was a triple Olympic champion and a global celebrity. Wilma ended 1960 by placing second to Olympic decathlon champion Rafer Johnson in the voting for the Sullivan Award, the AAU's annual award to the nation's outstanding amateur athlete. After her 1961 season, however, Rudolph was a hands-down winner of the Sullivan.

Wilma won the national AAU 100-yard title in 10.8 seconds to earn a place on the U.S. national team which would contest three international dual meets during a whirlwind two-week visit to Europe. The first meet was the titanic confrontation with the Soviet Union, staged July 15-16 in Moscow. On the first day, Wilma sped 100-meters in 11.3 to match her own World Record set the year before in the Olympics.

Later that same day, Wilma finished off the efforts of teammates Willye White, Ernestine Pollards and Vivian Brown in the 4 x 100 relay as the U.S. squad trimmed one-tenth off the World Record with a 44.3 clocking.

Only two days later, the American team met the West Germans in Stuttgart. In the 4 x 100 relay on the meet's first day, the U.S. was disqualified after passing the baton out of the exchange zone. Wilma returned for the 100 the next day, July 19. Maybe the disqualification of the relay team had something to do with it—or maybe Wilma just felt faster than ever before.

Regardless of the reason, Rudolph dashed over the 100-meter straightaway in Stuttgart's Neckarstadion in 11.2 seconds to cut one-tenth off her own World Record. Her mark would not be equaled for more than three years and would not be bettered for four seasons.

Three days later, the U.S. team met Great Britain in London, and Wilma ran only the relay. She ended her season on a winning note as the Americans outran the British in the 4 x 110-yard relay, 45.5 to 46.3. Rudolph then was the overwhelming winner of the Sullivan Award, and also was named World Athlete Of The Year by the Associated Press.

Even though she barely was 22 years old at the height of the 1962 season, Rudolph had decided to retire after the early-July dual meet between the U.S. and USSR. The meet was scheduled for Stanford Stadium and Rudolph qualified for the American team by successfully defending her AAU title over 100 yards. It was her fourth consecutive victory—a feat yet to be matched by any American (although Evelyn Ashford won five non-consecutive titles and Stella Walsh claimed four non-consecutively).

In the Soviet dual meet, Rudolph went out a winner as she took the 100-meters (11.5) and anchored the winning American 4 x 100 team (44.6). Then it was over. She related in her autobiography, "I went over to a bench to take off my shoes. A little boy I had noticed hanging around the whole meet hoping to get an autograph was there again. But sometimes the little kids get pushed aside.

"So the little boy came over and asked me for my autograph. I told him, 'I'll go you one better than that.' I took off my shoes, signed both of them with a ballpoint pen and gave them to him. So I didn't end my career by hanging up my spikes. I gave them away."

Rudolph now lives in Indianapolis, where she heads the Wilma Rudolph Foundation, a non-profit amateur athletics program based in the city. "I have always felt it is important that I give something back to sports and to people," she said. She also is a lecturer and motivational speaker, and was named track coach at DePauw University early in 1987.

"If there is a legacy to come out of what I accomplished, it is that I give something to the youth of America," she has said. "Young people need to hear and learn positive things and those are the kinds of things I stress to children. My own life is an example of what a person can achieve, even if he or she comes from a family of 22 children and had to overcome illness and hardship.

"I stress that having self-determination is very important in life, and that athletes can provide very important lessons in that kind of self-determination. Hand-in-hand with athletics must be a strong emphasis on academic achievement. They complement each other in the attainment and maintenance of self-worth and productivity in life itself. My life is proof of that."

Rudolph and coach Ed Temple, 1977.

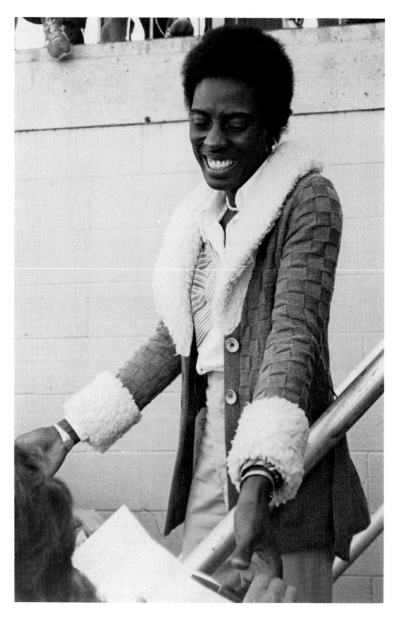

Autograph hunters caught Tyus at the 1976 Olympic Trials.

WYOMIA TYUS

Until late in the afternoon of October 15, 1968, no sprinter—man or woman—had ever successfully defended an Olympic Games crown over 100 meters. Not great men like Jesse Owens, Harrison Dillard or Bobby Morrow. Nor superb women sprinters like Fanny Blankers-Koen, Betty Cuthbert or Wilma Rudolph.

Shortly before six o'clock on that cold, rain-swept day at the '68 Mexico City Olympics, however, a tall 22-year-old American dashed into the history books. Wyomia Tyus not only sped over the metric century in 11 seconds flat to set a new World Record, she became the first sprinter ever to retain an Olympic 100 title.

And in the two decades since, Tyus has remained the only two-time champion in the history of the Olympic short dash.

Tyus was born August 29, 1945, in Griffin, Georgia, the only daughter in a family of five children. "Some of my earliest memories are playing games with my four brothers," she recalled. "Our father always encouraged me to play—and always made it clear to my brothers they better include me in whatever games they played. Otherwise, they would have to answer to him."

When Wyomia began serious sprinting in her early teens, father Willie kept up his encouragement. Any social conventions of the day which discouraged women from competing in athletics didn't wash with the strong-minded Mr. Tyus. Wyomia first made a mark on the national scene at the 1961 national AAU Girl's championships when she placed second in the 75-yard dash and third over 100 yards. The winner of the longer race was another fleet Georgian, Edith McGuire from Atlanta. The careers of Wyomia and Edith would be intertwined through the early 1960s, from their early battles in the national Girls meet to their college days at Tennessee State to their races at the '64 Tokyo Olympics.

Fortunately for both Tyus and McGuire, they competed at the national level for the Tennessee State Tigerbelle Track Club, a club formed and coached by TSU coach Ed Temple. It was one of the few well-organized women's clubs in the country and the experienced Temple had guided the careers of such sprinting luminaries as Mae Faggs, Barbara Jones, Lucinda Williams and most recently, Rome triple gold medalist Wilma Rudolph. Any young woman sprinter in the early '60s in the U.S. couldn't train under and compete for a better coach than Ed Temple.

At the 1962 AAU Girls's meet, the then-16-year-old Tyus scored a triple win over 50, 75 and 100 yards. Her times at the shorter distances of 5.8 and 8.3 were American Records, period, regardless of age classification. The next year, Wyomia was just graduated from high school when she got her first taste of international competition.

Tyus finished second to McGuire at the '63 National AAU championships as both clocked 11.0 for 100 yards. Then it was off to Europe for the annual tour with the U.S. national team. Wyomia was still 17 years old. In the four matches—versus the Soviet Union, Poland, West Germany and Great Britain—Tyus finished as the number-two American behind McGuire in every 100-meter race. She also handled the second leg on the 4 x 100-meter relay team.

It was a summer of gaining valuable experience for Tyus. She had the chance to compete against such veteran international sprinters as Maria Itkina of the USSR, Jutta Heine of West Germany and Dorothy Hyman of Britain. Heine and Hyman had won medals at the '60 Olympics behind Rudolph. By now, Tyus knew every bit of experience would be important, because the next year would culminate with the Tokyo Olympics.

Tyus had completed her frosh year at Tennessee State by the time of the 1964 national AAU outdoor meet. She was 18 years old and reversed the finish with McGuire from the '63 nationals; both sped 100 meters in 11.5, but the victory was Wyomia's. Edith won the 100 in the dual meet with the USSR several weeks later, clocking 11.5 with Wyomia one-tenth-of-a-second behind. Finally, in the August Olympic Trials just two weeks before she turned 19, Tyus placed third to earn her spot on the Tokyo team as McGuire won from Marilyn White. Their respective times were 11.3, 11.4, 11.5, all aided by a wind over the allowable limit of two-meters-per-second.

By the time the U.S. Olympic squad arrived in Tokyo in mid-October, Tyus had turned 19. If one of them was considered more of a favorite, it probably was the 20-year-old McGuire after her wins in the Soviet dual meet and the Olympic Trials.

"Coach Ed even told the press over there that he felt he had a girl to fill Wilma Rudolph's shoes," Tyus remembered. "He felt Edith would be the one to win in Tokyo, while my time would come four years later in Mexico."

As wise and experienced a coach as Temple was, he was proven wrong in Tokyo by Tyus. In her first-round qualifying heat on October 15, Wyomia sped 11.3 seconds to tie the Olympic Record set four years earlier in the Rome semifinals by Rudolph. Then in her quarter-final later the same day, Tyus showed exactly which sprinter would be the 100-meter star in Tokyo.

Wyomia sped 11.2 in her quarter-final to set a new Olympic Record—and tie the World Record. In her semifinal the next day, Wyomia was only a step behind her record-matching clocking; her 11.3 outran Poland's Ewa Klobukowska (11.4) and U.S. teammate White (11.5).

For the final later in the afternoon of October 16, Tyus drew lane 6—and with McGuire in seven and White in eight, she would have most of her prime rivals in nearby lanes. Klobukowska was across the track on the inside in lane one.

The eight sprinters were off virtually together when the starter's gun sounded, but a surge around 30 meters put Tyus into a lead she never relinquished. Even though she led by two meters at the finish tape, Wyomia dipped into the string with the lean which would become her finishing trademark. Her clocking of 11.4 easily gave her the gold medal ahead of McGuire (11.6). Klobukowska barely edged White for third, both also timing 11.6.

Tyus (r) wins the '64 Olympic 100 from teammate McGuire.

Wyomia Tyus

With the 1-2-4 finishers in the 100 (and McGuire the champion at 200 meters), the United States rightly could have been expected to rate as the favorite in the 4 x 100 relay. But Poland had both the speed and smooth baton passes and clicked to a World Record 43.6 to beat the Americans by 0.3 for the gold medal. Several years later, however, the Americans retroactively claimed the global best after Klobukowska became a *cause celebre* when she failed a sex test and all her individual and team World Records were stricken from the record books.

During the 1965 season, Tyus underscored her place among sprinting's super-elite. She first defended her national AAU title, this time over 100 yards. Then during a two-week span in July, Tyus again put her name into the log of World Records. First in Kingston, Jamaica, on July 17, Wyomia zipped over 100 yards in 10.3 to match the mark first set back in 1958 by Australia's Marlene Mathews-Willard.

Two weeks later, in the U.S.-USSR match in Kiev, Tyus sped over 100 meters in 11.1. That tied the mark set earlier in July in the same race by both Klobukowska and Irena Szewinska of Poland.

Tyus retained her national AAU 100-yard title in 1966, and added the 220-yard crown for a sprint double, even though she openly admitted she never liked running the longer distance. The next year, however, she finished only third in both sprints and in the 100 meters, up-and-coming young Barbara Ferrell served notice of her talent by matching the 11.1 World Record. Later in the summer, however, Tyus won the Pan-American Games 200 gold medal and then beat both Szewinska and Ferrell in the 100 at the dual meet between Europe and the Americas.

The 1968 Olympic season found another new, young challenger rising up in husky Oregonian Margaret Bailes. Her 11.1 at the AAU Championships beat Tyus (11.3), although Wyomia came back to cover the 200 in 23.5 and earn places on the Olympic team in both events. The Mexico Games would, like Tokyo four years earlier, be staged in mid-October—timing which somehow seemed to bring out the best in Tyus.

61

The 100-meter competition in Mexico was scheduled for October 14-15, just one day off from the timetable in Tokyo. In the first-round heats on the 14th, Tyus threw down her gauntlet to the field right away as she won the first race in 11.2 to equal her own Olympic Record. Bailes in heat two and Ferrell in heat six responded with 11.2s of their own. Szewinska clocked 11.3 in heat four and it was clear that fast times would abound thanks to the rarefied atmosphere. Mexico's 7300-foot altitude meant there was less air resistance pushing against runners and quick efforts resulted.

Later that day, the quarter-finals saw the heat turned up a notch. Ferrell was blown to an 11.1 clocking by a six-meter per second wind, three times the allowable. Tyus won the second quarter-final in 11.0 with an over-the-limit 2.7mps breeze behind her. The wind died down by the time of the third race and young Australian Raelene Boyle claimed a share of the Olympic Record with her 11.2. Boyle's glory was short-lived, however, as Szewinska blazed 11.1 in the fourth race to equal the World Record and set a new Olympic mark.

Overnight, torrential rains doused Mexico, but the rain had let up by the time of the mid-afternoon semi-finals in the 100. Szewinska clocked 11.3 to take the first race from Ferrell (also 11.3). The downpour returned as the sprinters took their marks for the second semi, but Tyus sped through the rain to win in 11.3, with Boyle second (11.4) and Bailes third (11.5).

The rains had again stopped by the time of the final, set for 5:50 p.m. Tyus, Bailes and Ferrell drew lanes 3-4-5, with Boyle in 2 and Szewinska in 7. The tension was palpable as the eight finalists stood behind their starting blocks—so what did Tyus do to cope with the pressure? She danced.

"Up in the stands, the athletes from Jamaica and Trinidad were playing tambourines and bongos. We could hear all that going on, and I just got into the enthusiasm of the crowd," Tyus related to Scott Ostler of the *Los Angeles Times*. So Wyomia loosened up with some steps of a current dance. Spectators, officials and even fellow athletes looked askance at Tyus' antics; some even wondered if she was making some sort of black power protest, like those which had occurred after several men's events.

But Tyus was just trying to stave off the crushing tension in the moments before the field of eight settled into their starting blocks. Ferrell false-started, then Tyus herself got away early on the second start. At the third crack of the starting gun, the group sprang as one off the line, but Tyus inched to the lead after only a few strides. And she just kept going. Her margin was two feet at the finish, but Tyus took no chances and dipped just before the finish in case there were any foes breathing down her neck.

There weren't as Tyus crossed the line in a World Record 11.0, which was automatically timed at 11.08, also the fastest ever. Ferrell followed ahead of Szewinska, both clocked in 11.1, and Boyle finished fourth also in 11.1. Imagine poor Boyle: matching the old global best and having nothing to show for it. Bailes clocked 11.3 for fifth place. Such was the class of the field which had been dominated by Tyus.

Tyus related to Ostler, "I can see it in my mind like it was yesterday. We came out of the blocks, I could hear the crowd cheering and all that. But my main thought was, 'Stay relaxed and lean at the finish.' It's amazing all the things that went through my mind in 11 seconds. I had time to say to myself, 'Gosh, you got a good start. Now you gotta go; you *gotta* go. Stay relaxed and keep your knees up. Don't tighten up at 90 meters because Szewinska will be coming. She always comes on at the end, so that's where you have to be your strongest.' "

The rain which had held off during the race—darkening the skies over the *Stadio Olimpico* with roiling, threatening clouds—unleashed its full fury during the awards ceremony for Tyus. She received her second gold medal in a torrent, and as she watched the Stars and Stripes run up the flagpole and heard the "Star-Spangled Banner" played in honor of her victory, she wiped away both tears of joy and the rainwater which cascaded down her cheeks.

There was time only for two days rest before Wyomia had to return for the heats and semi-finals of the 200 meters. Just before Tyus' appearance in the fourth heat, Boyle had matched the Olympic Record of 23.0 in heat two, and Ferrell sped a new record of 22.9 in heat three. Tyus cruised 23.4 to take her heat; odds-on favorite Irena Szewinska also easily won her heat with 23.2.

In the first semi, Boyle matched the Olympic best of 22.9, with Tyus second at 23.1 and Szewinska third with 23.2. Ferrell responded in the second semi with another Olympic Record of 22.8, a clocking matched by young Aussie Jennifer Lamy. Margaret Bailes clocked 22.9 in third place, so all three Americans qualified for the next day's final.

For the first 100-meters of the final, it looked like Tyus was gunning for a double victory. She blasted the curve and led Boyle into the homestretch, with Szewinska and Ferrell equal third. But then Tyus' stride shortened as she began to tire and the field swept past her. Szewinska went on to win in a World Record 22.5, from Boyle (22.7), Lamy (22.8), and Ferrell (22.9). Tyus clocked 23.0 for sixth place, one-tenth ahead of Bailes in seventh.

Forty-eight hours later, Tyus, Ferrell and Bailes were joined by Mildrette Netter for the heats of the 4 x 100 relay. As in Tokyo four years before, the U.S. looked to be the favorite since the 1-2-5 finishers from the 100 handled the first three stints and Tyus, of course, anchored. Passing on U.S. relay teams traditionally tends to be indifferent at best, since team members work with each other on baton exchanges for only a short time. European teams often consisted of the same members for several years, thus exchanges were much more polished.

But in heat one, the U.S. clicked and set a World Record of 43.4. A surprise in the second heat came from the unheralded Dutch, who matched the 43.4 clocking. In the final, though, the Americans ran away and hid from the field. Despite one terrible exchange—leadoff runner Ferrell overran the slow-starting Bailes, who took the stick while virtually standing still—the U.S. team passed well enough.

Besides, the Americans had leg speed to burn—and burn they did, to a World Record 42.8. Cuba was a far-back second (43.3), while the USSR matched the old record of 43.4 in third. Holland and Australia also ran 43.4, but all they got for it was fourth and fifth place.

After her golden efforts in Mexico, Tyus announced her retirement and she stayed retired until 1974. Early that year, she returned to the sprint wars of the newly-established International Track Association professional circuit. She ran with ITA for two seasons, clocking a 100-yard best both years of 10.3 and a fastest 100-meters of 11.3 in 1975. When the pro circuit folded in 1976, Tyus retired again, this time for good.

In looking back on her climactic year of 1968, Tyus commented, "Even after winning the Olympic 100 in 1964, I felt that '68 really would be my best year. I was very confident and in great shape. I was very fortunate to go through my entire career without suffering a major injury.

"I was completely loose that day of the 100 final in Mexico. All of my thoughts were positive; there was nothing negative about it to me. I felt that the gold medal was just there waiting for me. A lot of other athletes were shooting for it, but I just had the belief that it was *mine.* I never told anyone how I felt, but deep inside, I felt that it was my race and my medal and I just had to go get them. I did, and that was a wonderful feeling."

Szewinska: an athlete for the ages.

IRENA SZEWINSKA

For much of her career, Irena Szewinska of Poland was known as "The Queen of the Track." It would be so simple just to list the seven medals she won while competing in five consecutive Olympic Games. Or the 10 medals she won in four European Championships appearances. No woman ever has won more medals in either of those supremely important championship tests than Szewinska.

Or one could talk about the eight individual World Records she set, plus another equaled and one relay mark set, during an international career which stretched from 1964 through 1980. Or that she was the first woman ever to set World Records at all three sprint distances (100, 200 and 400 meters).

That was the greatness of Irena Szewinska which was easy to observe and a privilege to witness. But there also was another side to Szewinska, and perhaps it is best revealed by those who knew her, loved her and competed against her.

Said Australia's Raelene Boyle, second to Szewinska in the 1968 Olympic 200 meters, "Irena was a model athlete: aggressive, determined, she knew what she had to do and how to achieve it. She worked very hard, yet off the track, she was perfectly charming: quiet, easy to talk with, a lovely person. I just wish I had her *talent.*"

Renate Stecher of East Germany won both sprints at the 1972 Munich Olympics, defeating Boyle and Szewinska over the 200. "Irena was my idol when I was a youngster," Stecher commented. "I had read of her great competitions in Tokyo and Mexico City, but I never dreamed that one day I would compete in the same race with her, let alone beat her. Irena Szewinska is the model for all sportsmen and sportswomen who aspire to compete in the Olympic Games."

Gerard Mach was Poland's national sprint coach during

the early years of Szewinska's career. Of her single-minded tenacity in training, he once observed, "She trains only to win. She not only knows what she is doing, but why she is doing it."

Of his wife of some 20 years, Janusz Szewinski has said, "She is a very quiet, pensive sort of person. Sometimes it is difficult to guess what she is thinking. But in spite of all her successes, she has managed to keep a balance in her life."

Even when she was the premier woman track and field athlete in the world, Irena Szewinska maintained a wonderfully well-rounded life. Her sport didn't push out other important facets of her being: as a wife; as a mother to her young son Andrzej; as a student while obtaining her graduate degree in economics and now in her career as an economist with the Institute of Economic Transport in Warsaw; or even today as a member of the Women's Committee of the International Amateur Athletic Federation, track and field's worldwide governing body. Even now that she has moved to the administrative side of the sport, she continues to contribute to the advancement of track—just as she did so brilliantly when she was a peerless competitor.

Szewinska was born Irena Kirzenstein on May 24, 1946, to Polish parents in the Soviet city of Leningrad. When she was still quite young, her family moved back to Poland. She was a quiet, studious youngster who took no interest in any sort of athletics until her early teens. Her mother recalls having to force Irena out of the house just to take a walk. Her mother added a telling afterthought: "I also remember that Irena never walked to school—she always ran."

Irena first competed around age 15, and by the age of 17 she was winning national Junior titles. That was in 1963 and her talents caught the eye of Polish national coach Andrzej Piotrowski. "I saw hundreds of girls compete," Piotrowski recalled, "but I felt only a couple of them had the abilities to try to make Poland's Olympic team for the Tokyo Games the next year. There was only one I *knew* could do it: Irena. She had a persistence to reach goals she had set for herself."

Irena trained long and hard with Piotrowski and was

chosen to represent Poland in the 200 meters, the long jump and as a member of the 4 x 100-meter relay. The Tokyo Olympic Games would be the first international competition of her life.

Even at the age of 18, Irena acquitted herself brilliantly. In the long jump, contested on October 14, "I hoped to just make the finals," she later admitted. Szewinska did better than that. She moved to second place in the competition with her jump of 21'1¼"/6.43 in the second round of jumping. That put her ahead of Tatyana Shchelkanova, the World Record holder at 21'11¾"/6.70. Great Britain's Mary Rand paced the competition with her opening-round leap of 21'7½"/6.59.

Then in the fifth round, Rand sailed out to 22'2¼"/6.76 for a new World Record. Irena showed she was nothing but competitive as she responded with 21'8"/6.60, her best of the competition (and just 2¾" shy of her lifetime best). So international newcomer Irena Szewinska won the silver medal—and the track and field world would see her on many more victory rostrums before her career was over.

"It was thrilling to be in my first Olympic competition," Irena remembered. "Then to place second, win a silver medal and defeat the former World Record holder. . . it was more than I ever would have dared to dream."

But her Olympics were far from over. Next came the 200 meters. Favored over the half-lap distance was the young American Edith McGuire, who earlier had placed second in the 100 to teammate Wyomia Tyus. McGuire lived up to her billing as she set an Olympic Record of 23.0 seconds to win from Szewinska and Marilyn Black of Australia, both of whom also bettered the previous Games best with their clockings of 23.1.

With sprint gold medalists Tyus and McGuire on the team, the United States could naturally have been expected to run away with the 4 x 100 relay. But the smooth-passing Polish quartet, with Szewinska handling the second leg down the backstretch of the one-lap race, had speed aplenty. Despite a damp track, Poland clocked 43.6 seconds to come home well under the 44.3 World Record. The runner-up U.S. team (43.9) and third-place Great Britain (44.0) also beat the former record.

So Irena Szewinska came home from her first Olympics with a gold medal, two silvers and recognition as one of the world's brightest new young stars on the track. Her performances in following seasons confirmed her position as one of the sport's superstars. Irena enrolled at the University of Warsaw in 1965 to study economics, and set the first two of her individual World Records. She clocked 11.1 in the 100 meters and 22.7 over the 200. In the latter race, Szewinska defeated American McGuire in the U.S.-Poland international meet—and Irena also contributed victories in the 100, long jump and 4 x 100 relay to Poland's point production.

In 1966, Szewinska competed in her first European Championships; in Budapest, she won the 200 and long jump and ran on the winning 4 x 100 team, plus finished second in the 100. She ranked first in the world in the 200, repeating her top placing from the previous year. And she rated No. 1 in the long jump and second in the 100. In 1967, she topped the ratings in all three events.

But the most significant event of 1967 for Irena came off the track: after a five-year courtship which began when they met at a sports club, Irena Kirzenstein married Janusz Szewinski on Christmas Day. But even while adding the responsibilities of family life to the rigors of her academic work, Irena was equally as determined to train for the 1968 Olympic Games in Mexico City.

Szewinska planned to compete in both sprints, plus the long jump and sprint relay. "Training was difficult because I had to split my time among several events," Szewinska told American writer Bud Greenspan. "I was not like other girls who could concentrate on just one event. But I felt ready by the time of the Games, prepared to meet what I knew would be stiff competition."

But her first competition in Mexico rocked Szewinska with a major disappointment: she failed to qualify for the finals of the long jump. Irena rebounded in the 100, however, matching the World Record of 11.1 seconds in her quarterfinal, which also set a new Olympic Record. For the final, she knew she would have to get a perfect start because another sprinter was in the race who was just as motivated to win as was Szewinska. American Wyomia Tyus was trying to become the first 100-meter champion, man or woman, to win the short dash in successive Olympics.

Szewinska didn't get the good start she needed; Tyus did, and led U.S. teammate Barbara Ferrell and Szewinska at the halfway mark. Irena closed fast on Ferrell, but neither of them could collar the flying Tyus, who crossed the line in a World Record of 11.08 to defend her title. Ferrell clocked 11.15 in second place, ahead of the 11.19 which gave Szewinska third place and the bronze medal.

"After the 100, I was more determined than ever to run my best and win the 200 meters," Szewinska recalled. And Irena rolled, despite another mediocre start. The extra length of the 200 compared to the 100 allowed Szewinska's long legs to unwind—and rev up. She blasted the World Record down to 22.58, comfortably ahead of the Australian duo of Raelene Boyle (22.74), and Jennifer Lamy (22.88). American Ferrell placed fourth (22.93), while 100 champ Tyus ran out of gas after a strong start and placed only 6th (23.08).

Szewinska's final competition in Mexico, the 4 x 100-meter relay, produced another disappointment: after a ragged exchange on the second pass, Irena herself dropped the baton and Poland didn't finish its qualifying race. The United States team went on to win the final in a World Record 42.87, with anchor runner Tyus thus claiming her second gold medal of the Games.

The inevitable post-Olympic letdown hit Szewinska after the intense preparation and competition for the Mexico Olympics. She concentrated more on her studies in 1969 than on training and competing, yet she had good enough seasons to world rank first in the long jump (a best for the year of 21'6¼"), second in the 200 (23.0 best) and sixth in 100 (11.3 best). Her season was short compared to previous years—but for the best possible reason. Irena was expecting. Son Andrzej arrived in February, 1970, so yet another ball was added to Szewinska's already-considerable juggling act in life.

As 1971 began, Szewinska looked toward the European Championships, scheduled for August in Helsinki, Finland. She began strenuous training under a new coach, Gerard

Mach, and often trained with men sprinters and 400-meter runners. Thus, she worked to develop the strength she knew she would need to carry her through the Munich Olympics in 1972.

Coming back after childbirth was tough work, even for an athlete as determined as Szewinska. After the Helsinki Europeans, Szewinska knew she still had a ways to go. Irena placed third in the 200, fifth in the long jump and sixth in the 100. Before Helsinki, she commented, "While I was recovering from the baby's birth, many of my competitors continued to train and improve. The level of competition moved higher."

She knew Munich would be tough. It was not made any easier when she suffered an ankle injury several weeks before the Games. Then, while she was warming up for the long jump qualifying round at the Olympics, Szewinska felt the injury flare back up. She had to face the bitter reality: withdraw from the long jump if she wanted to have any chance in the sprints.

Irena finished second in both her qualifying heat and quarterfinal round races in the Olympic 100, but then suffered more disappointment by finishing sixth in her semi-final and out of the final. East German Stecher dashed a World Record 11.07 to take the gold medal in the climactic race.

Like Mexico four years earlier, Szewinska was left with the 200 as her final chance to salvage some respectibility out of the Munich debacle. The hurt ankle continued to plague her, but Szewinska's mighty effort netted her third place, barely. Irena sprinted 22.74 to just nose out East Germany's Ellen Streidt (22.75) for third. Stecher won her second sprint title with another World Record (22.40), while Boyle (22.45) again finished second.

Any athlete could have retired contented after compiling a career like Szewinska's. But after Munich, Irena still had the nagging feeling that her deepest athletic potential remained untapped. She looked for a new challenge.

The 1974 season would culminate with another European Championships, this one scheduled for Rome's *Stadio*

Olimpico in late August. Szewinska had already made a major adjustment in training: Mach had emigrated to Canada and there wasn't another coach in Poland with his experience to be able to plan Irena's training.

So, Irena and Janusz talked it over for quite some time before arriving at their decision: Janusz would supervise Irena's training. "I was nervous at first," admitted Szewinski, a sports photographer by profession. "I had been just an adequate athlete myself [personal best of 53.4 in the 400-meter hurdles], I had never come close to setting a World Record or competing in the Olympics."

Irena gave her husband more credit than he gave to himself: "Janusz competed in the 400 hurdles, a very demanding event. And he studied physical education and knew how to develop scientific approaches to training and competition which would be the most effective. I always had complete confidence in his guidance."

Her results early in 1974 showed the husband-wife team was doing something right. On June 13, Irena regained the World Record over 200 meters, slicing the mark down to 22.21 in East Germany. After the race, Janusz was asked the inevitable question: might Irena concentrate on the 400 and could she break the big barrier in the event of 50 seconds?

Janusz replied, almost casually, "Absolutely no problem." Irena had run the first 400 of her career in September of 1973, a 52.0. The second one-lapper of her life came in 1974, in Warsaw's Kusocinski Memorial meet on June 22.

If there ever was any doubt where the next challenges for Szewinska could be found, Irena dispelled them with her stunning run: 49.9 seconds to slash 1.1 seconds off the World Record and leave the 50-second barrier a memory. Irena rocketed the first 200 in a stunning 22.9 seconds and even though she faded in the second half of the distance, she nevertheless opened up a whole new era for women's one-lap sprinting.

"I knew I was fully capable of getting under the World Record of 51.0," Irena said. "But the 49.9 still surprised me. And I don't plan to run another 400 for a while. I want to concentrate on the two sprints and both relays at the European Championships."

In Rome, Szewinska was stellar. Twice she faced '72 Olympic champion Renate Stecher. In the 100, Szewinska scored her first-ever European title with an 11.13 dash, which turned back the quick-starting Stecher (11.23) by a full tenth-of-a-second, a wide margin in any sprint race. At twice the distance, Stecher again started fast and ran a hard curve to enter the homestretch with a lead of three meters.

But the Irena Szewinska of 1974 was—incredibly—a Szewinska like no one had ever seen before. Irena turned on the power just after the sprinters came out of the curve, collared Stecher and sped away to win in 22.51, ahead of the 22.68 by the East German. Notably, the race was run *into* a headwind of almost three meters per second.

Irena carried Poland to third place in the 4 x 100 relay, but perhaps her most breathtaking performance didn't win any medal. Poland was next-to-last in the eight-team race at the final pass in the 4 x 400-meter relay—so Irena proceeded to scorch a 48.6 for her anchor circuit, the fastest ever run by a woman up to then. She brought Poland up to fourth place— besides raising her legendary status a notch or two in the process.

All in all, during 1974, Szewinska won all 23 of her races over 100 meters, won 19 of 20 at 200 (losing only one qualifying heat), set the 400 World Record and was the unquestionable star of the European Championships. She was named Athlete of the Year in every major poll, including *Track & Field News* and *Women's Track & Field World* in the U.S. and *Athletics Weekly* in England.

"In years before the 1974 season, I never had good training in the spring," Szewinska commented. "But early in '74 I had the best training of my life. Plus I did special work for the 200, which also helped me in the 100. Next, I had to decide between running the 200 or the 400 at Montreal."

The schedule for the 1976 Olympics in the Canadian city would not permit Irena to double in the 200 and 400. She would have to make a choice. She ran the 400 well enough in 1975 to retain her No. 1 World Ranking, although Stecher edged her out for the top spot in the 200.

"Before I learned of the conflict in the schedule, I felt

confident that I could perform well in both events," Szewinska reflected. "But having to choose just one event made me worry that I wouldn't have anything to fall back on."

In considering the choice, Szewinska had the added knowledge that 18-year-old Christine Brehmer of East Germany had lowered the 400 World Record to 49.77 in May of 1976. A month later, Irena herself reclaimed the record with 49.75. It would be a classic confrontation: the experienced veteran vs. the rising new face. Irena and Janusz decided in late June: the 400 it would be.

"Once the decision was made, I was very excited," Szewinska told Greenspan. But in Montreal, Szewinska's efforts in the first two rounds of qualifying raised same questions about her status. She ran a sluggish third in her qualifying heat; in the quarterfinals, with the first four finishers in each of five races moving on to the semifinals, she clocked only 52.00 to place 4th and barely advance.

But Szewinska was nothing but clever. Janusz had told her to run slowly on purpose. "He told me to ease through the qualifying races. There would be four rounds and there was no need to run fast in the early ones," Irena said. In her semi, Szewinska came alive, cutting the Olympic Record to 50.48. Brehmer finished an easy second in the other semi behind American Rosalyn Bryant. The stage was set for the final.

Szewinska drew lane 4 for the final on July 29; Brehmer was inside her in lane 2. So the East German could try to cover any moves made by Irena. Brehmer ran a fast 23.3 for the first half of the race, while Szewinska's low-slung strides brought her past the 200 in 23.5. Irena didn't take full command until 90 meters remained, but once she gained the front, she was off to the races.

She hit the line in 49.29 to blast nearly half-a-second off her own World Record and leave Brehmer (50.51) almost 1½ seconds back. A more commanding, crushing victory wasn't to be found anywhere in women's races in Montreal. "That race was very important to me because everything came together perfectly: the gold medal and the World Record," Szewinska said. She had her third Olympic gold medal and she won it at age 30 to become the oldest winner in women's

Szewinska allows a smile after taking the 1976 Olympic 400.

track at Montreal. She also had become the only woman to win medals at four successive Olympics, and at *five* different events, to boot.

Was Irena now content? Hardly. In 1977, at the age of 31, she again ranked first in the world over both the 200 and 400. Her crowning moment—perhaps of her career—came when she stepped forward as captain of the European Select team to accept the winner's trophy at the inaugural World Cup. On the track in Dusseldorf, Szewinska won both the 200 and 400. She beat Montreal Olympic winner Barbel Eckert over the shorter distance, and East Germany's rising 400 star Marita Koch at the longer.

The next year, however, at the 1978 European Championships in Prague, Koch provided unquestionable proof that Szewinska's skein as The Queen of the Track was finally unraveling. The East German, then just 21, won the continental title in 48.94, her third World Record clocking of the year. Teammate Brehmer just edged Szewinska for second, 50.38 to 50.40. The defeat marked the first 400 loss for Szewinska, after chalking up 34 consecutive wins dating back to her debut in late 1973.

The 1979 edition of the World Cup brought Irena back to Montreal's *Stade Olympique*, the scene of her brilliant Olympic 400 three years before. But Koch again held the upper hand as Szewinska finished third, also trailing the USSR's Maria Pinigina.

And suddenly, the Olympic Games had come back around, the 1980 version to be staged in Moscow. Although hurt by a boycott of western nations, the Games still saw Koch meet the challenge of all comers, the East German taking the gold medal in an Olympic Record 48.88 ahead of the emerging Czech Jarmila Kratochvilova (49.46).

In an ironic twist, Szewinska had finished last in her semi-final after pulling a muscle during the race. Four years earlier, the same fate had befallen Koch in Montreal; she pulled a muscle in her quarter-final. That injury kept her out of the semi-final won by Szewinska.

This time, the handwriting on the wall was too clear for Szewinska to ignore. She was 34 years old, the younger challengers were faster than ever and the inevitable had arrived. It was time to retire. Szewinska's last competition came in Tokyo at the Eight Nations meet. In a way, her career had come full circle, ending in Tokyo where she had first appeared on the international stage some 16 years earlier in her first Olympics.

In 1983, after setting World Records at both the 400 and 800 and winning World Championships titles at each distance, Kratochvilova commented, "My first hero was Irena Szewinska. I learned from her that being 30 years old doesn't mean being over the hill in terms of athletic ability."

An American observer wrote that Szewinska's impact on the sport "cannot be counted just in the medals she won or the records she set. She thrives on the joy, the beauty and the exhilaration of sport." And a British journalist commented, "Even after Szewinska had to yield to a new generation, she continued to demonstrate those qualitites of modesty and ability that set a standard for all to follow."

The last word goes to Irena herself. "Often during my career, I was asked if I ever got enough of track and field," she said. "I always answered with a curt, 'No.' The sport is my passion; I am never tired of it or from it. It brings me untold joy and pleasure."

RUTH FUCHS

It wasn't the usual place to find an athlete who had, only an hour earlier, successfully defended her own Olympic championship. Nevertheless, there stood Ruth Fuchs—on a traffic island in the middle of a busy Montreal street.

She stood all alone, notable enough for an athlete from an Eastern Bloc nation and especially one from East Germany. Eastern athletes often are shepherded everywhere by watchful team officials, even on a simple walk from the Olympic Stadium across a crowded thoroughfare to the Olympic Village nearby.

But there stood Ruth—out by herself, just as she was in her specialty, the javelin.

Up to that moment, a late July day in 1976, Fuchs had won the 1972 and '76 Olympic javelin gold medals, the '74 European title, and she had set four World Records and been ranked Number One in the world the previous four years. Her superiority in throwing the 600-gram (1.32 lb.) spear had made her as isolated far ahead of her competition as she appeared to be marooned on the traffic island, surrounded by Montreal motorists.

Then, a couple of American track fans joined her on the island. One recognized Fuchs and extended a hand to offer congratulations. "Sehr gut," he said in rudimentary German. Fuchs looked surprised for a moment, probably as much that she had been addressed in her native language by a total stranger, as that stranger had recognized her in the first place.

She smiled tightly and stiffly returned the handshake. Then she noticed the sign to walk was green and she briskly turned and strode across the street. For a moment, though, Fuchs standing on that traffic island summed up her position in the javelin world: out by herself, far away from her competition.

Fuchs: she threw the javelin like Zeus hurling thunderbolts.

Ruth Fuchs

Fuchs began throwing the javelin in 1960, at the age of 14. Born in Egeln, she was a schoolgirl in the East German city of Jena—famed for the scientific instruments manufactured in the renowned Carl Zeiss factory—and was coached virtually from the beginning by Karl Hellmann.

After she won the 1974 European title in Rome, Fuchs was asked if it was easy to learn to throw the spear. "Well, I have been throwing the javelin for 14 years," she replied. "I believe I *might* finally be getting the idea of it."

Throughout her career, Fuchs worked diligently to perfect her technique. Results in the javelin can be among the most inconsistent in track and field, precisely because the slightest variance in technique can spell the difference between a soaring throw that rides the air currents out to record distances, and a throw that rises high out of the thrower's hand, stalls out and plummets to the ground far too early.

Fuchs first emerged onto the world javelin stage when she improved from 168'4"/51.30 in 1966 to 184'0"/56.08 in '67 and 189'4"/57.70 in '68. She approached 200 feet in 1970 as she reached 198'10"/60.60, but it was not until the 1971 European Championships in Helsinki that Fuchs made her first appearance in a major championships.

She placed third at Helsinki and duplicated her second place in the '70 World Rankings in the 1971 ratings. But that was the last time in the decade of the 1970s that any other javelin thrower would rank ahead of Fuchs.

By mid-June in the Olympic year of 1972, the javelin best was the longest-surviving women's field event World Record. Global bests in the high jump, shot put and discus had been bettered the previous year, while the long jump mark had been extended in 1970.

But the javelin record stubbornly remained at the 204'9"/62.40 thrown by Yelena Gorchakova of the USSR in the qualifying round at the 1964 Tokyo Olympics. Gorchakova had returned the next day and placed only third in the final, but her record had survived—until June 11, 1972.

On that day, Gorchakova's record was bettered not once, but twice. First, Poland's Ewa Gryziecka threw 205'8"/62.70 in Bucharest, Romania. The Pole's glory was short-

81

lived, however, thanks to Ruth Fuchs.

Throwing in Potsdam less than an hour after Gryziecka had set her mark, Fuchs pummeled the World Record by hurling her spear 213'5"/65.06. It was the largest single improvement in the javelin World Record since women's records were first officially ratified, beginning in 1927.

Plus, she had another throw in her six-throw series of 207'0"/63.10. Either way, Fuchs was the World Record holder—and her run into the history books had begun.

Every time she threw her javelin a long distance, Ruth Fuchs loved to run out and retrieve her spear—after making certain that she was off the runway and her throw was completely valid. No stepping over the white end line for Fuchs, and thereby fouling her effort.

But in the one meet in which she *really* wanted to race after her flying javelin, efficient officials prevented her. "I just wanted my javelin as a souvenir," Fuchs said after she had won her first Olympic gold medal. She had been in command almost from the start of the competition in Munich. She took the lead in the second round with a throw of 197'6/60.20, ahead of the opening effort by 18-year-old American Kate Schmidt of 196'8"/59.94. Ruth improved in round 4 to 200'8"/61.16 and then in the fifth round hit an Olympic Record of 209'7"/63.88 to better Gorchakova's then-World Record from Tokyo.

It was only after she had collected her gold medal that Ruth revealed she had injured an ankle earlier in the summer. She had been running after a javelin. But all was right in Munich for Fuchs, just as it would be throughout the decade of the '70s virtually whenever she threw.

In 1973, Fuchs lengthened her own global record to 216'10"/66.10. In 1974, though, she combined a record throw with a major victory: her heave of 220'6"/67.22 gave her the European title. Teammate Jacqueline Hein, who also had finished second to Ruth in Munich, finished more than 16 feet behind for the silver medal.

Fuchs crowned her 1975 campaign by easily winning the European Cup. Then it was the Olympic year of 1976, and Fuchs again demonstrated her immense talent to reach her peak precisely in time for the biggest competition.

On July 14 in East Berlin, Fuchs armed 226'9"/69.12 to extend her own World Record yet again. And exactly two weeks later in Montreal, she never gave the other throwers even the slightest chance to challenge for her Olympic crown.

It was expected that American Schmidt could possibly mount a challenge to Fuchs. Schmidt had thrown 218'3"/ 66.52 before the Games to become the second-longest thrower in history. And West Germany's Marion Becker had claimed the Olympic Record in the Montreal qualifying round by throwing 213'8"/65.12.

Fuchs was the seventh thrower in the competitive order for the final, and she made seven her lucky number by regaining her Olympic Record with her opening toss of 216'4"/65.94. That was the battle, and the war, as Fuchs' third-round mark of 213'5"/65.06 also outdistanced the best offered by either Becker (212'3"/64.70) or Schmidt (209'10"/63.96). Fuchs had become the only woman in Olympic history ever to successfully defend a javelin title.

"I was overjoyed to win twice in a row," Fuchs reflected. "But Montreal was harder on me than it might have appeared. There always was an air of uncertainty throughout the competition: would my first throw hold up? I was especially concerned whenever Schmidt threw. But in the end, it all worked out."

Fuchs had a habit of making results "work out," thanks to her maturity and experience. In 1977, she won the European Cup again, just missing her own World Record as she reached 226'1"/68.92. She also won the inaugural World Cup.

Shortly after that Dusseldorf meet, however, Schmidt stunned the track world with a global mark of her own, 227'5"/69.32. The next year, Fuchs concentrated on defending her European title and in Prague, her concentration was impeccable. She threw a European Record 226'11"/ 69.16 to beat runner-up Tessa Sanderson of Britain by nearly 22 feet.

The 1979 season saw Fuchs regain the World Record when she threw 228'1"/69.52 that June. Two months later, she defended her World Cup title. And as the decade came to a close, her greatness brought another honor: *Track & Field News* selected her as the women's Athlete of the Decade for the 1970s, ahead of such superstars as Soviet discus thrower Faina Myelnik, East German sprinter Renate Stecher, Polish sprinter Irena Szewinska and East German high jumper Rosemarie Ackermann. A decade like Fuchs' was unbeatable: two Olympic titles, a pair of European golds, five World Records, and eight consecutive number one World Rankings. Indeed, Fuchs has found consistency in the most inconsistent of events.

Early in 1980, moreover, Fuchs indicated that she would be every bit as tough to unseat as Olympic champion at the Moscow Games. At the end of April, Fuchs upped her World Record for a sixth time, edging the closest yet to the event's next barriers of 70-meters (229'8") and 230-feet with her heave of 229'6"/69.96. She went to Moscow a solid favorite for her third Olympic crown.

But Fuchs injured her back shortly before the Games and no amount of talent can overcome such a debilitating injury. Fuchs was the second-longest thrower in the qualifying round with 210'10"/64.26, but East German teammate Ute Richter claimed Ruth's Olympic Record by throwing 218'8"/66.66.

Fuchs drew the lead-off position in the order for the final, an enviable position since a long opening throw would force the rest of the field to play catch-up. Fuchs managed only 196'6"/59.90 on her first throw; the very next thrower, Saida Gunba of the USSR, hurled 216'9"/66.06 and it was clear Fuchs was in for a long day.

An exponent of the Fuchs theory of getting a big first throw to force everyone else to catch you was Cuba's Maria Colon. So Colon opened with an Olympic Record 224'5"/68.40 as the 10th thrower in the order. All the other throwers tried to catch up after that, including Fuchs.

But none could, and the 22-year-old Colon was Olympic champion. Fuchs reached 201'8"/61.46 in the third round and then got her best of the day, 209'9"/63.94, in the fifth. That placed her eighth, far from a crowning end to a briliant career.

Fuchs faced facts, though. She had been training and

competing for two decades. She had compiled a career second to none in any event. Her injury would require a long period of recovery and rehabilitation, and even then there was no absolute assurance she would return to 100% health and strength.

So Fuchs retired at the end of the 1980 season. The mantle was passed to a new generation of javelin throwers— but whether anyone can ever approach Fuchs' career achievements remains to be seen.

Fuchs remained involved and influential in her sport, though, serving in various capacities with the East German track federation and eventually gaining appointment to the Women's Committee of track and field's world governing body, the International Amateur Athletic Federation. Once a mover and shaker on the competitive arena, Fuchs today is active in the policy-making and developmental aspects of the sport.

Fuchs once commented, "I always went into a competition with a specific distance in mind that I felt I would need to throw to win that competition. So my objectives always were clear. There were times, though, when I threw a record and really surprised myself."

Throughout her stellar career, though, Fuchs came to typify excellence through consistency. But she hardly was an unfeeling automaton, either. "I would sprint after my javelin to express my joy," she said. She gave herself plenty of opportunities for happiness.

Stecher won 6 medals in the Olympic dashes and sprint relay.

RENATE STECHER

After scoring victories in the 100-meters, 200-meters and as the anchor runner on her 4 x 100-meter relay squad, East German teenager Petra Vogt was rightly viewed as the star of the 1969 European Championships. Only 18, Vogt had rushed to the front of the band of youngsters looking to supplant such veteran East German sprint stars as Karin Balzer and Ingrid Tiedtke.

Running second to Vogt in the 200, as well as handling the second leg down the backstretch in the 4 x 100, was another teenager, 19-year-old Renate Meissner. Her thickly-muscled legs and low-slung arm action wasn't stylish, but nonetheless produced a quick turnover of powerful sprinting strides by the youngster from Jena.

While Vogt lorded over the continent's best sprinters in 1969, it was a short-lived supremacy. Less than a year later, Vogt—and the world—had been overtaken and surpassed by the churning power of the now-married Renate Stecher. It would be well into the decade of the 1970s—after a pair of Olympic Games, another two European Championships and numerous World Records—before the world's sprinters would catch Stecher.

Renate Stecher actually was a more-established sprinter than Petra Vogt when the both of them broke through internationally at the 1969 Europeans. Renate, born May 12, 1950 in Suptitz, had her first season of serious competition in 1963 at the age of 13 when she ran 12.9 seconds for 100-meters. From the beginning of her running career, she was coached by Horst-Dieter Hille—who later would direct some of East Germany's (and the world's) finest sprinters, such as Barbel Wockel, Marlies Gohr and Ingrid Auerswald.

Three years later, the 16-year-old Renate made her international debut at the European Junior Games, the forerunner of the continental Junior Championships. Stecher won a gold medal as a member of the 4 x 100-meter relay team. She also cut her 100 best to 12.0 and first attempted the 200, recording a personal low of 24.9 seconds.

At the 1968 version of the European Junior Games, Renate won a pair of silver medals in the sprints, thanks to career-best performances of 11.6 and 23.9. She claimed a third silver award on the 4 x 100 team. By this time, coach Hille realized that Stecher could be a viable force at the full-scale European Championships in Athens the following year. So the coach set about to methodically plan Renate's training and competition for 1969 so she would reach a mini-peak at the selection races for the East German team and then so she would reach her all-out best at the title meet itself.

But that age-old bugaboo of all athletes—injury—hobbled Renate during the crucial preparation time before the selection meets. Her leg ailment kept Stecher out of her national championships, where young Vogt signalled the rise of a new generation of sprinters in East Germany with her national record dash of 11.3 seconds, barely ahead of the veteran sprinter-hurdler Balzer.

Just a few days before the East German team was to leave for Athens, Renate had regained enough strength and conditioning to be able to run in a special trial race over 200 meters. Her personal best time of 23.3 seconds secured her a ticket to Athens, and when Balzer suffered a slight leg muscle strain and decided to concentrate solely on defending her title in the hurdles, Stecher was deputized into the sprint relay. So it was that Renate claimed her silver medal in the 200 and gold in the 4 x 100.

In the first year of the 1970s, Stecher set about producing the performances which would make her the top sprinter of that decade. Indoors, she went undefeated and won the European Indoor Championships 60-meters, her first of three successive victories in the indoor dash. She also took time to marry 400-meter hurdler Gerd Stecher.

During the outdoor season, Stecher sprinted all the way to the top of the world. On August 2, in Berlin, she dashed the 100 in 11 seconds flat to tie the the World Record first set in 1968 by Wyomia Tyus of the U.S. and matched in July of 1970 by Chi Cheng of Taiwan. Renate seemed primed for stellar performances at the major European meeting of 1970, the team-championship European Cup, scheduled for Budapest.

But Renate's appendix knew nothing about her sporting timetable and several weeks before the late-August Cup, Stecher suffered an attack of appendicitis. She had to rest almost totally after emergency surgery, but shortly before the meet, she cajoled her doctor into letting her compete.

Going almost literally from a hospital bed to international competition, Stecher was barely edged in the 100 by West Germany's Ingrid Mickler. Stecher won the 200, though, and anchored the winning 4 x 100 relay and helped lead East Germany to its first Cup victory. She ended the year ranked second in the world in both sprints behind the astounding Chi, who was undefeated in all 83 of her races at the three sprint distances during 1970.

Although no one knew it at the time, that loss in the European Cup 100 signaled the beginning of an historic string by Stecher. Following that race in August of 1970, until she was beaten in the early-June Olympic Day meet in 1974 by the peerless Irena Szewinska, Stecher never lost to another woman over 100 or 200 meters. By the time Szewinska snapped the string, Renate compiled a record of 90 consecutive outdoor victories. No other sprinter—and few other women athletes—had approached such domination.

When asked to what she attributed her rise to prominence in 1970, Stecher quickly acknowledged her coach, Horst Hille. "He worked with me from the very beginning of my career," she said. "Not only did he teach me all the fundamentals of sprinting—how to start, how to carry my arms to get the most power from my stride, how to handle a relay baton—he also taught me something else that is so important for an athlete. He taught me to be patient; to work hard for good results and to be patient for them to happen."

89

Stecher's patience was rewarded in 1971. She went undefeated indoors and defended her European Indoor title over 60-meters. Outdoors, another European Championships beckoned in mid-August in Helsinki. Two weeks before the big meet, Stecher underscored her position as the world's fastest sprinter (a leg injury had ended Chi Cheng's season early in the summer) by matching her own World Record of 11.0 in the 100. She went to Helsinki as solid a favorite as there could be.

In the Finnish capital, Stecher swept all before her. In the 100, she sped 11.4 seconds to claim the gold medal, turning back West Germany's Mickler (11.5) to avenge that European Cup defeat from the previous year. Renate then emulated Petra Vogt by taking the 200 title, sprinting a meet record 22.7. And what of defending champion Vogt? She ran seventh in the 100 and didn't even contest the 200. The former champion and the new titlist teamed up in the 4 x 100 relay as East Germany finished second behind their German counterparts from the Federal Republic. Stecher ended 1971 ranked No. 1 in the world in both sprints, the first of three consecutive years she would rate as the best on earth over both dashes.

An Olympic year dawned with the coming of the 1972 season, and Stecher picked right up where she had left off in 1971. Indoors, she won her third consecutive European Indoor title, this one coming over 50-meters. Early in the outdoor season, she showed she was as fast as ever.

On June 3, Renate again sped the 100 in 11-flat to tie the World Record for the third time. Several weeks later, as Olympic fever really began to heat up performances, the 11.0 global best was matched by Renate's teammate Ellen Stropahl, plus Eva Gleskova of Czechoslovakia. Finally, just 11 days before the start of Olympic track and field competition, Stecher plowed to another 11.0 clocking.

In Munich, however, there really never was any doubt about who was the best sprinter—not only the fastest, but also the *best.* It was Renate Stecher. Sprinters who had produced fast hand times leading up to the Games couldn't reproduce such quick clockings, due in part to the strict procedural controls in force at every Games, as well as the use in Munich of far more accurate electronic timing. Stropahl failed to advance past the quarter-finals; Gleksova made the final but pulled a muscle early in the race and limped home in 8th, and last, place.

Stecher so dominated the 100 that her *smallest* margin of victory was 0.15-of-a-second in her first-round qualifying heat. She won her second-round quarter-final by a massive 0.22 with 11.27, leaving the great Szewinska second at 11.49. Renate won her semi-final in 11.18, with Iris Davis of the U.S. second at 11.36; Australia's Raelene Boyle (fourth in Mexico City) just edged Cuba's Silvia Chivas by 0.01 in the other semi with 11.32.

After an even start in the final, Stecher simply pulled away before the distance was half-covered. She used all the power in her 5'7¼", 157-lb. frame to widen her margin all the way to the line, which she crossed in 11.07 seconds as Boyle (11.23) followed ahead of Chivas (11.24) and Davis (11.32). Stecher produced the fastest time ever run, one-hundredth quicker than the World Record time of Wyomia Tyus at Mexico City.

Stecher was no less-dominant a figure over 200-meters. She won her heat, quarter-final and semi unpressed; Boyle and defending champion Szewinska were beaten by Stropahl in their semi. For the final, lanes three through six were occupied by Strophal, Boyle, Szewinska and Stecher.

Renate powered around the curve and headed into the homestretch in front, but with Boyle just a step behind. The tough Aussie hung on tenaciously, but never could overcome Stecher's strength. Boyle's unexpected challenge certainly helped push Renate to a World Record 22.40, Boyle clocking 22.45. Szewinska squeaked passed Stropahl by 0.01 for the bronze medal with 22.74.

Thus, Stecher joined an elite group of sprinters, those to win both Olympic dash titles: Fanny Blankers-Koen, Marjorie Jackson, Betty Cuthbert and Wilma Rudolph. And all but Jackson of that golden quartet went on to anchor her 4 x 100 relay team to victory. Could Stecher emulate Blankers-Koen, Cuthbert and Rudolph?

In a seeding oddity, the two fastest teams heading into

Munich—East Germany and West Germany—were drawn for the same qualifying heat (proper seeding should produce only one meeting between the two fastest entrants in an event, in the decisive final). Both teams ran flat out, probably anxious to score a psychological victory.

The three sprinters preceding Stecher for East Germany were Evelyn Kaufer, Christina Heinich and Barbel Struppert, not exactly household names. Kaufer didn't advance in the 100 behind the quarter-finals, Heinich had tied for fifth in the 200, and Struppert was only running the relay. The West German squad consisted of Christiane Krause (substituting for the injured national 100 champion Elfgard Schittenhelm), the veteran Ingrid Mickler (though not in the crack form of her '70 and '71 seasons), Annegret Richter (fifth in the 100) and Heide Rosendahl, the darling of the West German fans and already the long jump winner and runner-up in the pentathlon.

But in the heat, the East Germans whipped to an excellent 42.88 clocking to win, a time just 0.01 shy of the World Record set by the United States four years earlier in winning the Mexico Olympic title. The West Germans clocked 42.97. The rematch in the final was a heart-thumper. The first leg was even, but great running by Mickler and Richter sent Rosendahl away for the anchor with a lead of one meter on Stecher.

Considering Renate's superior speed—not to mention her two sprint gold medals—it wasn't unusual to expect Rosendahl to succumb to Stecher's powerful finish. But the gritty Westerner yielded only half of that one meter. It seemed that Rosendahl was carried along by the thunderous storm of cheering from the home crowd and she crossed the finish line a winner in a World Record 42.81, with East Germany following at 42.95. That relay loss was the only real glitch in Stecher's superb '72 season. After her World Records and Olympic victories, she naturally ranked first in the world at each sprint distance.

"The Olympic 200 was my biggest race ever," Stecher commented at the end of the season. "It was very hard to win. For the first time in many years, I wasn't aware of whether I had won or lost."

For the first half of 1973, Stecher concentrated on finishing her university studies in education. But she quickly showed she had not neglected her sprinting, either. On June 7, Stecher sped to a place in the history books: she clocked a World Record 10.9-seconds, the first sub-11-second 100 ever. Little matter if it was hand timing; Stecher had broken *the* big time barrier in women's sprinting.

Twice more in the next six weeks, Renate blazed to clockings of 10.9, her third clocking coming in her semi-final at the East German Championships in Dresden on July 20.

Then in the final, Stecher surpassed even herself as she roared to a 10.8 clocking for another World Record. The automatic clocking was 11.07, equal to her winning time in Munich, but auto times would not become mandatory for World Records until 1977, so the hand-timed 10.8 stood as the new global standard.

Not surprisingly, Stecher won both dashes at the European Cup in rainy, wind-swept Edinburgh. She again ranked first in the world in both events and capped a brilliant season with her selection as Athlete Of The Year by *Women's Track & Field World* magazine. Always a quiet, taciturn person, Renate commented only, "I must be certain to maintain my form through to the next Olympics in Montreal. There are many good athletes who are improving all the time."

One of the most improved athletes in all of the 1974 season turned out to be the indomitable Irena Szewinska. The Pole started her outdoor season fast, and got only better. At the Olympic Day meet in East Berlin, Szewinska ended Stecher's near-four-year undefeated string when she sped a World Record 200 of 22.0 to Renate's 22.5.

Renate never made excuses though, and she certainly could have used an injury in March or a debilitating case of the flu which hit her in April. Both set back her training considerably. Outside of Szewinska, however, Stecher beat all her major foes, so the stage was set for the deciding battle between the two star sprinters. The major campaign would be waged at the European Championships in Rome's *Stadio Olimpico.*

Szewinska showed her sharpness by winning her semi-final in a meet record 11.15, while Renate placed only third

93

in her semi in 11.38. In the final, Stecher got away first, with Szewinska fractionally behind. Renate led until the 70-meter mark when the relentless momentum Szewinska had built up throughout the race carried her to the front. Irena swept passed and won by a clear meter, lowering her meet record to 11.13 as Stecher finished a full one-tenth-of-a-second back at 11.23.

The pair met again in the 200 final, where Renate ran a fabulous curve to emerge into the final straightaway with a lead of three meters. But the 200 allowed Szewinska to really get her long legs unwound and revved up. Irena collared Stecher midway in the stretch and won going away in 22.51, another meet record and an effort made all the more notable since it was run into a headwind of nearly three meters per second. Stecher again claimed the silver medal, clocking 22.68.

Stecher salvaged some degree of glory in the 4 x 100 relay. She was back running the second leg of the race down the backstretch, the best position to utilize her speed to build an early lead. Teaming with Doris Maletzki, Christina Heinich and Barbel Eckert (later Wockel), Stecher and her mates slashed the World Record to 42.51; another East German squad, with Stecher also handling the second carry, had twice run 42.6 previously.

It was fitting that Szewinska succeeded Stecher as World Athlete Of The Year after her all-conquering '74 season, which ended with Irena ranking first globally in both sprints ahead of Stecher. Said Stecher, "Irena had a great year and being named Athlete Of The Year was a natural conclusion. The injury and flu I had in the spring caused a break in my training, but they really didn't bother me that much. I really don't feel I 'lost' this past year; Irena just won and I finished second."

As an historical footnote, Stecher's gold and two silvers in Rome brought her career total of European Champion-ships medals to eight. Szewinska's pair of sprint golds, plus a short relay bronze, also gave her eight, and they matched Fanny Blankers-Koen as winners of the most medals in meet history. Szewinska would place third in the '78 400 and 4 x 400 relay to swell her total to 10, but Stecher remains tied

94

with Blankers-Koen as the second-greatest medal winner ever at the continental title meet.

That 1-2 finish order between Szewinska and Stecher was reversed in 1975. Stecher won both sprints at the European Cup, as Szewinska placed second in the 200 and third in the 100. Renate's seasonal bests of 11.13 and a World Record 22.38 naturally paced the world and she regained her No. 1 ranking positions.

So suddenly another Olympic year had arrived and Montreal would host the 1976 Games. Stecher paced the entrants in the 200 with her 22.44 yearly best, although West Germany's Inge Helten had nipped the 100 record down to 11.04 shortly before the Games. But Stecher was considered a solid favorite at both distances.

The 100 was up first. Stecher finished second in her heat to Annegret Richter from West Germany, who had placed fifth four years earlier in Munich. Other heat winners included Helten, old foe Raelene Boyle and teammate Marlies Oelsner (later Gohr), the latest young star in the East German sprint stable.

Richter indicated in her quarter-final that she would put up a tough challenge to the defending champion, her 11.05 cutting Stecher's Olympic record by 0.02. In the semis, Richter went even one better: a World Record 11.01 to lower Helten's fresh mark by 0.03. Stecher won her semi in 11.10, so Renate was growing faster with every race.

For the final, Helten drew lane 1, Stecher lane 4 and Richter lane 7. They took command of the race after the 20-meter mark and moved away from the field. Richter pulled ahead in the second half of the contest to win in 11.08, to Stecher's 11.13 with Helten third at 11.17.

In the 200, Stecher rightly could have expected Boyle to be her prime adversary. Boyle had pushed Renate over both dashes in Munich and had won a Commonwealth Games double in 1974. In the heats in Montreal's 200, Stecher posted the fastest time with 22.75. In the quarter-finals, it was young teammate Eckert who moved fastest at 22.85. The semi-finals saw Stecher win the first race in 22.68 as Boyle shockingly was disqualified for two false starts. Eckert easily won the other semi in a personal best 22.71 from 100 champion Richter (22.90).

The reigning queen and the young pretender to her throne were separated by the entire track for the final, as Stecher lined up on the outside in lane 8 while Eckert knelt in lane 1 on the inside. They were even around the turn, although Eckert opened a bit of daylight early in the home-straight. And Richter suddenly was flying in a desperate attempt to emulate Stecher's Munich double.

Stecher faded at the end to finish third in 22.47, while Eckert and Richter dipped across the finish almost as one. But young Barbel was the winner by 0.02 in 22.37, an Olympic Record. The bronze medal gave Stecher a complete set of Olympic medals; she and Szewinska remain the only women sprinters ever to win gold, silver and bronze medallions in the Games dashes.

The final Olympic appearance for Stecher came, as usual, in the 4 x 100 relay. The East German quartet of Oelsner-Gohr, Stecher, Carla Bodendorf (fourth-placer in the 200) and Eckert would have to outrun their West German counterparts, who had set an Olympic Record of 42.61 in the heats. Oddly, however, Richter ran the third leg of the race around the final curve, rather than the anchor which one would expect of the Olympic 100 champion.

For three of the four 100-meter stints in the final, West Germany held a slim lead. But anchor Annegret Kroninger was no match for Eckert's closing rush and East Germany claimed the gold medal with its own Olympic Record of 42.55.

So ended the Olympic career of Renate Stecher. And shortly after the Games, the now-26-year-old Stecher announced her retirement from running altogether. "There are many fine young sprinters now," she said, obviously referring to Eckert and Oelsner-Gohr in her own country. "I have been fortunate since 1969 to be able to compete at the level of the world's best sprinters. But I cannot run as fast over the first 30 meters of the 100 as I used to, and if you cannot do that you won't win many races. So it is time to retire."

Now a housewife and mother of two daughters,

Stecher was once asked about her development into the world's premier sprinter in a relatively short time. "A 'sensational explosion' one writer described my emergence," she recalled. "I was often asked in my younger days if I thought I was especially talented. Sure, I was talented, certainly more than the average person on the street.

"At the same time, though, I had a very carefully-planned, systematic training scheme. But the main thing for me always was that I simply loved the sport. I loved to run fast, and worked to get even faster. Most of all, I loved the sensation of speed."

Kazankina: the first to defend an Olympic 1500 title.

TATYANA KAZANKINA

Up until the afternoon of August 1, 1980, no Olympic 1500-meter champion, man or woman, ever had successfully defended a Games championship. That really wasn't too surprising for the women, since the 1500 had been added to the Olympic program only in 1972. The USSR's Lyudmila Bragina won that inaugural title in Munich, and was succeeded four years later in Montreal by a frail-looking, gauntly-featured teammate, Tatyana Kazankina.

The '76 season had seen Kazankina stamp herself as a runner of record-setting caliber. Six weeks before the Montreal Olympics, the Leningrad-bred Kazankina had run a World Record in the 1500 meters of 3:56.0—her previous best had been a 4:05.9 in 1974. A last-minute addition to the USSR team at 800-meters, she proceeded to win the gold medal in the Canadian city with another World Record, 1:54.9. Her previous fastest had been year 1975 when she ran 2:01.7.

What a difference a year had made for Kazankina back in 1976. But as she toed the line for the 1980 Olympic 1500 in the Soviet capital, Kazankina was a far different athlete: world-renowned, a veteran of major international championships, a World Record setter, not to mention defending champion at 1500.

Kazankina also had made it known she didn't believe in the idea that history wouldn't repeat itself in Moscow's 1500: she came to her second Olympics buoyed by supreme confidence. "It was only natural," said the soft-spoken Kazankina. "Just like before Montreal, I had run a World Record. I had won in Montreal after setting a record, so I felt that was a good sign of good fortune for Moscow."

Less than a month before the Games, Kazankina had cut exactly one second off her own World Record with a 3:55.0

clocking. And in the qualifying heats in the Games, Kazankina had shattered the Olympic Record of 4:01.4, set in Munich by Bragina when the time also was a global mark. Kazankina had run 3:59.2, easing up in the homestretch. She was at the peak of her form when she needed it the most.

In the Moscow final, Kazankina let teammate Nadezhda Olizarenko, the 800-meter champion, set the early pace. Tatyana settled into sixth place for a lap, and then steadily began to work her way up through the pack of eight other runners. Fifth place, then fourth, then third.

With a lap-and-a-half to go, the 5'3¼", 110 lb. Kazankina flowed powerfully into the lead, and it suddenly became a race for second place. "I was thinking first of keeping my Olympic title and not of fast times," Kazankina said later. "I realized this year that I had lost some speed, which is why I didn't run the 800 in the Olympics. I had to change tactics—I started my finishing kick much sooner. I used to kick only well into the last lap."

It hardly mattered where she started to sprint. Kazankina had a lead of 1.4 seconds at 1200 meters, well ahead of Christiane Wartenberg of East Germany. By the final curve, she had a margin of 15-meters and she crossed the finish line at 3:56.58, nearly 1½ seconds ahead of Wartenberg (3:57.8). Naturally, Kazankina's clocking set another Olympic Record.

And her effort made Kazankina a history-maker: the first 1500 champion ever to defend an Olympic title.

One of the most exciting features of the sport of track and field is its unpredictability. Who would have thought in 1975, for example, that a 23-year-old unknown from the USSR would be the next Olympic champion and World Record setter at both the 800 and 1500?

Sure, Tatyana Kazankina had ranked fourth in the world in both 1974 and '75—but to cut more than seven seconds off her 800 best and almost *12* from her personal best at 1500? Then win both Olympic gold medals and be selected women's Athlete of the Year for 1976 by *Track & Field News?* Sounds like the staple of Hollywood's B-grade melodramas.

Kazankina didn't even first appear on yearly lists of Soviet performances until 1971, when she ran a 4:19.0 1500 at age 19. The next season, she clocked 2:05.2 in the 800 and 4:13.6 in the 1500. A year later, she improved to 2:03.5 for the two-lap distance, but ran only 4:14.2 for 1500. Then in 1974, she cut her bests in both events, to 2:03.1 and 4:05.9. She ranked fourth worldwide at the longer distance, and duplicated that rating in '75; in the pre-Olympic year, she once again lowered only her 800 best (to 2:01.7) but not her 1500 personal record (best of 4:07.9).

But the Olympic Games do funny things to athletes: the Games often bring out performances athletes never knew they had in them. In early June of 1976, Soviet Valentina Gerasimova—who had ranked No. 1 in the world in '75 at 800—sliced the World Record down to 1:56.0. At that same meet in Kiev, Kazankina clocked a career-best 1500 of 4:05.2.

It seemed a logical assumption that Soviet selectors would name Gerasimova, Svetlana Styrkina (second in Kiev with 1:56.7) and the experienced Tatyana Providokhina as the USSR entries in the Montreal 800. That probably would have been fine with Kazankina. After all, she wanted to concentrate on the 1500.

Ten days after the Kiev meet, Tatyana cruised 1500 in 4:02.8 in Helsinki and then at the end of June, she made the *big* breakthrough: a World Record 3:56.0. The Soviet Olympic team headed to Montreal shortly after and along the way stopped in France for a dual meet against the French. Kazankina threw a wrench in the Soviet plans by winning the 800 in 1:56.6 to become the second-fastest two-lap runner in history.

So, in a way, Kazankina painted herself into the corner. The Soviet team hierarchy told Tatyana she would run both the 800 and 1500 in Montreal. She didn't think much of the edict. "I wanted to think only of the 1500," she said. "I didn't want to be the second-string runner in the 800. With Gerasimova the strong favorite in the 800, I ran the risk of not doing well in the 1500 because I had to run the 800. I loved the 1500, but I didn't feel at all comfortable in the 800.

Not to worry, Tatyana. You placed second in your semifinal behind Styrkina, with Gerasimova only sixth and out of the final. Then in the final, Styrkina set the pace for 600 meters, but you waited—comfortably and confidently—until the middle of the final turn to unleash a devastating burst of speed which carried you to the front midway down the homestretch and to a winning margin of more than three meters at the finish. Oh, don't forget that you also broke the World Record by 1.1 seconds.

In her quiet, reserved manner, Kazankina insisted her victory was just a matter of luck: "I was able to accelerate on the outside while the others fought on the inside. On the final straight, everyone was wearing themselves down, while I was coming on with a full head of steam. They all wilted and I caught them unawares."

Why, then, did the field in the 1500 final run so slowly in the early going? Did they hope to lull Kazankina to sleep and then outkick her? A 2:15.8 split at the 800-meter mark played right into Tatyana's strength. With 250 meters to go, East Germany's Gunhild Hoffmeister and Ulrike Klapazynski sprinted after leader Lyudmila Bragina. The defending champion had begun a long drive for home with one lap to go. The elbows flew as the leaders tussled, but nestled out of harm's way in sixth place was Kazankina.

It was just a matter of time before Tatyana unleashed her kick. In the middle of the last turn, she had moved to third and with 50 meters to go, Kazankina collared Hoffmeister and won by three meters in 4:05.5. Many fans had hoped for history's first sub-3:55, so were disappointed by the "slow" time. But was there any question about Kazankina's speed? How could there be, after she ran the last 800 of the race in 2:03.5 and her last lap in 56.9.

No one would ever again doubt the speed of Kazankina—nor would she ever enjoy the anonymity of being relatively unknown in international circles. Kazankina was a star.

Unpredictibility means not knowing what is coming next. It works for the athletes as well as fans. After her Montreal double, Kazankina was asked if she would defend her titles in Moscow. "I will have to talk with my husband," she said after the 800. Mr. Kovalenko must have had a talk with his wife, for after the 1500 she said, "I hope to be in Moscow and still be on top."

But the question of whether or not she would move up to the newly-instituted international distance of 3000 meters elicited this response from Kazankina: "That is mighty long for me. I have no taste for it right now." Then, she hedged—perhaps deciding not to burn all her bridges behind her too quickly. "At least for now," she added.

The sharp-eyed follower of the sport might have noted that Kazankina had run 3000 meters in 8:57.8 in 1975 and ranked eighth in the world. The 1.8-mile distance would not be added to the Olympic program until the 1984 Los Angeles Games, but it became an official World Record distance in 1974. Shortly after the Montreal Olympics, in fact, Bragina—perhaps seeing the handwriting on the wall in the 1500—clocked a record 8:27.14 in the 3000, a mark that would survive for nearly six years.

Kazankina, however, kept her eyes fixed on the 1500 in 1977 as she won the inaugural World Cup and repeated her ranking of No. 1 in the world. She raced sparingly in 1978 and later in that year revealed it was for the best of reasons: she was expecting. Her daughter arrived early in 1979, so Tatyana just set her sights on the coming 1980 Olympics in Moscow.

She was getting close to her 29th birthday at the 1980 Games, so Kazankina focused only on the 1500, feeling she had lost enough speed to make too chancy a successful defense of her 800 title. But the 1500 was hers all the way. Her 3:55.0 global record before the Games merely served to underline her favorite's role, and she lived up to the expectations—and then some.

But her historic successful defense of her Olympic 1500 title was not her greatest race in 1980. She saved that for Zurich's renowned Weltklasse invitational meet in August. Much of the pre-meet talk had centered on the possibility of a 1500 World Record from Moscow men's champion Sebastian Coe of Great Britain.

Kazankina proved the pre-meet prognosticators were

looking at the wrong 1500. Teammate Tatyana Providokhina, bronze medalist in the Olympic 800, set a 58.3 pace for the first lap with Kazankina second at 58.5 and American star Mary Decker third (59.0). The Soviet pair shared the lead at 800 meters in 2:04.5—stunningly, 0.4 faster than the pace had been in the men's 1500 final in Moscow.

Providokhina dropped out after 900 meters, leaving Kazankina to shoot for the world mark on her own. Decker was now 10 meters behind and the rest of the field another 60 meters back. Kazankina steamed around the final 600 meters, the incessant roar of the packed stadium urging her on. During the final lap, the stadium announcer informed the throng that Kazankina's splits were ahead of the pace in her 3:56.0 record race. The knowledgeable, appreciative Swiss fans clapped in unison as Kazankina pushed on.

Tatyana held her form in the homestretch and stopped the unofficial stadium clock at 3:52.45. Her official time ended up at 3:52.47. She had run her final two laps in 2:05.0 and her final 400 in 60.5 to lower the record to the rough equivalent of a 4:09 mile—Decker's official outdoor mark stood at 4:21.68. Kazankina had run faster than any men's Olympic 1500 champion before 1932, and 0.2 faster than the immortal Finn Paavo Nurmi ever ran in his life.

Kazankina's effort was voted Performance of the Year for 1980 in the annual *Track & Field News* poll, and she placed third in the Athlete of the Year voting, just six points out of first place.

Kazankina took it easy in both 1981 and 1982, although she gave a glimpse of things to come in '82 when she clocked 8:36.54 to lower her best for 3000 meters by more than 20 seconds. And there would be a new goal in 1983, the inaugural World Championships, to be staged in Helsinki. Tatyana would be close to 32 years old then, but knowing how she responded to the lure of a major championship, the question begged to be asked: would she play a major role in yet another race for medals?

Many observers felt if she ran in Helsinki at all, it would be in the 1500. She had run 4:03.48 before the championships and even though there were three other Soviets faster, Kazankina clearly was the most experienced.

Kazankina finishes her historic 1500 World Record in 1980.

But, when the runners lined up on August 8 for the heats of the 3000 meters, there was Kazankina. Her main rival in that second heat was none other than Decker, who was attempting a 3000-1500 double. Tatyana and Mary traded strides the entire distance, Decker even putting on a little sprint at the end to cross the line virtually even with Kazankina.

The two other Soviet entries, two-time European champion Svetlana Ulmasova and the young Natalya Artyomova, also qualified for the final. Speculation was rife that the Soviets would employ some sort of "team tactics" against Decker in the final. But the American never gave them the chance, leading all the way. Midway down the last backstretch, Kazankina was boxed on the curb behind Decker. Ulmasova, however, swung out from fifth place and sprinted to the lead; Kazankina pulled even with Decker with 150 meters left.

Then the American simply shifted gears and ran away from them both. Decker's burst so dispirited Kazankina that she slowed and thus allowed West Germany's Brigitte Kraus to close fast for second place. Kazankina held third ahead of Ulmasova.

Just 11 days later, though, Kazankina was back on the winning track as she claimed the title in the European Cup 3000. Her fine season ended up ranking her second in the world behind Decker; the American also paced the 1500, with Kazankina fifth (she had run a seasonal best of 4:01.23 in July).

With the 3000 now on the Olympic program, Kazankina looked ahead to the '84 Games in Los Angeles. But, like Decker in 1980, Tatyana fell victim to political expediency when the Eastern Bloc nations boycotted Los Angeles, ostensibly because of worries over the safety of their athletes while in the United States.

Would she have played a major role in the Olympic 3000? Just consider that, first, Kazankina won the Eastern Bloc's alternative meet to the Games in 8:33.01. The Olympics had been won by Romania's Maricica Puica in 8:35.96. Then 10 days later, on August 26, Tatyana blasted the World Record down to 8:22.62.

Tatyana Kazankina

Unfortunately, the biggest headlines Kazankina was to make in 1984 came shortly after her 3000 record. Tatyana traveled to Paris for an international meeting; she won the 5000 with her debut effort over the distance of 15:23.12. She then was ordered—per the rules of the International Amateur Athletic Federation which allow for random drug testing at selected meets—to report for doping control.

Kazankina said no. The official heading the Soviet delegation at the meet also refused to allow her to submit to testing without a Soviet doctor present, although there is no provision in IAAF doping regulations for such presence of a physician from an athlete's nation.

What *is* provided in IAAF doping rules is that if an athlete refuses to report for testing, he or she is presumed to be guilty of the use of a banned substance. Therefore, the athlete is suspended from competition; the usual sentence is 18 months.

IAAF officials initially felt Kazankina's refusal was due to a misunderstanding on the part of the Soviet official. But the world governing body of track and field stuck to its guns and Kazankina was suspended for 18 months.

It was an ignoble chapter in a career of such brilliance, a career which transformed the middle distance events. But not even the dark spectre of a drug suspension could keep Kazankina totally down. She regained her international eligibility in March of 1986 and first showed up in results in early September when she won a five-kilometer road race in Finland.

But had Kazankina resigned herself to just competing in small-scale events, willing to run out the remainder of her career? Hardly. Two months later, she finished fifth in the IAAF Women's World 15-kilometer Road Race Championships in Portugal, clocking 49:12 for the distance.

Will even longer distances, like the 10,000-meters, beckon the talents of Kazankina in the future? No one knows for certain, even Tatyana herself. Regardless of the distance she runs, though, the sport can always be certain of the type of effort Kazankina will give: nothing but her best.

Ashford: twice sped to Athlete of the Year honors.

EVELYN ASHFORD

Both women bounced up and down in excitement and glee. They easily could have been two children in front of a gift-laden tree on Christmas morning. They laughed and squealed with joyful abandon, oblivious to the stream of reporters, cameramen, sound technicians and officials who passed them on the way to a nearby interview tent. The facade of the Los Angeles Memorial Coliseum loomed darkly above them in the night sky.

"Let me see it! Let me see it!" shouted Pat Connolly to Evelyn Ashford. The slim, dark Ashford—who had won the 1984 Olympic 100-meters only an hour earlier on the Coliseum track—stood with the effusive, blonde Connolly, who had been her coach for nearly a decade. In the late afternoon of an early August day, Ashford had achieved the goal both of them had lived for, dreamed about and worked toward with a singular passion and dedication since Ashford ran her first competitive races back in 1975 at age 18.

Now, both admired the reward: Ashford took the shiny golden medallion from its black leather case and held it up by its pastel-striped ribbon. "Isn't it beautiful?" Ashford said in a hushed voice, but one still bubbling with childlike joy. Connolly cupped the medal in her hands, inspecting it with a mixture of awe, reverence and pure glee.

Their moment of shared delight was interrupted by a West Indian television crew asking for an interview. Ashford quickly returned the medal to its box and her countenance changed from that of an excited child to one of a serious, thoughtful adult. The lights went on and the interviewer got as far as, "Evelyn..." when Connolly, watching from off-camera, said loudly, "Put the medal on. Put it on! That's what you worked so hard for so long to win!"

Ashford was embarrassed only momentarily. Connolly's

109

outspokenness, seemingly about any subject, had been a fixture of their relationship from the beginning. Then Ashford took out the medal again, draped it around her neck and adjusted it as it dangled in front of her chest. The interview was then completed without further interruptions.

When reminded later of the incident, Connolly said with a laugh, "Why shouldn't she have worn the medal? Evelyn worked for it, she earned it and it capsulized her victory. No, better than that, it symbolized the struggle."

To see Ashford in full flight over a sprint straightaway of 100 meters, or around a curve and down the homestretch of a 200, it is difficult to conceive that moving so quickly ever was a struggle for the American. Twice during the 1980s, Ashford set a World Record at 100-meters—10.79 in 1983 and 10.76 in '84, a few weeks after her Olympic triumph. In every race, Ashford, is power personified, yet with a fragile, doelike grace which belies the brute strength she possesses.

But the struggles Connolly mentioned were not simply the contests on the track against the world's fastest women. There were inner struggles and doubts to overcome; injuries which struck seemingly at the worst possible times, but over which Ashford ultimately triumphed. Ashford's rise to become the fastest woman sprinter in history often meant conquering her own self-doubt before she ever stepped on a track.

Evelyn Ashford was born April 15, 1957, in Shreveport, Louisiana, the first of five children in a military family which followed the father on his various assignments with the U.S. Air Force. The shy, quiet Evelyn didn't show any athletic ability until her final year of high school; by then she lived in Roseville, near California's capital of Sacramento.

It was a case of "girl-faster-than-all-the-boys" when Ashford recorded times of 11.5 seconds and 24.2 for the 100 and 200 as a high school senior. Then she moved on to the University of California at Los Angeles in the autumn of 1975. The next summer, the 1976 Olympic Games would be staged in Montreal and once the '75 season was over, athletes everywhere focused their attention toward the Games in the

French-Canadian city. At that time, though, Evelyn Ashford knew basically zero about the Olympic Games—or even competing at the collegiate level, let alone the national or international plateau.

Ashford would learn quickly, because the women's track coach at UCLA was Pat Connolly. A three-time Olympian herself in the 1960s, and a setter of American Records in a variety of events, Connolly knew the Games and the sport well. And she also knew she had something special walk into her life the day Ashford came out for the UCLA team. Connolly recalls timing Ashford on the first day of practice—and then refusing to believe her own watch, so fast were Evelyn's times.

It was clear that Ashford was one in a million. Connolly, an intense and strong-willed woman even in the best situations, kept telling the young teenager she had the talent to become the best sprinter ever. But it would take hard work, *very* hard work. Connolly would devise all of Ashford's training, then supervise it. No distractions—like press interviews—would be allowed. Athlete and coach set a single-minded course toward the future.

Ashford took a lot of convincing about her own talent. "There were a lot of tears and a lot of self-doubt on her part in the beginning," said Connolly. "She would cry and say, 'Do you really think I can run as fast as you say I can?' Gradually, through her own efforts and results in races, she saw that she really did have the talent. She just had to gain experience--and the more anyone gains experience in anything, the greater her self-confidence becomes."

Ashford's future arrived in June of 1976 when she placed third in the 100 meters at the U.S. Olympic Trials to earn a berth on the American team for Montreal. The Olympics would be Ashford's debut in international competition. At the Games, leading American Brenda Morehead was hobbled by a leg muscle injury and didn't qualify for the final. Besides Ashford, the U.S. was also represented by Florida teenager Chandra Cheeseborough, who had set an American Record at 200- meters of 22.77 the previous year at the Pan-American Games in Mexico City.

When the sprinters flashed across the line at the finish of

the 100 final on July 25, it was Ashford who placed highest among Americans. West Germany's Annegret Richter had set a World Record 11.01 in her semi-final, and Richter turned back defending champion Renate Stecher of East Germany in the final, 11.08 to 11.13. Back in fifth place in 11.24 ran Evelyn Ashford.

Later, Ashford was interviewed by radio reporter Sam Skinner, who asked the youngster, "Well, Evelyn, do you feel like the fifth-best sprinter in the whole world?" The tone of Ashford's answer was one of pure incredulity: "No," she said with a definitive gulp to her voice as though she were thinking, "You have *got* to be crazy! Me, one of the world's best? You *are* crazy."

Years later, Ashford reflected, "It all was so new to me. Everything was just for fun. I mean, it was an honor to compete in the Olympic Games, but I didn't go in with the attitude of winning as being the prime thing. My attitude was, 'Let's see what you can do. Let's see if you can compete against the best in the world.' "

Ashford proved at Montreal that she could compete with the best. The next season, and one meet in particular, provided the first of several critical turning points in her career.

For the 1977 season, the all-important competition was the inaugural World Cup, a team-oriented event which featured teams from various regions of the world including the United States. Ashford compiled a fine record during the year, winning both sprint titles at both the AIAW women's collegiate championships and the TAC national championships. Ashford would be the U.S. representative in both dashes in the Dusseldorf World Cup.

Chief among the contenders in the 100 was East Germany's Marlies Gohr, who had placed eighth and last in the Montreal Olympic 100 the year before. But in the course of 12 months' time, Gohr had matured into the world's leading sprinter by dashing a World Record 10.88. She outran Britain's Sonia Lannaman in the World Cup, while Ashford got a rude awakening internationally as she placed only fifth.

In the 200, Ashford had to face not only Montreal Olympic winner Barbel Wockel of East Germany, but also the legendary Irena Szewinska, a heroine in the past four Olympics. Szewinska defeated Wockel with Ashford fourth, but Evelyn felt she may as well have finished dead last.

"At that first World Cup, I was humiliated," Ashford admitted. "I told myself I never would let that happen to me again. I decided I had to find out if I had what it took to become a true world-class sprinter. I *had* to answer that question for myself."

Connolly added, "She really became a top sprinter in 1979, but the decision to work for it was made after the '77 World Cup. Evelyn's strongest attribute as an athlete is her ability to concentrate. I would hate to have to compete against her, in anything. Her intensity is that fierce."

So the single-minded athlete and her like-minded coach worked and worked. In 1978, Ashford clocked a personal best in the 100 of 11.18, ranked fourth in the world and first among Americans (even though she placed second in the AIAW race and third at TAC). Plus she clocked 22.66 in the 200, just shy of her 22.62 career low; she ranked third globally and was first again in the U.S. after scoring an AIAW-TAC double victory.

The big breakthrough—to true world class—came in 1979. At the TAC Championships, Evelyn zipped an American Record 10.97 in her 100 semi-final, finally getting the sub-11-second time that she and Connolly knew lay within her. She won both TAC sprints and then claimed both dash gold medals at the Pan-American Games. Her biggest tests, though, came in the second World Cup, staged coincidentally on the same Montreal track where she had debuted internationally three years earlier.

Her first test came in the 200 when she faced East Germany's Marita Koch, who had climbed to the top of the world at 400 meters. Koch was close to the world's best over the 200 as well, but Ashford churned the turn and held off Koch's surge in the homestretch to win in an American Record 21.83 from Koch's 22.02. Then in the 100, Ashford faced Gohr, who still claimed the 100 World Record and had ranked No. 1 in the world the past two seasons. But the slim Ashford outran her compact rival, 11.06 to 11.17.

Evelyn had arrived at the center of the world's athletic

stage, but she still was the shy, reclusive woman-child she had been back in 1976. Connolly reluctantly allowed Ashford to answer questions from the press after her competition was finished in Montreal. Ashford did so courteously, but with short, terse answers. It was plain that Ashford was uncomfortable dealing with her own thoughts or having to express them in public.

And when she tried to leave the podium from which interviews were conducted, reporters converged on her like steel to a magnet. Everyone wanted to know more about this young star, the one who could run so fast—either away from her competition or from the press and the public.

Ashford was trapped against a pillar and for a few moments resembled a cornered fawn, eyes darting from side to side seeking a route of escape. Connolly pushed her way through the crowd and finally plucked her protege from the melee, to the protesting howls of the member of the fourth estate.

Again, the passage of time imparts perspective on those days from both athlete and coach. "In my view, reporters never were sensitive to the moment," Ashford said. "I always was a nervous wreck before a race and some writer would come up and say, 'You're going to win, aren't you?' right at the time I was trying to psych myself to a peak. So, the way to avoid that was to not talk to the press at all."

Said Connolly, "The main reason I kept Evelyn away from the press was that it seems that after anyone gains a certain amount of success, everyone around wants a piece of it. And the press can write about and emphasize the wrong things. I am very much one who wants to control as many of the variables of a situation as possible. And I felt very strongly that we were doing all the preparation for the 1980 Olympics by ourselves. There wasn't anybody helping us—financially, or otherwise. If we were going to go to Moscow and beat the Eastern European sprinters in 1980, we had to do everything ourselves. So I felt we had to control the situation as much as possible, and eliminate all unnecessary distractions."

Ashford's generally shy personality, coupled with the enforced aloofness imposed by Connolly, caused her to be unfairly saddled with a reputation as an uncooperative loner. But she and Connolly didn't care because there was a new goal: the 1980 Moscow Olympics.

The new decade of the 1980s was only a few days old, however, when events totally outside the realm of sport intruded into the athletic world. A few days into 1980, U.S. President Jimmy Carter announced that if the Soviet Union did not withdraw military troops from Afghanistan, the U.S. would boycott the Moscow Olympics and would urge as many Western nations as possible to follow.

What did follow in the next four months—until the U.S. Olympic Committee voted in mid-April to go along with the government's boycott proposal—was a lurching period of uncertainty for all American athletes: Will we boycott or won't we? What will happen? Should I put in the mental and physical intensity to prepare for an Olympics if we end up not going? Ashford was not immune to the feelings of confusion.

"I will always look back on the 1979 season with good feelings," Ashford said. "But the boycott ripped out my soul. I had put all my emotional eggs in that one basket and when it was yanked away from me, I felt totally empty. I just stopped caring."

Connolly related, "There is a story I tell about a tree Evelyn brought me from Montreal after the '76 Olympics. I planted it and took care of it; it was my Olympic tree. It really sprouted and started to grow in 1977, just like Evelyn did. In 1979, that tree must have shot up three feet. It was beautiful.

"I never told this to many people because I thought they would think I was crazy. But that tree was healthiest when Evelyn was running her best. Then early in 1980, when I first heard about the possibility of a boycott, I took extra care of the tree, as if that would prevent a boycott. But about the time the boycott was officially announced, our dog ripped off a branch from the tree and it started to die.

"All this time, Evelyn still refused to believe a boycott would happen—she believed some miracle would enable her to run in the Olympics. I told her she had to face facts and she would snap back, "I don't want to hear that!'.

"The tree never sprouted one leaf that spring. We went out to Japan for a meet, which we never would have done if the Games had been on. We never would have gone so far outside our strict training plan Just after we got back, I pulled on the tree trunk it just came right out of the ground. It was just a twig in the dirt, but it was very symbolic of the whole terrible situation.

"Then at the Pepsi meet in May, Evelyn was injured and I was actually relieved. It made it clear to her that there would be no Olympics for her; she could forget about them totally. Our whole approach, really, reflected the belief that we wouldn't go: we did television interviews, we didn't ice down her legs after workouts, we didn't even do hard training sometimes. The intensity, the meticulous attention to detail, just wasn't there."

From being ranked the world's No. 1 sprinter in the 100 in 1979, Ashford hardly ran at all in 1980. She rested an injured leg muscle the remainder of that year, but returned to competition during the indoor campaign of 1981. Gradually, like a sprinter gaining momentum throughout a race, Ashford got faster and better as the season rolled along.

She won both sprints at the TAC Championships; she won 17 of her 18 outdoor sprint finals; she lowered her American Record in the 100 to 10.90, just 0.02 behind Gohr's 1977 global record. Ashford ranked first in the world in each dash, and the frosting on the comeback cake came when Evelyn was voted Athlete of the Year by *Track & Field News.*

"My whole attitude was one of uncertainty as '81 began," Ashford remembered. "I didn't know if I wanted to run fast or not. I just started training and as the days passed, the old spark inside started coming back. In 1980, I felt so dead inside. But I had a good year in 1981 and I decided that what I really wanted was to win two gold medals at the '84 Olympics in Los Angeles. I wanted that for myself."

Ashford scaled down her 1982 season a bit, although she repeated as TAC 100 champion and ranked No. 1 in the U.S. in both sprints (and second in the 100 and third in the 200 worldwide). The 1983 year would provide another new goal: the first-ever World Championships, scheduled for

Helsinki, Finland.

"One reason I slipped a little in '82 was that Pat took time off from coaching me, so I was pretty much on my own," Ashford said. "She felt she owed it to her family." Athlete and coach reunited to prepare for Helsinki, however, and all proceeded well: Evelyn won both sprints at the TAC Championships to qualify for the U.S. team to Helsinki. She was edged by Gohr in the 100 a week later in the U.S.-East Germany dual meet.

But Ashford rebounded from the loss to her rival by achieving one of the goals she and Connolly had aimed for since the beginning of their collaboration. At the U.S. Olympic Festival, a national-level multi-sport festival staged in Colorado Springs, Ashford surged to a World Record of 10.79, snipping 0.02 off Gohr's month-old record. Evelyn was so overcome when her time was annouced, she fell to the track and sobbed in joy and relief. It mattered not that the time came in the helpful mile-high altitude of the Rocky Mountains; what mattered most is that the record time came, period.

Heading to Helsinki, Ashford and Gohr were rated virtually even in the 100, while Ashford was a slight favorite in the 200. Two-time Olympic champion Barbel Wockel was expected to be Evelyn's main challenger in the 200, although 400 superstar Marita Koch was rumored to be considering the distance after an injury had left her short on training for the one-lap contest.

In Helsinki, the 100 went true to form in the early rounds. Ashford won her heat as did Koch, who was entered in the shorter sprints after all. Gohr finished second in her qualifying heat. Then in a seeding surprise, Ashford and Gohr squared off in the fourth quarter-final race. Evelyn dashed 11.11 to win from Gohr's 11.16. But just beyond the finish line, Ashford hobbled to a stop, her face reflecting concern. First reports claimed she suffered from back spasms, but later were amended to say she suffered a slight recurrence of the injury from back in 1980. Scar tissue had sloughed off, but she was expected to be back strong for the next day's semi-finals and final.

In the semis, Gohr sped 11.08 to win her race, while

Brilliant moments in '84: Ashford wins the Olympic 100. . .

. . . and beats Gohr in Zurich with a World Record of 10.76.

Evelyn showed she would be tough by clocking a victorious 10.99. For the final, Ashford lined up in lane two, with Gohr on the outside in lane eight. Koch got the best start, with Gohr next and Ashford third. Gohr accelerated at 30 meters to take the lead and Ashford appeared to make a strong move at 40 meters to catch the East German.

Suddenly, at 50 meters, Ashford shot up into the air, hoppled a few steps and then fell to the track in a heap. Gohr went on to win the global title from Koch, 10.97 to 11.02. All Ashford could do was pound the track with her fist. Her season was over; Ashford went home. Connolly had commented in Helsinki, "I feel the injury was not caused by the stress of competition but rather from emotional stress due to personal problems not related to track at all."

The off-track problems *were* serious: the marriage of Evelyn and Ray Washington, who were wed in the spring of 1978, was on the brink of falling apart. So the injury sent Ashford home, to heal her physical hurt but also to deal with the personal trauma in her life.

"Ray and I were forced to talk things out," Ashford revealed, a tone of confidence and self-assurance bolstering her voice as never before. "It was hard, emotionally-wrenching work, but we did it. We worked out those deepest feelings between two people. I really felt that after we did that, I never would be afraid of a mere footrace again."

That new personal confidence was Ashford's secret weapon as the 1984 Olympic year dawned. She returned to competition in mid-April and showed a seemingly new turn of speed in Modesto in mid-May as she zipped a 10.78 100 with an illegally-aiding wind. She looked sharp and crisp and fast.

For two rounds of the Olympic Trials in late June, Ashford was the Evelyn of old. But then while warming up for the semi-finals the next day, Ashford felt a twinge in her right hamstring muscle. "I advised her to pass on the 100 and run only the 200, so she wouldn't put as much strain on her leg," said Connolly.

Ashford said no; it would be the 100 or nothing. She finished only a struggling third in her semi. "I thought for a moment, 'Oh, no, not again.' I wondered if the fates were determined that I never ran in another Olympic Games," recalled Ashford. However, her long-time trainer Vicky Vodon massaged, treated and wrapped her leg so Ashford could shoot for her dream.

For the final, Ashford's right leg was swathed in elastic bandages and tape from buttock to knee. And over all the wraps, she wore a pair of skin-tight leggings. But the muscle held firm and Ashford overhauled early leader Alice Brown at 70 meters to edge ahead for the victory in 11.18 to Brown's 11.20. "I was going to run no matter what. I couldn't get to the Olympics any other way," said Ashford, who threw her hands to her face beyond the finish to hide her tears of relief. It hardly mattered that the leg injury caused her to stop in her heat of the 200 meters after covering hardly 20 meters. It wasn't worth the risk—and, besides, Ashford already was on her way to the Olympics.

Ashford went to Los Angeles, of course, a very different athlete from the young, inexperienced teenager of Montreal eight years before. Now she was the World Record holder, vastly experienced, and the favorite. If the Olympic Trials had been a nightmare, the Games were like a dream.

Her leg had healed and was strong. A boycott of the Los Angeles Games by Eastern Bloc nations removed her toughest competition. Plus, Ashford was ready; she *wanted* that gold medal in the 100. "It *was* easy," said Ashford. "I hated to say that about the other sprinters, but it really was easy, mentally and physically.

"When I first crossed the finish, I was mad at myself because I thought it wasn't a fast time. Then the Olympic Record of 10.97 was announced and I thought, "Is that all there is to it? What was all the anxiety about all these years? Let's do it again!' "

Ashford's life-long dream came true on the victory rostrum when the gold medal was draped around her neck, the same medal she later showed Connolly in their gleeful reunion. And Ashford collected a second medallion as the anchor runner on the winning U.S. 4 x 100-meter relay team.

But Ashford's greatest moment of 1984 was still to come. After the Games, Evelyn and Ray headed to Europe; Connolly stayed home to accompany her family on a long-promised vacation. The coach also felt it was time for Evelyn to get along on her own on the summer European circuit.

Victory in the Olympic 100 had been Phase One of Plan Ashford for 1984; Phase Two would be a rematch with Gohr. "I wanted to run my best race of the year against Marlies," said Ashford. The rerun came in Zurich's Weltklasse meet. Recalled Ashford, "I felt very nervous when we were on the starting line. That was how I expected to feel when I raced Gohr in an Olympics. In Zurich, I just told myself, 'Okay, this is it. You either do it or you don't.'"

Evelyn did. Gohr got out first, but Ashford was right behind and assumed command with 40 meters to go. Gohr hung tough and Evelyn had to produce another surge in the final 10 meters to cross the line first. And her time said it all: a World Record 10.76. "I usually never felt this way about such a big race, but the time could have been 11.9 for all I cared," she said. "I just wanted to beat Gohr."

Ashford went undefeated in eight 100-meter finals in 1984, beat all challengers, won the Olympic title and set the World Record in beating her prime foe. That sort of season could only be rewarded with her second Athlete of the Year selection by *Track & Field News.* And the 10.76 was named Performance of the Year.

The track world did without Ashford in 1985, though. She discovered shortly after Zurich that she was pregnant with her and Ray's first child. She was, in fact, pregnant in that race. "Fastest 100 ever by a pregnant sprinter," she joked.

On May 30, 1985, Evelyn and Ray welcomed Raina Ashley Washington into the world. On February 8, 1986, at the Vitalis/U.S. Olympic Invitational indoor meet in East Rutherford, New Jersey, Ashford returned to racing with a 6.68 victory over 55-meters ahead of Jamaica's Merlene Ottey-Page.

Ashford split her time during the '86 indoor season between racing and, surprisingly, reporting on racing. Ashford had developed a mature, professional persona as a broadcaster and confidently handled athlete interviews on a number of telecasts.

When the outdoor season arrived, though, the only things to occupy Ashford's mind on the track were the usual:

racing and winning. There were some things which were different, though, the main one being that Ashford and Connolly had parted ways. Rather than find a new coach, Evelyn decided to coach herself and have Ray help administer the workouts ("I realized I knew a lot more than I ever thought I did.") When she first got back in training after Raina's birth, Ashford admitted she did nothing but hurt.

"I just wanted to get reacquainted with running again in 1986," said Ashford. "I expected to lose a lot of races. The first few months of training were terrible. I really didn't start feeling like an athlete again until the Goodwill Games in Moscow."

Ashford won the Soviet sports festival by beating the hottest new sprint star of the day, East Germany's Heike Drechsler. World-renowned as a long jumper (World Record setter at 24'5½"/7.45 in 1986), Drechsler had been sprinting sub-11-second 100s before Moscow. And in her race immediately prior to facing Drechsler—at the TAC Championships in Eugene—Ashford had been upset by Pam Marshall in the 100. Evelyn had, in fact, placed third in the championship race, despite dashing a wind-aided 10.85.

"So I was pretty unsure of myself in Moscow," she admitted. "Then Pam strained a muscle and pulled out of the 100 and I was able to run." She closed fast to edge Drechsler at the line as both ran 10.91. "That gave me a tremendous boost in confidence," she added, "and got me rolling for the rest of the summer season."

In 1986, Ashford won 14 of her 15 finals in the 100 and sped the fastest time of the year, 10.88. She won eight of nine finals in the 200, including a victory at the Van Damme meet in Brussels over Drechsler (who had twice matched the 200 World Record). She ranked first in the world in the 100 for the fourth time in her career, and second in the 200. Evelyn Ashford was back better than ever.

And Ashford knows she now has an even deeper and wider view of life itself, thanks to the birth of her daughter. "Before Raina, I just wanted to be 'Evelyn Ashford, athlete.' That's all. I had tremendous tunnel vision," she commented. "After Raina, I decided I wanted to be more in my life than just a runner.

Evelyn Ashford

"Before, I didn't let anyone into other facets of my life to see my character, to see what I was like off the track. I'm more relaxed now, and I don't mind letting people see who I am."

Ashford scoffed at the idea of quitting running, however. "Retire? I'll run until these legs fall off," she laughed. "I'll run until it's not fun anymore, but I can't imagine running ever not being fun. It's such a part of my life—not *all* of my life, but a very important part of it.

"I will continue to run because I love the feeling of running fast. When I run a good race, it feels like I'm flying and I *love* that feeling."

Raina Ashley Washington and mom, February 1987.

The greatest woman track and field athlete ever?

MARITA KOCH

No one knew it at the time, of course. But in the fourth quarter-final of the 400-meters at the 1976 Montreal Olympic Games, the track world saw the first-ever meeting between the then-current "Queen of the Track" and the future monarch.

In that race, 19-year-old Marita Koch of East Germany covered the lap in 51.87 to finish in third place, one slot ahead of Poland's Irena Szewinska. The peerless Pole—a world-class competitor for a decade, a veteran of three Olympics and a multiple World Record setter at a variety of events—clocked an easy 52.00. Both advanced to the semifinals and were scheduled to meet again in the first semi the next day.

But Koch was forced to withdraw from the semi-finals because of the flare-up of an old leg injury. Szewinska went on to win the semi in an Olympic Record 50.48 and the following day, she took the gold medal with a World Record 49.29 victory in the final. The injury-hobbled Koch could only sit and watch.

Now, fast-forward your time machine to the 1986 European Championships in Stuttgart. Barreling around the Neckarstadion oval in 48.22, Marita Koch wins her third consecutive continental 400 title—this one by the staggering margin of 1.43 seconds. Several days later, she anchors the East German 4 x 400-meter relay team to victory, her third consecutive gold medal there. No other woman besides Koch has ever won three straight golden doubles in the history of the European Championships.

Watching Koch sprint her way to yet-another history-making performance at this 1986 event is a Polish member of the Women's Commission of the International Amateur Athletic Federation, track's worldwide governing body. That delegate is Irena Szewinska.

During her stellar career, which spanned 16 years at the highest international level, Szewinska won seven Olympic medals in five different events. She set 11 World Records: two at 100-meters, four at 200, three at 400 and two in the 4 x 400 relay. Her selfless sportsmanship made her the *grande dame* of the track world from the mid-1960s until her retirement after the 1980 Olympics.

At those '80 Moscow Games, Szewinska was succeeded as Olympic champion in the 400 by Koch—and the roster of achievements produced by the East German makes her every bit as royal a "Queen of the Track" as Szewinska. Through the end of 1986, Koch set seven World Records over the 400, four at 200, two each in the 4 x 100 relay and 4 x 400 relay and one in the 4 x 200 relay.

Add to those 16 official outdoor World Records another 15 unofficial indoor bests at distances ranging from 50-meters through the 200 and Koch tallies up an amazing total of 30 career global bests. By way of comparison, her prolific teammate, sprinter Marlies Gohr set 13 outdoor records and eight indoors for a total of 21.

Can Koch compete? She won the '80 Olympic 400, of course, and anchored East Germany to second in the 4 x 400. At the 1983 World Championships, Koch won the most medals of any woman: three golds (200, 4 x 100, 4 x 400) and a silver (100). She owns her "triple double" at the European title meet. That totals a dozen medals in the sport's three most-prestigious championship meets—10 of them gold.

Further, since 1978 when she set her first official World Record, Koch has won 31 of 35 races at 200-meters, losing only to Evelyn Ashford ('79), Jarmila Kratochvilova ('83), Valerie Brisco-Hooks ('85) and Silke Gladisch ('86). In the 400, Koch has lost only two of the 32 one-lappers she has run since '78. Kratochvilova ('81) and Barbel Wockel ('82) are the fortunate pair to beat her.

But if she had stuck with her original sport, Marita Koch would be a team handball player today. And, believe it or not, she still might be only a substitute.

That Koch would distinguish herself throughout such a

career of unparalleled excellence wasn't immediately apparent when the child Marita first turned to running around the age of 11. She was born February 18, 1957, in Wismar, near East Germany's Baltic coast. Her first sport was, in fact, team handball but she was deemed—can you imagine?—too short and too slow. So Marita played only sparingly as a substitute.

Then at a school sports day, Koch competed in some sprint races against her schoolmates. "I knew right away that I had speed," Koch recalled in her quiet, almost embarrassed manner. "I was the fastest girl and I beat all the boys, too."

In 1972, at the age of 15, Koch won a regional all-sports day 400 in 60.3 seconds, and also sprinted 100-meters in 12.2 and 200 in 25.5. The next year, she sped 12.1 and 24.5 and showed her versatility by winning nine events in a regional youth championships, including the long jump and pentathlon.

Throughout her career, Koch was coached by Wolfgang Meier, a maritime engineer and former sprinter. Meier knew that for the talented youngster to develop her obvious abilities, she would have to improve her speed.

So Meier consulted with Horst-Dieter Hille, the renowned coach of '72 double Olympic sprint champion Renate Stecher, World Record holder Marlies Gohr and Olympic champion Barbel Wockel. Hille suggested various workouts and, as it turned out, as Koch developed strength in the 400, she also cultivated her speed. Her big breakthrough came in 1975 when she clocked bests of 11.7, 23.92 and 51.60.

Marita finished second in the European Junior Championships 400 with that 51.60, but was overshadowed by teammate Christine Lathan, who took the final with a World Junior Record of 50.84. And the next year at the Montreal Olympics, Koch was sidelined by that leg injury and watched not only Szewinska win the gold medal, but Lathan take the silver (and also win a gold in the 4 x 400 relay).

Koch was well-recovered from the injury when the 1977 season began. Indoors, she won the European Indoor 400 title with an undercover World Record of 51.15. Outdoors, Marita slashed her sprint times to 11.28 and 22.38, and became the second-fastest 400 runner of all-time with her

Koch: the stride of a champion.

49.53 best. Only Szewinska's 49.29 record from Montreal was faster.

The '77 season also produced the first real meetings between Koch and Szewinska, "real" in the sense they both were healthy and running at the top level, unlike at Montreal. On August 21, at the Nikaia meeting in Nice, France, Koch sped 22.55 in the 200 to best Szewinska's 22.63. But their biggest meeting was their second, in the 400 at the inaugural World Cup in Dusseldorf on September 4.

Koch went out fast and ran a hard first 200, opening up a lead of several meters over Szewinska. But Irena stuck close and began a drive coming off the final turn into the home-stretch. With 50 meters to go, Szewinska took command of the race and she went home a winner in 49.53 to the 49.76 by Koch.

Szewinska later reaped more glory in Dusseldorf when, as captain of the victorious European Select women's team, she stepped forward to receive the winner's World Cup. Irena ranked first in the world at 400 in 1977—but it was the last time Szewinska would claim the top spot. Marita Koch would see to that. And never again would Szewinska beat Koch in a 400. The mantle of "Queen of the Track" began to shift.

Seven was a lucky number for Marita Koch in the 1978 season. It was her seventh season of competitive running. She competed in just seven meets the entire outdoor season. But what a seven they were. In her first meet, she sped a personal best 100-meters of 11.19 and then the next day, Koch blazed to the first official World Record of her career. Her 22.06 for 200 hacked down Szewinska's global mark by 0.15-of-a-second.

In her second meet a week later, Koch started out the same way, zipping to a 100-meter best on the first day. This time, she clocked 11.16 for the straight sprint. Then the next day, June 4, she again covered the 200 in 22.06, matching her own World Record. Koch suffered a slight leg injury in training shortly after, and missed nearly an entire month of competition.

But she was healthy by the time of the East German Championships on July 2, and was eager to run her first 400 of the season. No other 400-meter sprinter in history would have wanted her to be quite so eager, for Marita sped 49.19 to trim 0.10 from Szewinska's global standard.

Then it was back into training for nearly six weeks, intense preparation for the season's summit meeting at the European Championships in Prague. On August 19, Koch emerged for a trial meet and exploded again: 49.03, putting Koch at the very brink of the 49-second barrier. At the time, only Koch, Szewinska and Lathan had ever ducked under even 50 seconds.

Then on August 22 in Stuttgart, just one week before the start of the European title meet, Koch set the stage for her Prague showdown with Szewinska. Marita churned the 200 in 22.18 for the third-fastest time ever run—and crushed Szewinska herself by a massive 0.80. So all roads converged in Prague and Koch's stunning new speed clearly put her in the driver's seat.

Marita was entered only in the 400—so she didn't have to split her mental and physical efforts between the 200 and 400—plus the long relay. "I felt very easy and controlled in both my heat [52.95] and semi-final [51.76]," Koch recalled. "I felt confident for the final to try to start very fast."

She blazed the first half of the 400 final in 22.9, held her form superbly over the closing half-lap and ushered in a new era in 400-meter sprinting as she became the first woman to run under 49 seconds with her World Record 48.94. She also became the first athlete, man or woman, to produce three 400 World Records in the same year. Koch ranked first globally at both the 200 and 400, and was named Athlete Of The Year by *Track & Field News.* It was the first of her unprecedented four selections.

In reflecting back on her season, Koch realized the key: her sprint speed had improved dramatically. "It always has been connected with me," she explained. "In order to run fast in the 400, I have to have good performances in the 100 and 200. The starts in the 100 help my 400, and the endurance of the 400 helps the 100 and 200."

Marita also spoke of her grand rival, Szewinska: "She won so many important meets and medals before I even thought about running. I always marveled at her durability.

Plus, she always was so likable and friendly; never rude or critical. I knew that about Irena long before I ever became known as a sprinter. I always wanted to emulate her."

As she gained experience and maturity, though, Koch only set standards for others to try to emulate. In her first outdoor meet of 1979, she merely burned a 21.85 200; it was aided by a wind over the allowable limit of two meters-per-second, but such a stunning debut effort showed that Koch was better than ever.

In her second meet shortly after, she cut her World Record, legally this time. It was a clocking of 22.02 and the effort made clear that the 22-second barrier in the 200 could fall to Koch at any moment.

That barrier-shattering moment arrived on June 10 in Karl-Marx-Stadt when Koch churned to a stunning clocking of 21.71. Never mind 21.9 or 21.8; Koch simply bypassed those clockings altogether. And Koch still was more than six weeks away from running her first 400 of 1979 as the short sprints made up the bulk of her early-season efforts. (Remember what she said about improvements in one event being linked to better times in another?)

The historic day ended up being July 29, when Koch sped over the full lap in 48.89 to slash her World Record from her winning effort the previous year in Prague. And that 48.89 was just a warmup—one week later in the European Cup final in Turin, Marita blasted her mark down to 48.60, a mark which would survive as the global best for three years. The USSR's Maria Pinigina was second, more than one second behind, at 49.63. Szewinska ran third at 51.27.

"Actually, I was surprised to run so fast in that first race," Koch recalled. "Honestly, I just wanted to get under 50 seconds in my first 400 of the year. And in the European Cup race, I just wanted to win in order to score the most points for our team."

Don't make the mistaken assumption, based on such comments, that Koch is an egotistical sort. She answered matter-of-factly, that's all. Most likely, that trait grew out of a way of life which placed prime emphasis on the keenest possible preparation of both physical and mental abilities. Honest assessments of progress and work still to do enabled

Koch to express her views frankly, but with the quiet certainty which marked her personality.

Koch's quiet confidence always was displayed on the track. At the climactic meet of 1979, the second World Cup, Koch returned to the Olympic Stadium in Montreal where she had watched Irena Szewinska win the Olympic 400 three years earlier. In her first World Cup race, Koch was defeated by American Evelyn Ashford in the 200, but she rebounded in the 400 with a crushing victory. Marita's 48.97 again left Pinigina (50.60) and Szewinska (51.15) far back in second and third.

Koch retained her top positions in both the 200 and 400 in the '79 World Rankings. Almost as astounding as her performances on the track were her performances in another demanding arena, her medical studies at the University of Rostock. Koch studied the extremely demanding field of pediatric medicine all the while she was training and competing as one of the finest athletes in history.

"Pediatrics demands 11 years of study, with five years of specialization," Koch explained. "I was in class about six hours each day, and then I trained between two and three hours every day, too. I couldn't waste one minute." She is too modest to add that she passed her final examinations in 1982 with grades only slightly below the highest score possible.

The 1980 Olympic season was diluted by the boycott by Western nations, but that really hardly mattered to Koch. The world's best 400-meter sprinters came from behind the Iron Curtain anyway: Marita herself and Christine Lathan from East Germany; the vastly-improved Czech Jarmila Kratochvilova; and Irina Bagryantseva and Nina Zyuskova from the host USSR.

Just nine days before the heats of the 400 in Moscow, Koch won the East German title in 49.55, second-fastest time of the year behind only her own 49.15. Marita had been slowed by a thigh muscle injury in May, but was strong and healthy by the time of the Games. Barring a total physical collapse due to serious injury, there seemed to be no way Koch wouldn't win the gold medal.

All the favorites cruised through their heats, Koch

actually finishing an eased-up second to Kratochvilova, 51.04 to 51.06. In the first semi-final, Koch was assigned lane one but again won easily, clocking 50.57. Koch watched teammate Lathan win the second heat in 50.16, just ahead of leading Soviet Bagryantseva (50.18).

The second semi-final also witnessed the end of an era. The eighth and last place in the race went to none other than Irena Szewinska. The defending champion was out of contention early in the race after suffering a leg muscle tear. She limped home in 53.13 and announced her retirement shortly thereafter.

In the final, Koch proved she was an undisputed "Queen of the Track." Marita was well-positioned, having drawn lane four. Lathan ran in lane five, Kratochvilova in six and Bagryantseva ran on the outside in lane eight. Koch never gave anyone else a chance and rocketed down the backstretch of Moscow's Lenin Stadium. Heading into the final turn, she had made up the distance on Kratochvilova two lanes ahead, and by the mid-point of the final curve, Koch had caught Bagryantseva on the outside.

Marita just added to her massive margin all the way to the finish as she clocked an Olympic Record 48.88 to easily defeat Kratochvilova (49.46), Lathan (49.66) and Bagryantseva (50.07). Three days after her triumph in the flat 400, Koch anchored East Germany's 4 x 400 relay team to an easy win in the heats of the baton event. The USSR won the other heat, running more than three seconds faster than East Germany, so the stage was set for a fast final.

The final *was* fast, but acrimonious as well. The USSR used one lineup of runners in its heat, and then produced a required medical certificate before the final, claiming two of the runners couldn't contest the final. The two "substitutes" turned out to be Bagryantseva and Zyuskova, the two best Soviets. The East Germans bristled at the Soviet chicanery, but maintained their team of Gabrielle Lowe, Barbara Krug, Lathan and Koch.

The USSR's Tatyana Prorochenko (50.2) outran Lowe (50.6) on the opening leg of the final but Krug (50.5) beat Tatyana Goyshchik (51.5) by a full second on the No. 2 stint. Lathan began the third leg with a five-meter lead, but

Zyuskova—fresh after not having to run the heats—roared after her, catching up by the beginning of the final turn. Lathan battled for the lead, but then accidentally stepped on the curb of the track. She limped home with a 51.0 leg, to 49.7 by Zyuskova.

When Lathan passed the baton to Koch for the climactic anchor leg, East Germany trailed the USSR by six meters. Koch blazed the first 100 meters to catch up to Bagryantseva, and Marita then tucked in behind the Soviet down the backstretch. Coming out of the final turn, Koch drew even with the Soviet, but never could edge ahead and Bagryantseva held on by the slim margin of two-tenths-of-a second to win in 3:20.2. Koch's anchor leg timed 48.3, a half-second faster than the Soviet's.

The difference in the race clearly had been a fresh Bagryantseva versus a recovering Koch. East German officials railed at the outcome, but the Soviet action was within the rules then in force. Whatever Koch felt, she remained silent and collected her silver medal. At the season's end, she also collected her third consecutive No. 1 rating in the World Rankings.

Koch's streak of top rankings ended in 1981, however. The bulky, powerful Czech Kratochvilova burst to world prominence early in the year with an indoor World Record of 49.64, the first sub-50 ever indoors. Outdoors, Kratochvilova ran six sub-50s during the season.

Meanwhile, Koch suffered a leg injury in early summer and then a bout of flu. But she had regained form by mid-August, in time for the European Cup final in Zagreb, Yugoslavia. Marita sped 49.43 to score another massive victory, outrunning second-placer Gaby Bussmann (50.83) of West Germany by a huge 1.40 seconds.

The summit meeting between the year's two best at 400 came at the third World Cup, staged in Rome in early September. It was all Kratochvilova this time, as the Czech rumbled to a decisive victory in 48.61, a mere one-hundredth off Koch's World Record. Marita herself finished second in 49.27, but there was no doubting that Kratochvilova was No. 1. The Czech naturally claimed the year's top spot in the World Rankings, pushing Koch to second.

The 1982 season, which would culminate in the European Championships in Athens, started off on an uncharacteristic note for Koch. In her first race of the season, a 400 in Erfurt on May 30, Koch was defeated by two-time Olympic 200 champ Barbel Wockel, 49.56 to 49.87. Coupled with the World Cup defeat by Kratochvilova at the conclusion of 1981, it marked the first time Koch had lost two 400s in a row since 1976.

But after that initial defeat, Koch never lost again. She got down to 49.49 in the late-June match against the USSR. A week later, Koch zipped the 200 in a year-leading 21.76 to win the East German Championships (Wockel didn't compete). In another week, Marita sped the 400 in 48.77 to win the inaugural dual meet with the United States.

All efforts, of course, pointed toward Athens in early September. Kratochvilova had been compiling a fine season, too; she brought a 48.86 seasonal best to the Greek capital. The clash of The Mighty Ks seemed certain to produce a revision of Koch's 48.60 World Record.

It turned out to be "the race that never happened," as Koch crushed Kratochvilova. That isn't meant to belittle the Czech; it's just that Koch was that good. Marita ran in lane three for the final, with Jarmila in lane four. Koch rushed over the opening 200 in 22.7, three-tenths ahead of the Czech—and then Marita kept on going. She rolled over the finish in 48.16, well ahead of Kratochvilova (48.85) and the global best.

Her run had looked almost, well, easy. "Oh no, don't think that," Koch said. "It was very hard. *Every* 400 is hard." But Kratochvilova vocalized what was there for all to see: "Frankly, I didn't think Marita, or anyone else, could run that fast. I have no regrets, though, because Marita was far too strong for all of us."

And Marita wasn't finished. The 4 x 400 relay was run as a straight final, with no preliminary heats necessary as only eight teams entered. Koch had three days of rest between the 400 final and the relay. Much pre-race speculation centered on whether or not the East Germans could lower the 3:19.23 World Record which had stood since the '76 Olympics. The mark had survived assaults in an Olympics, another European

Championships and three World Cups in the intervening six years.

For three-quarters of the Athens final, run on a damp evening of September 11, it looked like the record would survive yet again. Kirsten Siemon (51.0), Sabine Busch (50.0) and Dagmar Rubsam (50.2) gave Koch a comfortable lead, but Czechoslovakia was running third at the final exchange, making a Koch-Kratochvilova rematch a remote possibility at best.

Koch started her anchor leg needing one of the fastest concluding runs in history to snare the global mark. Kratochvilova had blasted a 47.8 earlier in 1982 for the quickest relay leg ever; Marita herself had clocked a 48.0 during the '82 season. Her fluid smoothness deceptively masking her raw power, Koch proceeded to stride around the oval in 47.9 to finish East Germany's 3:19.05 World Record. Back in second, Kratochvilova uncorked a 47.6 to bring her team home in 3:22.17, which made Czechoslovakia the third-fastest nation in history.

After her disappointing 1981 campaign, Koch had climbed back to the top and she was selected Athlete Of The Year by *Track & Field News* for the third time. "I was very disturbed about 1981," she admitted. "I really wanted to quit running. But Wolfgang Meier urged me to continue. He gave me the courage to keep at it."

Koch sold herself short, again. Her '82 season wasn't simply a matter of being talked back into competing. Meier revealed another strong point of Koch's when he commented, "Marita always has been very ambitious. Whatever she takes on, she pursues with a total commitment. In fact, she always does far more than ever is asked of her." In other words, Koch never would be satisifed with giving only a half-hearted effort, at anything. Thriving on challenges, she simply *had* to give her absolute best in whatever she attempted.

Track fans welcomed the inaugural World Championships in Helsinki, Finland during the 1983 season, and rightfully could look forward to another Koch-Kratochvilova confrontation in the 400. However, Marita's preparations were hampered by a leg injury during the winter. Then, she suffered a twisted ankle in the mid-June dual meet against the U.S. Kratochvilova, meanwhile, had clocked 48.45 by the middle of July.

So with her base training for the 400 well behind schedule, Koch announced she would contest only the 100 and 200 at the World Championships, as well as both relays. Kratochvilova added the 800 to her schedule, and she cracked the World Record in July (1:53.28). But history's two finest 400 sprinters would compete in the same Helsinki race only in the 4 x 400 relay.

In the 100 at the World Championships, Koch sped 11.02 to claim the silver medal behind teammate Marlies Gohr, as their prime challenger—American Evelyn Ashford—suffered a leg muscle injury halfway through the final, fell and failed to finish. "I ran an optimum race for me," Koch said "I couldn't have run any better."

Koch had moved into the second slot on the 4 x 100 relay team earlier in the summer when an injury knocked out Barbel Wockel. Along with Silke Gladisch, Ingrid Auerswald and Gohr, the East German team had cut the World Record to 41.53 shortly before the global meet. And in Helsinki, the crack foursome won by miles in 41.76; silver medal-winning Great Britain was a full second behind.

Next up for Koch was the 200, an event which was considerably weakened by the injury to Ashford, by Wockel not even being entered in the meet and by a general lack of emphasis during the season. Koch got a stirring battle from Jamaica's Merlene Ottey-Page, but Marita triumphed in 22.13 to 22.19 for Ottey-Page. "I got a bad start and had to put everything I had into the final 100 meters," Koch recalled.

But Marita's work wasn't quite finished on that August 14 day. She still had the 4 x 400 to go. Instead of her usual anchor position, Koch was switched to the third leg, probably to give her team as big a lead as possible heading into the final stint, where Kratochvilova would run for the Czechs.

Czechoslovakia countered by starting off with Tatiana Kocembova, runnerup to Kratochvilova in the 400 (where Jarmila had just gotten under 48 seconds with her World Record 47.99). Kocembova's 48.93 gave the Czech's the lead after the first leg, Kerstin Walther having run 50.95 for East Germany. But Sabine Busch's 49.46 gave her team a lead it never would surrender after the second leg.

As Koch began her third carry, the USSR was second and Czechoslovakia third, about a half-second back of East Germany. Marita simply blew the race wide open with her 48.55 carry to send Dagmar Neubauer away on the final leg with a margin of better than two seconds. Neubauer was fully aware of who was behind her, but ran a controlled 50.78 as East Germany won in 3:19.73, the fourth-fastest time in history. Kratochvilova bulled to a 47.75 closing lap to bring Czechoslovakia home in second place.

"We really didn't think we could win this race," said Koch, as spokesman for the East German victors. "So naturally we are very happy. As for me, this is the second race I have won today—and that is fantastic."

For the second consecutive Olympics, Koch was affected by a boycott. The Eastern Bloc nations pulled out of the 1984 Games in Los Angeles, forcing Koch to stay at home. But her season was no less brilliant. In early June, Koch anchored a 4 x 400 relay team with a 47.70 in Erfurt as the squad cut the World Record to 3:15.92. She won the July Olympic Day meet in 21.71 to tie her own World Record for the 200. Then in the mid-August Friendship Games, the Eastern Bloc's alternative to the Olympics, Marita sped 48.16 for the year's fastest 400. She went undefeated at both distances, ranked No. 1 in the world in each and finished second in the balloting for Athlete Of The Year. Evelyn Ashford, who won the Olympic 100 and set a World Record in beating Gohr, won the *Track & Field News* honor for the second time in four years.

So Koch approached the 1985 season standing at a kind of crossroads in her life and career. She was nearly finished with her medical studies; she was 28 years old and engaged to her coach, Wolfgang Meier; she wanted to marry and have children. The big meet of the '85 season would take place late in the year with the staging of the World Cup in Canberra, Australia, in October. There were rumors in the track world that the East German track hierarchy promised Koch she could retire after the World Cup—*if* she set a World Record in Canberra.

Marita concentrated on the sprints for much of the summer. She finished second in the East German Championships 100-meters in a career low of 10.97, Gohr winning in 10.94. Koch won her national 200 title in 21.78, the year's fastest half-lap clocking. She won the European Cup 200 several days later, running 22.02. Three days later, Koch suffered a rare defeat at 200 as American Valerie Brisco-Hooks—who had won both the Olympic 200 and 400 in Los Angeles—outran Marita at Zurich's Weltklasse meet, 21.98 to 22.16.

Then Koch returned to training for more than a month, re-emerging on September 22 for a trial meet in East Berlin. She ran her first 400 of the year, a 48.97. All appeared well as Koch headed for Australia. After a 23.07 200 in a tuneup meet in late September, Koch was ready for her fourth World Cup.

On the meet's opening day, October 4, Marita first made a shambles of the 200-meter field. It didn't matter that she was running in the tight lane one; Koch simply blasted the half-lap in 21.90 to win with consummate ease from the 22.61 of Jamaica's Grace Jackson.

The 4 x 400 relay was contested on the first day of the meet, rather than on the final day. Three strong legs by the USSR, including a 48.7 third carry by Pinigina, left East Germany with a slim lead of one-tenth-of-a-second as Koch took the baton for the anchor. Soviet Olga Vladykina spurted into the lead around the first turn, while Koch cannily bided her time. Marita broke the Soviet around the final turn and pulled away with a 47.9 carry to finish East Germany's 3:19.49 winner.

Koch then enjoyed a day off before returning for the 400 on October 6. Marita simply mauled the competition—and the World Record. She rocketed through the first 100 in a stunning 10.9, as timed by Wolfgang Meier. She controlled the power flowing out of her 5'7¼", 141-lb. frame and flashed past the 200 mark in 22.4—a time that probably would have won the flat 200!

She kept up the speed and control around the second

Koch acknowledges her 47.60 record at the 1985 World Cup.

curve and cruised by 300 meters in 34.1. Marita maintained her control until just a few meters remained, but it hardly mattered that she faltered a little because she had recorded a stupendous 47.60, slicing 0.39 from Kratochvilova's World Record and giving her a seventh one-lap best.

"That race probably was the first time I ever felt fresh after the 300 mark," Koch recalled. "I knew it was a very fast race, but I also realized I had enough strength for the final 100. Yes, this was the greatest race of my career."

So great that it was voted Performance Of The Year, a fitting complement to Koch's fourth Athlete Of The Year selection. Of her remarkable World Cup performances, Koch commented, "Even after I ran 21.90 in the 200 and 47.9 to anchor the relay, I didn't feel I had proved all I could. Because I had a day's rest before the 400, I felt exceptionally fresh.

"On the way to the stadium for the 400, I joked with Wolfgang about running a very fast time. I said to him, 'Why not 47.11!' It was a joke and I have no idea why I picked those numbers. Maybe I just wanted to be beat my old best of 48.16 by more than a second. To tell the truth, I felt that 47.65 was reasonable, but I would have been happy with 47.98.

"After the race, I had the feeling I had reached my limit in the 400. It was my perfect race—if such a thing exists. Now, I'm going to find it difficult to be motivated to prolong my career."

Even if Marita's priorities appeared to be shifting, she was persuaded to return for the 1986 season, which would be highlighted by the Stuttgart European Championships. But she missed much of the outdoor season due to an injury to her Achilles tendon. She ran her first 400 only two weeks before the Europeans, but it still was a world-leading 49.24.

In Stuttgart, there never really was any doubt that Koch would win. She covered the first half of the final in 22.8, in spite of the cold weather and puddles on the track from heavy rain. Her year-pacing 48.22 was the No. 5 performance in history—and give her a massive margin of 1.45 seconds over Soviet Vladykina.

Koch assumed her standard anchor position in the 4 x 400 relay, but by the time she got the stick, the outcome of the race was an accomplished fact. Sub-49-second legs by Sabine Busch (48.3) and Petra Muller (48.9) gave Koch a huge lead. Marita could have strode around comfortably to her sixth European gold medal, but that never was her style; she sped 48.3 to finish East Germany's meet record 3:16.87, the second-fastest time in history.

"Because I was hurt at the start of the season, it was very difficult coming back," Koch commented. "We had to change my style of training, but my form returned bit by bit. When my times started coming around, I felt very relieved. I don't know if this meet will end up being my farewell to the sport. I will decide probably by the end of the year whether or not I will continue competing."

Her decision came early in 1987: retirement. But Koch's place in track history is secure. As Vladykina said after the Canberra record, "She is simply the best ever." Kratochvilova, who competed in the 800 for the European Select team, said, "I felt a little sad to lose my record, but I always considered Marita to be the best."

Perhaps the final word goes to Kratochvilova's coach, Miroslav Kvac. His comment is a fitting summation of Koch's brilliant career: "Marita Koch is the most remarkable woman sprinter of our time."

JOAN BENOIT SAMUELSON

Asked to describe the trait which most contributed to the evolution of Joan Benoit Samuelson into the 1984 Olympic champion in the marathon, Bob Sevene replied, "She is Dr. Jekyll and Mr. Hyde."

Sevene advised Benoit through much of her distance running career, particularly during that dramatic '84 campaign. During that year, Joan suffered a crippling knee injury less than a month before the U.S. Olympic Trials in the 26-miler. She succumbed to surgery just 17 days before the race, quickly returned to training and then went out on the day that mattered most and buried the Trials field to earn her ticket to Los Angeles.

Then, as if to underline her dogged determination and iron-willed competitiveness, Benoit spurted away from her Olympic challengers after only three miles—and kept going. She outran 1983 World Champion Grete Waitz by nearly a minute-and-a-half to become the inaugural women's Olympic marathon victor.

A year later, Benoit did it again: in the 1985 America's Marathon in Chicago, Joanie slugged it out for 20 miles with World Record holder Ingrid Kristiansen before pulling away to win by nearly two minutes in 2:21:21. Her effort missed Kristiansen's global best by only 15 seconds.

Sevene's portrait of Benoit continued with writer Larry Colton: "She is like an animal; her mother hates me to call her that, but I can't think of a better way to describe her. Besides, Joanie doesn't mind the description.

"When you first meet her, she seems so very soft and gentle. She has nothing bad to say about anyone. But put her in a pair of track shorts and she is one of the most vicious

143

Guts personified: Benoit in the '84 Trials marathon.

people you will ever come across. That viciousness isn't directed toward other people, because Joanie runs her own race—yet, in a way, it is. The better another runner is, the more Joanie wants to beat her. The intensity of her approach to running isn't reflected at all in her life away from running.

"But if she is running right and feeling her best, Joanie will die before she will let anyone beat her."

Joan Benoit was born May 16, 1957, in Portland, Maine. Her first sport was cross country skiing, a natural athletic endeavor in a part of the world where cold, snowy winters are the rule. She remembered one Christmas as a child receiving skis—when, she claimed, she had asked for running shoes and a sweatsuit.

In her early teens, she suffered a leg injury in skiing and turned to running after the injury had healed in order to regain her fitness. Skiing soon was relegated to the status of a leisure-time pursuit. In her sophomore year at Cape Elizabeth High, Benoit first ran cross country. She ran with the boys' team, since her school didn't have a girls' team.

Joan played field hockey, skiied and ran through the rest of her high school years. As a senior in the spring of 1975, she won the Maine class-B state title in the mile run. Her field hockey stick had become a relic of the past, too.

She entered Bowdoin College and gained her first real national recognition when she finished seventh in the TAC National 3000-meters in 1976. A year later as a sophomore at Bowdoin, she finished sixth in the TAC 10,000. Benoit transferred to North Carolina State in 1978, but missed the bucolic solitude of her beloved Maine countryside and returned to Bowdoin to finish her final two years of college.

Early in January of 1979, Joan decided to satisfy a curiosity she had long felt about the marathon distance of 26.2 miles. She entered the Hamilton, Bermuda, Marathon and finished second with a clocking of 2:50:54. Whatever mystery the classic road distance might have held for Joanie was dispelled.

For her second outing over 26 miles of macadam—and her first real competitive effort, since the Bermuda race had been hardly more than a training run—Benoit chose the granddaddy of American marathons: Boston. It was almost like a hometown race for her, since she ran in the summer for the Boston-based Liberty Athletic Club. The environs around Hopkinton, Wellesley, Natick and Boston were familiar haunts to Benoit.

Joan didn't let her unfamiliarity with real racing over the marathon distance unsettle her in the Boston contest. Nor was she disturbed by the competitive presence of another rising Boston-based runner, Patti Catalano. Despite a sore foot, Catalano paced Benoit with a 2:28 tempo for better than half of the race. Joanie caught Patti on Heart-break Hill around the 18-mile mark and went into the lead for good one mile later.

Benoit cruised home to slash the American Record by 68 seconds. With her Boston Red Sox baseball cap askew on her head, Joanie crossed the finish in 2:35:15 to chop down Julie Brown's 2:36:23 in becoming then the fourth-fastest woman in marathon history. *Track & Field News* cautiously ventured, "If she applies herself to the marathon, Joan appears capable of running a sub-2:30."

Two months after her rousing marathon, Benoit gave another display of her gritty racing ability when she ran the 10,000-meters on the track on the first day of the TAC Championships, held in Walnut, California. Lap after lap of the 25-circuit race, Benoit traded strides with North Carolina high school senior Mary Shea. The pair provided a stark con-trast—the tall, angular Shea locked in step with the short, stoic Benoit.

Shea outsprinted Joanie on the final homestretch to win the race with an American, and World Junior, Record time of 32:52.5. Joan finished just two-tenths of a second behind.

Her toughness in the heat of combat provided a total contrast to a vision of a more whimsical Benoit seen at lunch earlier that same day: sitting quietly with a group of runners, chatting occasionally or tossing in a droll Down East witticism. It was only if you watched her carefully that you would have seen what occupied Joan—it was a pancake restaurant and she kept interchanging the tops of the syrup pitchers. Maple on raspberry, strawberry on coconut, peach on blackberry.

It was a view diametrically opposed to her on-track persona: the tenacious, fierce determination not to let go of her prey until every last ounce of energy had been sapped from her 5-foot-3, 105-pound frame. The marked difference between Benoit on the track and off seemingly always was present.

Benoit had one more appointment with the marathon in '79. In the September Nike-Oregon Track Club race in Eugene, she won in 2:35:41, less than a half-minute behind her Boston record. She ended the year ranked No. 1 in the U.S., and third globally, in the marathon. Not bad for her inaugural season.

The 1980 season started well for Joan, as she trimmed her American Record down to 2:31:23 in early February in Auckland, New Zealand. But soon after, Joan was laid low first by an emergency appendectomy, and then surgery on a shoulder. In the meantime, Catalano finished second at Boston in 2:35:08, second all-time among Americans only to Joanie's record.

Returning to action in early August, Benoit clocked 2:38.42 to place fourth in the Avon Marathon. One month later, however, Catalano made her own entry into the record rolls with a victory in Montreal in 2:30:58. Six weeks later, Patti ran brilliantly in New York, becoming the first Ameri-a woman under the 2:30 barrier with her 2:29:34. Catalano ranked first in the U.S. ahead of Joan (and second globally).

In 1981, America's best woman marathoner was Patti Catalano. She won her biggest race of the year at Boston, cutting the American Record to 2:27:51—and pulling second-placer Benoit to her own career best of 2:30:16 in the process. Joanie did some winning of her own, however, taking the TAC 10,000 title on the track and winning seven of the 13 road races she contested over a variety of distances.

The once-esoteric world of road racing had taken a quantum leap into being a full-fledged sport of its own, and Benoit was one of its stars. She twice set American road bests for the half-marathon and once at 25-kilometers. In the year-end World Rankings for the marathon, Joan rated sixth globally; she was ranked second in the U.S. behind Catalano.

147

Patti ranked No. 2 worldwide behind Norwegian star Grete Waitz.

Suddenly in 1982, the shoes of America's best woman road runner switched back from Catalano's feet to Benoit's. Patti was sidelined by the first in a long series of injuries, but Joanie had a superb season. She concentrated her efforts more on the roads—and of the 11 distances—she contested, she won nine of the races. The distances ran the gamut from 7.1-miles and 10-kilometers, through the half-marathon and 25-kilometers.

Her finest effort, though, came in the mid-September Nike-OTC marathon in Eugene. Running masterfully through a cool Oregon drizzle, Benoit sliced Catalano's American Record to 2:26:11 to become the then-second fastest woman in marathon history. Only the 2:25:29 by New Zealand's Allison Roe was faster.

Joanie motored past the 25-kilometer mark in an unofficial 1:25:20—exactly 61 seconds faster than her official American Record for the distance. She related, "Soon after that, I caught up with one of the men runners and asked if we could run together to catch a pack ahead of us. I said it would make it easier for us both.

"He gave me this crazy look and asked if I knew how fast we were going. I said I didn't because I never run with a watch. He said, '2:20 pace.' I was shocked, and thought, 'Oh-oh,' and slowed down.

"But the whole race felt so good; it felt easy, like a track race. I had too much left. I don't know if I could have gotten the World Record—but I'm sure I could have run 20 seconds faster at least. Actually, I was susprised by the American Record. Running a sub-2:30 was my only real goal."

Benoit ranked first among Americans and second in the world for the '82 season, positions she duplicated in 1983. She had surgery on both Achilles tendons early in the year—but no woman ran faster than Joanie in 1983, or ever. Her crowning race came "at home" in Boston on April 18. Just two days earlier, in London, Waitz had matched Roe's global best of 2:25:29 and after her own race, Benoit admitted she hoped to run "2:23 something" in Boston.

She did that all right, with 17 seconds to spare. Her

Joan Benoit Samuelson

Benoit wins the 1983 Boston Marathon with a World Record.

149

stunning 2:22:43 destroyed the World Record by a staggering two minutes and 46 seconds. She started fast; her 10-kilometer split of 31:50 had been bettered up to then only twice in open races—both times by Joan herself. Her half-marathon time of 1:08:23 was 39 seconds faster than her official American Record.

"The men I passed in the race kept telling me, 'Lady, watch it. Slow down,'" Joan recalled. "But I always felt in control. I kept listening to what my body told me and I felt in complete control the whole time." Then, in her quiet, understated manner, she added, "I just felt great and I thought, 'What the heck, go for it.'"

Benoit had pushed out the boundaries of women's marathoning as never before. Since World War II, ten Boston men's races had been won with times slower than hers. In 1975, the women's World Record had been 20 *minutes* slower.

Joanie also got in her licks on the track that season. She finished sixth in the TAC track 3000 in 8:53.49, which remains her career best. In late August, she won the Pan-American Games 3000 gold medal in Caracas, Venezuela. Despite her brilliant Boston run, though, Benoit ranked second globally in the marathon to Waitz. Grete had followed up her London win in record-matching time by defeating all challengers by three minutes to win the first World Championships race, and then won her fifth consecutive New York Marathon in November. Boston was Joanie's only 26-miler of '83.

Benoit knew she would run at least a pair of marathons in 1984, however. First, it would be the Olympic Trials to qualify for the U.S. team for Los Angeles. Then would come the Olympic marathon itself, the first women's 26-miler in Games history. Joan purposely scaled down her competitive schedule, competing in a few indoor meets during the winter and then one road 10-kilometer race early in March.

Then one day in late March, Benoit went out on a 20-mile training run. After 14 miles, her right knee suddenly just locked up. It simply refused to work. She had to walk home. For the next two weeks, Joan tried everything to solve the knee problem: cortisone, pain-killers, steamy saunas, baths in ice-cold water, even rest.

All of it did exactly zero good. On April 25, a distraught Benoit underwent arthroscopic surgery; the plica band, a tendon deep inside the knee, was cut. There were just 17 days left until the Olympic Trials marathon. Five days after the surgery, Joanie ran for 55 minutes without pain. Several days later, she ran for nearly two hours straight, again pain-free.

But then she developed a strained hamstring muscle in the back of her left thigh from overcompensating for the injury and during recovery. "I ran so much because I always like to go into a race feeling strong and charged up," explained Benoit. One week before the Trials, Joan couldn't run at all. Then she was treated by a machine called an Electro-Accuscope, a new-fangled device which was reputed to administer a low-level electrical stimulus to a muscle.

Regardless of exactly what the machine did, Benoit benefitted. Four days before the marathon, Joan ran 17 miles at a reasonable tempo. "After that run, I knew I could go the distance. What I wasn't sure about was whether or not I could compete with whatever pack of runners were left by 20 miles," she said. "It was the worst possible mental state for me to be in for a marathon."

Once the race started, though, Joanie was all guts and bravery. Benoit and Betty Springs moved into the lead early and shared the front through the first dozen miles. By 20-kilometers, though, it was Joan's race. She was ahead of Springs by two seconds at the halfway mark, clocking 1:13:18. Benoit continued to drive forward, as Julie Brown, Lisa Larsen and eventually Julie Isphording caught and passed Springs. It had become a race for second place.

"The last six miles were tough," Benoit admitted. "I was fine on cardiovascular terms, but my legs just wouldn't go any faster. I knew if anybody came up on me, I would have a tough time holding them off." No such problem, Joanie. She crossed the finish line with arms raised in 2:31:04, the fastest American time ever on a loop course in an all-women's race. Brown and Isphording joined Benoit on the Olympic squad.

"I came here to place in the top three and run as easily

as I could," Joanie explained after her heroic effort. I held back until 20 miles, but I won't hold back in the Olympics."

Benoit got an early look at the Los Angeles Memorial Coliseum, where the Olympic marathon would finish, when she ran in the mid-June track and field Olympic Trials. A 10,000-meter track race was scheduled as an exhibition, and Joan felt she needed to hone her pacing skills. She won by half-a-minute in 32:07.41, still her fastest ever.

Then she buckled down for some serious training leading up to the Games. It was expected that the clash between Benoit and the talented Norwegian duo of Waitz and Kristiansen would be one of the highlights of the Olympics. Joan and Grete had met only once before in the marathon: Joanie had finished third in the 1981 Boston race while Waitz had dropped out. Kristiansen, meanwhile, had twice run under 2:27 in 1984 and her 2:24:26 from London in May was the fastest time of the year. The Eastern Bloc boycott of the Los Angeles Games kept away no real gold-medal threats. It would be a titanic clash.

Joanie never let it happen. The 50-runner field trotted away from the starting line at Santa Monica College on an overcast August 5 morning. The race course started out near the Pacific Ocean, west of Los Angeles proper, and then wound inland until it concluded at the Coliseum.

For a little more than two miles, the runners watched each other, as well as the warming sun, the rising temperatures and the thickening air. Just after three miles, Benoit had had enough. She moved into the lead and began to increase her pace. Nobody knew it then, but the race for the gold medal was essentially over.

Even the great Waitz didn't go after Benoit. Everyone must have thought Joanie would wilt eventually in the heat and smog, and then she could be reeled back in by her pursuers. Everyone thought wrong. Joan kept going. . . and going and going. She had a margin of nearly 90 seconds by the 20-kilometer mark over the pursuing pack leaders of Kristiansen, Waitz, Rosa Mota of Portugal and Lorraine Moller of New Zealand.

All her pursuers realized too late that Benoit was not

Benoit is just strides away from her 1984 Olympic triumph.

about to cave in. Waitz had moved out to a solitary second place by 35-kilometers, but Joanie still had a lead of better than one minute. She entered the Coliseum in solitary splendor and completed one lap of the track to win in 2:24:52, still the fastest time ever in an all-woman race. Joanie was on her victory lap waving an American flag when Waitz finished second in 2:26:18. Mota (2:26:57) outlasted Kristiansen (2:27:34) and Moller (2:28:34) for the bronze medal.

"I promised myself months ago that I would run my race and no one else's," Joan said. "That's exactly what I did—even if I didn't want to take the lead. I didn't want to look like a showboater in the Olympic marathon if I led early and then fell apart halfway through. I always felt in control but I kept telling myself, 'You feel too good to blow this, so stay on top of your game.' "

Benoit admitted that, in retrospect, the knee injury probably was a blessing in disguise: "I decided that I probably would have run my best race at the Trials to make the team, and then had little left for the Olympics. So the injury and the timing worked out perfectly. I mean, I felt like I was following the yellow brick road. I hate to sound cocky, but it really was a very easy run."

Millions of Americans saw her gritty, brave triumph and then took Joan to their hearts. The quiet, reclusive New Englander was a star. As Jack Welch wrote in *Track & Field News,* "The race itself made history. It also made Benoit finally famous. And fame probably will be her most difficult opponent."

Joanie's first race after her glory in Los Angeles came on September 16 in the Philadelphia Half-Marathon. She seemed to have not skipped a beat as she lowered her own American Record to 1:08:34. Thirteen days later, a radiant Joan Benoit became Mrs. Scott Samuelson in Bath, Maine, in the presence of 200 family members and friends. A guest observed of the wedding, "There was a clambake, Joanie was a beautiful bride and they were very much the happy newlyweds."

In many ways, life never would be the same for Joan. She was a celebrity; talk shows called, magazines, newspapers, businesses, causes. People recognized her everywhere, once even to the point of crowding around her in a grocery store to clamor for autographs. Being famous got in the way of being a runner. Joan treasured her training time, when she could take her black Labrador, Creosote, out with her and just run away from everything for a little while.

She told Welch early in 1985, "Before the Olympics, I scheduled my day around running. After the Games, I schedule running around my day. Before Los Angeles, nothing took precedence over running. Now I'm worn out and it's frustrating. I feel I can't do the work I need to do."

Joanie did enough to win nine of the 11 road races she ran that year, though. And, as she had shown was her style, she saved her very best for the biggest contest. The America's Marathon in Chicago on October 20 pitted Samuelson against Kristiansen, who had set a scintillating World Record of 2:21:06 in London in April. Olympic bronze medalist Mota would be there, for good measure.

Samuelson and Kristiansen broke away from the other women after two miles; their climactic struggle would be an isolated one. Yet they chatted back and forth occasionally and even traded water bottles. The pair split 1:09:33 for the half-marathon, 36 seconds faster than Kristiansen's pace in her record London race. They were running on a 2:15-2:16 pace—and when told that by observers in the lead car, Joanie only rolled her eyes skyward.

Otherwise, Samuelson kept her eyes riveted on the pavement, in sharp contrast to the Norwegian who glanced up and down and all around as they ran. Once, near 18 miles, Joan was visibly cheered by hand-painted signs held by onlookers which read, "Go Maine" and "Bowdoin College."

Samuelson made her first surge at 19 miles and Kristiansen quickly responded. But after two more surges at 20 and 21 miles, Ingrid had to let go. Joanie covered the final mile in 5:24 to come home in a brilliant 2:21:21, an American Record and the second-fastest time in history. Kristiansen, at 2:23:05, was just able to hold off Mota by 24 seconds.

"I didn't feel as much in control in this race as I did in others," Joan admitted afterwards. "It's a completely

155

different ballgame with someone right on your tail all the time—especially when that someone is Ingrid. I expected Ingrid to take off sometime after the halfway point. I had some stomach problems myself after 20 miles. But I was able to keep my bull head and push on.''

Joanie's sterling effort aside, Sevene frankly stated, ''I so wish she had broken 2:20. That's such a big thing for her. If she had done it, then maybe she would have given serious thought to retiring. She and Scott want to start a family—plus I don't know how much longer her body can take the physical pounding that a marathon inflicts.''

Shortly after Chicago, in fact, Samuelson had surgery on both of her feet. That partly helped to restrict her 1986 season to a few road appearances at shorter distances, plus a track 10,000. Many non-running activities also played a part: promotional work for Nike shoes, charity drives, work for the Bowdoin alumni association, and even some race commentary on television.

Even after she won the 1985 Sullivan Award, presented to America's leading amateur athlete by the Amateur Athletic Union, and ranked first in the world in the marathon for the second consecutive year, Joan's goal of a sub-2:20 is still there. Whether she ever breaks that barrier remains to be seen.

Her place as one of the toughest, most competitive runners ever is secure, though. But her husband points out, ''In races is where people see how tough Joanie is. Away from racing, though, people can't see what a happy person she is, what a great sense of humor she has, how close and warm with friends she is. Those are sides of her that are so beautiful to see, too.''

HEIKE DRECHSLER

At the 1978 European Championships in Prague, the Soviet Union's Vilma Bardauskiene dominated the long jump competition. The 24-year-old Lithuanian from Vilnius produced a surprise in the qualifying round when she spanned 23'3¼"/7.09 on her first leap. That extended her own World Record from the 23'2½"/7.07 she had jumped twice on the same day only 11 days earlier.

In the final, held on a cold, rainy day, Bardauskiene prevailed easily, even if the dismal conditions held her best to just 22'7"/6.88. After collecting her gold medal, Bardauskiene ventured a prediction: "The dream jump of the century for women probably will be at 24'7¼"/7.50. I hope to reach this distance myself."

That same 1978 season, a 13-year-old from the East German city of Jena reached a personal best leap of 18'8"/5.69. That jump by young Heike Daute added more than four feet to her longest jump of the previous year, 14'7½"/4.46. But, after all, Heike began jumping only in 1977 and she still was learning the event.

Heike turned out to be a fast learner: by 1980, she had reached 21'9½"/6.64; in 1982, she got out to 22'10"/6.98; the next year, the 18-year-old Daute won the World Championships and hit 23'5¼"/7.14; and in 1985, the now married Heike Drechsler scored her third consecutive No. 1 in the global rankings after putting the World Record out to 24'5"/7.44.

And in 1986? Drechsler merely came the closest yet to that "magic" jump of 7½ meters when she extended her own World Record to 24'5½"/7.45—and she did it twice. Furthermore, as if to explore new frontiers, she turned her considerable talents to the sprints.

Even though it was her first season to concentrate on

Drechsler's talent blossomed early in the 1980s.

the dashes (her previous bests of 11.75 and 23.19 dated back to 1981 and 1985, respectively), Drechsler raced over those new horizons in a flash: 10.91 in the 100, equal-second fastest time of the year and 21.71 in the 200. The half-lap time simply matched the World Record first set by her renowned teammate Marita Koch.

Oh yes, Drechsler ran 21.71 twice, too—the second one in Stuttgart to win the European Championships on a cold, raw day and *into* a headwind. Since Koch's pair of 21.71 clockings, as well as Heike's first, were aided by tailwinds, Drechsler's Stuttgart effort certainly is the fastest 200 ever run by a woman.

When the inevitable comparison was put to her—that she could potentially win four Olympic gold medals in the 100, 200, long jump and 4 x 100-meter relay, as one athlete did at the 1984 Los Angeles Games—Drechsler's response was dogmatic: "I am not Carl Lewis. I am Heike Drechsler." Obviously, that is more than adequate.

Heike Daute was born December 16, 1964, in Gera, East Germany. Her family soon moved to Jena, the city where she grew. As many athletes in Eastern Bloc nations do, Heike first began participating in athletics at school sports days. Observant coaches noted her ability, as well as her long-legged physique. She eventually came under the tutelage of Peter Hein, coach of Sport Club Motor Jena; he has been her coach throughout her career.

She began competition in earnest as a 12-year-old in 1977 with that best of 14'7½". As she grew and developed, her coaches felt Heike would become a heptathlon star. In 1980, at age 15, she accumulated 5855 points in the seven-event discipline, the second-highest total among East Germany's multi-eventers for that year. And her long jump best of 21'9½"/6.64 had come in another heptathlon.

Drechsler recalled, "My real home always was the combined event. From the beginning of my career, my coach saw to it that my training was versatile: it included distance running, sprinting and shot putting, as well as jumping.

"But it was increasingly clear by the time I was 15 or so that my real future would be in the long jump. So I began to concentrate most on that—but I still like to do a heptathlon once or twice a year, for fun."

In 1981, Drechsler showed the choice had been the right one. Her best jump of 22'8"/6.91 was equal-second longest for the season, she won the European Junior title and she gained her first worldwide ranking with a sixth-place rating. She scored 5891 heptathlon points, but it was clear that her future was rapidly arriving in the long jump.

Even at her young age, however, Drechsler was able to keep in perspective the rapid strides she was making. "My parents and my coach, Peter Hein, helped to keep my attitude relaxed," she explained. "When you reach the high international level so quickly in your career, you are put under great pressure to be successful. I simply approach every competition with the determination to do my very best. I feel if I do that, I should win. And if I jump a very long ways, all the better. But the first aim is to win."

Heike improved just 2¾" in 1982 to 22'10¾"/6.98, but claimed the World Junior Record with that leap. She just missed a medal at the European Championships in Athens, placing fourth, and ranked as the No. 5 jumper in the year-end global rankings. Some observers noted that she tended to perform at a lesser level outside East Germany; she still was young and a newcomer to the pressure cooker of international-level competition, seemed to be the thinking.

Drechsler got her chance to display her maturity in 1983 at the inaugural World Championships, staged in Helsinki. The favorite heading to the Finnish capital was Romania's Anisoara Cusmir-Stanciu, who had extended the World Record three times in 1983 to a best of 24'4½"/7.43. Her teammate Vali Ionescu, the '82 European winner and a record-setter herself early in '83, would be in the thick of the fight, as would top American Carol Lewis.

As luck would have it, the draw for the final put Stanciu fourth in the jumping order with Drechsler right behind her in fifth. Stanciu threw down the gauntlet to the field on her first effort when she reached 22'11¾"/7.00. Up next, Drechsler responded with a wind-aided 22'8"/6.91. Lewis, followed Drechsler, moved to second at 22'9"/6.93.

In the second round of jumping, Drechsler reached

23'½"/7.02 to take the lead. In the next sequence of jumps, however, Stanciu responded strongly with a wind-aided 23'5¼"/7.15. It was a short-lived lead, however, as Heike put everything together and hit the sand at 23'10¼"/7.27. Even if it was aided by a wind over the legal limit of two meters per second, Drechsler's jump put her in command to stay.

No one else could approach Heike, but in round four, Drechsler herself popped 23'6"/7.16 to give her two jumps better than the longest Stanciu could produce. So at the age of 18, Heike Drechsler was the World Champion. Stanciu finished second, Lewis third, but Ionescu managed only 21'8¾"/6.62 to place ninth.

"I knew that sometimes in important meets, I didn't feel very confident in the beginning of the competition," Drechsler reflected. "But when I jumped 6.91 on my first jump in Helsinki, I felt good and that boosted my confidence right away. Then I was able to put together a good series. I was very happy to win the world title, because then I could turn toward 1984 with great confidence. I looked ahead solely to the Olympic Games."

Sadly, there would be no Olympics in '84 for Drechsler, or any other athletes from Eastern Bloc nations. A boycott of the Los Angeles Games kept the athletes home. Ostensibly, the boycott resulted from announced doubts about security measures for athletes; many observers felt, however, the eastern boycott was a retaliatory move against the United States after the U.S.-led boycott of the 1980 Moscow Games.

Regardless, Drechsler must have felt a bitter irony when Stanciu collected the Olympic gold medal with a pedestrian leap of 22'10"/6.96. During 1984, Drechsler compiled a stellar year, winning all 10 of her outdoor meets, jumping beyond 22'10" in nine of them and matching that distance in the other.

She reached a best that year of 24'3½"/7.40, a slim inch behind Stanciu's World Record. That effort came on July 26, and two days later, Heike became Mrs. Andreas Drechsler as she married the star goalie of SC Motor Jena's soccer team. Three weeks later, she won the Eastern Bloc Friendship Games with 23'5½"/7.15. Heike was an unquestioned repeat

No. 1 in the World Rankings.

For the 1985 season, Drechsler had to plan for a late peak, since the team-oriented World Cup competition was scheduled for early October in Canberra, Australia. During the summer season, Heike twice leaped 24'3¾"/7.33 for the longest mark of the year. She won the dual meet competition against the Soviet Union, outjumping Soviet star Galina Chistyakova who had defeated Heike during the winter at the European Indoor Championships.

However, at the European Cup meet in mid-August, Chistyakova leaped her best of the year, 23'10¾"/7.28, to upset Drechsler who reached 23'8¾"/7.23. Heike wasn't overly upset about the loss, though. "From such defeats, you can draw conclusions about what you have to do in following competitions in order to win," she observed.

Three days later, at Zurich's Weltklasse meet, Drechsler hit a year-leading 24'3"/7.39; Chistyakova placed only third (23'7½"/7.20) behind Jackie Joyner of the U.S. (American Record of 23'9"/7.24). Drechsler then took a month away from competition, just training and getting ready for the World Cup.

East Germany's athletes reappeared on the competitive stage on September 22 at a tuneup meet in East Berlin. "It was a cold and rainy day, and it felt like just a usual day of competition," said Drechsler in looking back on what would become a very important day to her. "There were only four of us jumping in the competition, but I considered only Helga Radtke to be a real rival." Radtke had recorded a career-best jump of 23'8"/7.21 in 1984.

Drechsler made it no contest early on, hitting 23'5½"/7.15 on her first leap and 23'9"/7.24 on her second. She fouled her third and fourth tries and jumped 23'6¾"/7.18 on her fifth. Then Heike was up for her final jump. The wind measured the maximum allowable speed of two meters per second. The crowd loudly urged on Drechsler.

And Heike responded. She pounded down the runway, hit the takeoff board perfectly, soared up and out and sliced into the sand virtually even with the marker indicating the World Record. The fans roared, and then exploded again when the distance was announced: 24'5"/7.44. Drechsler had added one centimeter to Stanciu's former record.

"When the judge announced the distance, I was so relieved," admitted Drechsler. "I finally had set the World Record people had been expecting of me for so long. I was very relieved, but also not too surprised because the record had come on my final jump. Usually, my first and last jumps are my best, if I don't overstep the board and foul. I was overjoyed to finally set the record—even if it was by just one centimeter. But, then, a record is a record."

Drechsler closed out her '85 campaign by beating Chistyakova at the World Cup by nearly one foot with a 23'10¼"/7.27 effort. Heike claimed her third consecutive No. 1 World Ranking. "After I finally jumped a World Record, I felt much more at ease," Drechsler commented. "My self confidence increased so much. I felt a strong sense of certainty within myself."

Nowhere was her self-confidence better displayed than during the 1986 indoor season. Drechsler was named Indoor Athlete Of The Year after winning her first European Indoor title and claiming the indoor record with 23'11"/7.29. And as if to dangle a tantalizing carrot in front of the world's track fans, she sped the arcane distance of 100 yards in 10.24, one-hundredth-of-a-second faster than Marita Koch's indoor record.

That sprint mark equated roughly to 11.1 seconds for 100-meters—and recall that her best of 11.75 dated back to 1981. But Drechsler downplayed talk of her taking a serious try at the sprints: "The long jump is enough! I have enough difficulty concentrating on six long jumps, let alone adding something else to my mind.

"If my fortunes in the long jump drop off someday, then I might consider looking more seriously at the sprints. For now, though, there is no question of changing."

Notice that Drechsler specified *changing* to the sprints; she didn't say a word about *adding* them to her repertoire. So, it turned out in 1986 that East Germany produced another brilliant sprint talent—Heike Drechsler. In early June, she zipped 10.97 in the 100 to become the No. 7 performer in history over the distance.

Ten days later, on June 21 in the always-titanic clash

Drechsler emerged as a record-matching sprinter in '86.

between East Germany and the USSR, Drechsler erupted. First, Heike added half-an-inch to her long jump World Record as she spanned 24'5½"/7.45. The record leap came on her sixth and final jump; her third jump also measured beyond 24 feet at 24'1½"/7.35. She returned the next day to dash the 200 in 22.13, her career best.

Just eight days after that sensational pair of efforts, Heike contested her national championships. On the first day, an illegal wind pushed her to a long jump triumph of 24'1½"/7.35 and she also produced a legal leap of 23'11"/7.29.

She was up early the next morning, June 29, to endure one of those slice-of-life interviews by American television (she likes science fiction movies; classical music by Beethoven and Mozart and rock tunes by an East German band called "Karat"; she loves to cook and her husband Andreas has an especially soft spot in his appetite for her Thuringian dumplings).

Then it was off to the track for the final in the 200 meters. She tied her blonde-streaked brown curls into a pony-tail and then surged the half-lap in 21.71 to come home equal to Marita Koch's World Record. The aiding wind was a legal 1.2 meters per second. Suddenly, Heike was a record-setting sprinter, too.

"I never expected such a time," Heike admitted. "Coach Peter Hein said to wait until the last 100 meters to make my strongest effort. I was simply hoping for a time under 22 seconds. Now some people already are predicting a time of 21.60 for me, but I never want to categorize myself. I have to learn to run the turn better; I have so much experience to gain."

The confidence Drechsler gained from her sprinting breakthrough showed up in the long jump. On July 3, she again jumped 24'5½"/7.45 to tie her fresh World Record. "Since my sprinting has started to blossom, I have found myself able to give maximum efforts on all six of my long jumps," she said.

Several days later, Heike ventured to Moscow for the Goodwill Games, a made-for-television sporting festival concocted by American entertainment magnate Ted Turner as a kind of replacement-after-six-years for the boycott-diluted

Moscow Olympics. Heike ran only the 100 and expected to face American Pam Marshall, who had won the U.S. championship ahead of Olympic silver medalist Alice Brown and LA winner Evelyn Ashford, who was back after a year's maternity leave.

A sore groin muscle caused Marshall to withdraw from the race, though. That opened up a lane for Ashford and the Olympic champion would face what Evelyn herself called "*the* hot girl in the sprints this year." For 50 meters of the race, Drechsler led the field, but then Ashford's supreme effort pulled her even with Heike. They flashed across the finish together, but the photofinish picture showed Ashford a narrow winner as both clocked 10.91. It was Drechsler's personal best—and remember she had started the season with a best of 11.75.

But Drechsler was saving her best for the biggest meet, of course. Other than the Olympics and World Championships, there is no higher-quality meet in the world than the European Championships. Heike was entered in her two record events. She clearly dominated the long jump, winning with a meet record leap of 23'10¼"/7.27. Such was her superiority that her *fourth*-best jump of the day still would have won the gold medal.

So by the time Drechsler got to the 200, she had nothing to lose. She was a clear favorite, since teammates Marlies Gohr and Marita Koch concentrated on their specialties of the 100 and 400 (each won a record third consecutive title). The day of the 200 final was rainy and cold, with puddles spotting the track in Stuttgart's Neckarstadion.

Nothing stopped Drechsler, though. She rocketed off her starting blocks and appeared to take command after just a few strides of the race. With every step, she lengthened her commanding lead. She powered down the homestretch and surged across the finish line with her head down. France's Marie-Christine Cazier finished second a country mile back at 22.32 seconds.

Heike again clocked 21.71 seconds to match the World Record and give her an equal number of record times with Koch. The wind reading of minus 0.8 meters per second meant Heike matched the global best while running into a headwind; if a tailwind had been pushing her along, she certainly would have run the fastest 200 ever.

"If the weather had been better, I could have broken the record," Drechsler confirmed. "People have said I can run 21.60, and now I believe it. This still was a difficult title to win, because I had never run two qualifying races before a final in my career."

Drechsler became only the second athlete in history, man or woman, to achieve two or more running World Records and two or more field event records. The first was the immortal Fanny Blankers-Koen of Holland, who set marks at 100 yards and 100 meters, 220 yards, the 80-meter hurdles, high jump, long jump and pentathlon. And with her four global marks, Drechsler owns more current World Records than any other woman. To cap off 1986, Heike finished a close second to World Record-setting heptathlete Jackie Joyner in the Athlete Of The Year poll conducted by *Track & Field News.*

"Of course I would like to be the first woman to jump 7½ meters in the long jump," Drechsler confirmed. "I look most toward the 1988 Olympics in Seoul. After that, I will decide how much longer I will compete." Drechsler is studying to be an elementary school teacher as well.

Throughout her career, Heike Drechsler has had high expectations placed on her. Her masterful talent has allowed her to respond with unquestioned brilliance. "I feel the followers of track and field expect a World Record holder to always perform very well," she said. "That is a great obligation, to prove in every competition that you deserve the title. You might not win every competition, but you can never give up without a good fight." Despite her youthful age and brief career, Drechsler has proved she is a record-holder continually deserving of the honor.

PROFILES OF OTHER WOMEN'S GREATS: WORLD

KEY TO THE SYMBOLS

Athletes are listed alphabetically. A name in parentheses which follows the athlete's full name is a married name. A bracketed name is the athlete's maiden name.

The major honors achieved by each athlete are listed on the same line as her name, incorporating the following symbols (a number preceding any honors indicates the number of such honors won; each category is separated by semicolons):

G   = Gold medal in the Olympic Games or World Championships.

S   = Silver medal.

B   = Bronze medal.

r   = Medal won as member of a relay team.

WR   = An outdoor World Record, as recognized (from 1932) by the International Amateur Athletic Federation (IAAF), or by the Association of Track & Field Statisticians. (The ATFS recognizes World Record performances not considered by the IAAF prior to 1932.) Includes the marathon, but not relay records.

No. 1   = Number one selection in World Rankings. The Rankings began in 1956 as the brainchild of the brilliant Czech statistician, the late Jan Popper. They were published, mainly in Europe, up to 1967 when Popper's rankings were first published worldwide in *Women's Track & Field World*. Popper's ratings appeared in *WTFW* through 1975 and in *Track & Field News* from 1976-'85. The 1986 Rankings were prepared by *T&FN*.

AOY   = Selected as world Athlete Of The Year by *WTFW* (1967-'74) or *T&FN* (since 1974).

*   = Following "No. 1" or "AOY" indicates that, in the opinion of the author and *T&FN* Women's Editor Howard Willman, the athlete would have ranked No. 1 in an event, or been named Athlete Of The Year, one or more times (undeter-

mined unless preceded by a number) prior to the first Jan Popper World Rankings in 1956, and the first AOY selection in 1967.

The second line indicates event(s), years of major competition, date of birth (and death, when applicable), and height/weight when known.

All statistics as of June 1, 1987.

A

ACKERMANN, ROSEMARIE [Witschas] (East Germany) . . .
G; 7 WR; 4 No. 1; AOY
High Jump, 1971-80 . . . . . 4/4/52, 5'9¼"/130

The world's finest high jumper in the decade of the 1970s, Ackermann made history on August 26, 1977, in West Berlin when she scaled the event's formidable barrier of 2.00 meters (6'6¾") for a World Record. Earlier in the same competition, she had made 6'5½"/1.97 to equal her own global mark. Undefeated that season, Ackermann was selected Athlete Of The Year. She first emerged in '72 with a 7th in the Olympics, and produced her first WR in '74. She set 7 outdoor records in 4 years.

The last record-setter to use the straddle style, Ackermann won the '76 Olympics and '74 Europeans, placed 2nd in the '78 Euros and 4th in the '80 Olympics. Achilles tendon problems hampered her last two seasons and she retired shortly after the Moscow Games.

A quiet, self-effacing athlete, Ackermann said after her historic 2.00 leap, "I always thought that the first woman over 2 meters would be someone greater than me."

ASHFORD, EVELYN (USA)
See U. S. section.

B

BALAS, IOLANDA (Romania) . . 2G; 14 WR; 9 No. 1; AOY*
High Jump, 1955-66 . . . . . .12/12/36, 6'¾"/159
See chapter.

BALZER, KARIN (East Germany) . . . . . G, B; 6 WR; 4 No. 1
    80/100 Hurdles, 1960-72 . . . . 6/5/38, 5'7¼"/141
    The barrier-breaking hurdler after the 80-meter event was
extended to 100-meters following the '68 Olympics, Balzer
was the first to run under 13 seconds (12.9 '69). Twice she
ran 12.7 ('70, '71) and then sped 12.6 on July 31, 1971. One
of the three women hurdlers to make three Olympic finals
(Aussies Shirley Strickland and Pam Ryan are the others),
Balzer won the 1964 race, placed 5th in '68 and 3rd in '72.
She also competed in the 1960 Games, failing to make the
final.
    Balzer triumphed in three consecutive European Cham-
pionships ('66, '69, '71), after placing 2nd in 1962. Also an
excellent sprinter, she won a silver medal in the '71 European
4 x 100 relay.

Ackermann celebrates after her historic 2.00 (6'6¾") leap.

BAUMA, HERMA (Austria) . . . . . . .G; 2 WR; No. 1*; AOY*
        Javelin, 1936-52. . . . . . 1/23/15, 5'3¼"/150
The 4th-placer in the '36 Olympic javelin, Bauma returned 12 years later to take the gold medal. She set World Records in 1947 (158'2"/48.20, the lone officially-approved women's WR that year), and '48 (159'6"/48.62), placed 2nd in the '50 Europeans and 9th in the '52 Olympics.

BENOIT, JOAN (Samuelson) (USA)
        See U.S. Section.

BLANKERS-KOEN, FANNY (Holland) . . . .
        3G, Gr; 11 WR; W No. 1*; 3 AOY*
        Sprints/hurdles/jumps, 1936-52. . 4/26/18, 5'8¾"/139
        See chapter.

BOYLE, RAELENE (Australia) 3S
        Sprints, 1968-82. . . . . . 6/24/51, 5'5¾"/130
Boyle was a marvelously fast bridesmaid in the Olympics, finishing 4th in the '68 100 (career best of 11.20) and 2nd in the 200, 2nd in both dashes in '72 (11.23/22.45 personal best) and 4th in the '76 100 (11.23). She twice scored golden triples in the Commonwealth Games, however, winning the 100, 200 and 4 x 100 relay in 1970 and '74. She moved up to the 400 late in her career and won the '82 Commonwealth; her one-lap best was 51.08. She World Ranked 2nd in the 100 once ('72) and three times in the 200 ('68, '71, '72).

BRAGINA, LYUDMILA (USSR) . . . . G; 7 WR; 2 No. 1
        Middle Distances, 1969-77 . . . . 7/24/43, 5'5"/126
Already World Record holder heading to the '72 Olympics (4:06.9), Bragina made a shambles of the Munich field in the inaugural Olympic 1500, breaking her WR in her heat, semi-final and final (4:01.38). She returned in Montreal to place 5th and shortly afterward set her third WR over 3000-meters with 8:27.12. That mark survived for nearly six years. Bragina began serious training at the relatively advanced age of 21 and won in Munich at age 29.

BRIESENICK, ILONA [Schoknecht] (Slupianek) (EG).....
G, B; 2 WR; 5 No. 1; AOY
Shot Put, 1975- ......9/24/56, 5'10¾"/205
The dominant shot putter in the world in the late 1970s
and early '80s, Briesenick won the 1980 Olympics and threw
World Records of 73'4½"/22.36 and 73'8"/22.45 that season
to earn Athlete Of The Year honors. She was the world's top-
ranked shot heaver from 1978-'82; she missed much of the
'78 season due to a suspension for a positive drug test.
Briesenick won three consecutive World Cups ('77, '79,
'81) and a pair of European titles ('78, '82), and placed 3rd
in the '83 World Championships. Her second marriage was to
shot star Hartmut Briesenick ('71, '74 Euro champ; 3rd '72
Olympics) and she missed the '85 season and most of '86 due
to maternity.

BRISCO-HOOKS, VALERIE (USA)
See U.S. section.

BYSTROVA, GALINA (USSR) ... B; 3 WR; 3 No. 1; AOY*
Hurdles/multi, 1956-65 .....2/8/34, 5'7"/143
The USSR's multi-event star between Aleksandra Chudina and Irina Press, Bystrova set a pentathlon World Record
of 4846 points in 1957 and upped it to 4872 in '58. She
matched the 80-meter hurdles WR of 10.6 in '58, too. She
won both events at the '58 Europeans and retained her pentathlon title in '62. At the Olympics, she finished 4th in the
'56 80-meter hurdles and 5th in '60, and placed 3rd in the
'64 pentathlon. She was the world's top-ranked pentathlete
in '57 and '58 and led the hurdles in '58 as well.

C

CHENG, CHI (Taiwan).........B; 7 WR; 3 No. 1; 2 AOY
Sprints/hurdles, 1960-73 ... 3/15/44, 5'7¾"/137
The greatest Asian athlete in the second half of the 20th
century (Japan's Kinue Hitomi being the first, in the late
1920s), Chi is the only Asian woman to win a track and field

Chi Cheng

Lyudmila Bragina

Ilona Briesenick readies to throw at the '80 Olympics.

medal in a post-war Olympics. She placed 3rd in the 80-meter hurdles at the '68 Mexico Games. A multi-talented performer, Chi made her biggest headlines as a sprinter and hurdler. In 1969, she won all but one of her 67 outdoor competitions, set a WR over the 200-meter hurdles and matched the 100-yard record to be selected Athlete Of The Year. But her greatest year by far was 1970.

In that season, Chi went undefeated in all 83 of her competitions. She set or matched 7 World Records, including one-day doubles of 10.0/22.7 for 100/220-yards, and 12.8/22.4 for the 100-meter hurdles/200. Her other record times were 11.0 100-meters, 22.6 220-yards and 26.2 200-meter hurdles.

Her career was dogged by injury, however. She missed the '72 Olympic Games after an operation which removed some 9" of muscle from her upper left leg. Various leg miseries finally forced her to retire in 1973. She returned home to Taiwan early in the 1980s from southern California, where she had attended college and developed into a world-class athlete.

Always immensely popular in her island nation, she was elected to the national senate in 1981, gaining 67% of the votes while the remaining 51 candidates together claimed the rest. Besides being a successful politician and newspaper columnist, Chi also heads the Taiwan national track and field federation, and is a member of Taiwan's Olympic Committee.

CHIZOVA, NADEZHDA (USSR).... G, S, B; 9 WR; 7 No. 1
Shot Put, 1965-76...... 9/29/45, 5'8½"/198

The most prolific setter of accepted World Records in shot history, Chizova's 9 marks ranged from 61'3"/18.67 in 1968 to 69'6¾"/21.20 in 1973 and she also threw a never-accepted 70'4½"/21.45 in '73. That was history's first heave beyond 70 feet. Chizova won a complete set of Olympic medals, starting with a bronze in '68. She won in 1972 (with a WR 69'0"/21.03) and placed 2nd in 1976 (after missing all of the '75 season with a back injury). She also is the only woman ever to win 4 consecutive European titles in any event ('66, '69, '71, '74).

CHUDINA, ALEKSANDRA (USSR) . . . 2S, B; 6 WR; AOY*
Jumps/multi-event, 1945-56 . . . 11/6/23, 6'2"/161

The great Soviet multi-event talent immediately after World War II, Chudina first emerged with a 2nd in the '46 European high jump. She reached her peak in the early 1950s and won medals in three field events at the '52 Olympics (2nd long jump and javelin; 3rd high jump). She set 5 pentathlon World Records between 1947 and 1955, her highest total being 4750 points. In '54, she high jumped a WR 5'8" and won the European pentathlon and placed 2nd in the long jump (as well as 5th in the javelin and 6th in the high jump).

During her career, Chudina captured 31 USSR outdoor titles, the most Soviet titles ever won by any athlete. Her wins ranged from the 400 meters and 80-meter hurdles, through the high jump, long jump and javelin to the pentathlon.

CUTHBERT, BETTY (Australia) . . . .
3G, Gr; 11 WR; 4 No. 1; AOY*
Sprints, 1956-64 . . . . . . 4/20/38, 5'6½/126
See chapter.

D

DAN, SHIN GEUM (North Korea) . . . . WR; 8 No. 1
400/800, 1959-67 . . . . . . 7/3/38, 5'8"/137

One of the more mysterious, and controversial, athletes in the 1960s, Dan was the first runner under 52 seconds for 400 meters and two minutes for the 800. Her problem was that North Korea did not belong to the IAAF, or her performances came in non-IAAF sanctioned meets. So only her 51.9 in 1962, the first sub-52 400, was officially approved as a WR. Her one-lap marks of 53.0 ('60, '62), 51.4 ('63) and 51.2 ('64), and 800s of 2:01.2 ('61), 1:59.1 ('63) and 1:58.0 ('64) were never accepted as records. Dan ranked 1st globally in the 400 in 1960-'64 and in the 800 in '61, '63 and '64.

Dan's tall, slim stature—not to mention her fast times—gave rise to charges she was a man masquerading as a woman.

She was examined by Japanese doctors in Tokyo before the 1964 Olympics, though, and the doctors claimed she was "100% female." She was known by the Westernized "Shin Kim" Dan for years, before transliterations reverted to the traditional Korean.

DE LA HUNTY, SHIRLEY STRICKLAND (Australia) . . . . .
2G, Gr, Sr, 3B; 3 WR; No. 1*; AOY*
Sprints/hurdles, 1948-56 . . . . 7/18/25
See chapter.

DIDRIKSON, MILDRED ("Babe") (USA)
See U.S. section.

DRECHSLER, HEIKE [Daute] (East Germany). . . . .
G; 5 WR; 5 No. 1
Sprints/Long Jump, 1981- . . .12/16/64, 5'11¼"/150
See chapter.

DUMBADZE, NINA (USSR). . . . . .B; 7 WR; No. 1*
Discus, 1939-1952. . . .1/23/19-4/14/83, 5'10"/181
Dumbadze set 7 discus global bests between 1939 and 1952, but only 3 were accepted as official World Records as the USSR was not a member of the IAAF until 1947. Her unratified marks included 161'1"/49.10 and 162'6"/49.54 in '39, 163'8"/49.88 in '44 and 165'8"/50.50 in '46. Her accepted WRs were 174'8"/53.24 ('48), 175'1"/53.36 ('51) and 187'2"/57.04 ('52). The latter effort added 11'3"/3.44 to the former record (175'10"/53.60 by teammate Nina Ponomaryeva), the greatest improvement in discus history. Dumbadze was the first to win two European discus titles ('46, '50) and she finished 3rd in the '52 Olympics.

E

EHRHARDT, ANNELIE (East Germany). . G; 4 WR; 3 No. 1
100-meter Hurdles, 1970-76 . . . 6/18/50, 5'5¼"/128
The technically immaculate Ehrhardt was the master of the 100-meter barriers in the early '70s. She won the '72

Olympics in a World Record 12.59—a mark which stood for 6 years and was unapproached for at least half that period. Ehrhardt was undefeated from '72 through '74, ranked 1st in the world those years and won the '74 European title. She ran hand-timed WRs of 12.5 (twice in '72) and 12.3 ('73), but that historic 12.59 clocking kept her among history's 10 fastest performers as late as 1984.

F

FALCK, HILDEGARD (West Germany). . . G, Br; WR; No. 1
800-meters, 1970-73. . . . . . 6/8/49, 5'8"/126

Because North Korea was not a member of the IAAF, Shin Geum Dan never received official recognition of her 1:59.1 in November of 1963, nor her 1:58.0 in August of '64, as World Records for 800. But those were the first clockings under 2 minutes over the 2-lap distance. Falck claimed the honor of the first accepted sub-2:00 WR when she clocked 1:58.45 on July 11, 1971. She won the '72 Olympic title in Munich, running just 0.10 shy of her WR with an Olympic Record 1:58.55. She also won a bronze medal on the 3rd-place 4 x 400 team. Falck ranked 1st in the world in '72; she had rated 2nd in 1970 and 3rd in '71.

FIBINGEROVA, HELENA (Czechoslovakia) . . . .
G, B; 2 WR; 2 No. 1
Shot Put, 1972- . . . . . .7/13/49, 5'10½"/194

The Czech was a long-established talent (World Records in 1976 of 72'1¾"/21.99 and in '77 of 73'2¾"/22.32, plus an indoor 73'10"/22.50 which remained the longest women's throw for 7 years). But she had trouble winning the major outdoor titles: 3rd '76 Olympics, 3rd '74 Europeans and then 2nd in '78 and '82.

Fibingerova did win 8 European Indoor titles between 1973-85, but a major outdoor victory eluded her until the inaugural World Championships in '83. In Helsinki, she moved from 4th place to the gold medal on the last throw of the competition with her effort of 69'¾"/21.05. Then she brought roars of delight from the crowd as she pursued as

Marlies Gohr

Annelie Ehrhardt

many of the startled officials as she could catch and administered a bear hug and a big kiss to each. She ranked 1st globally in '83, as well as '77.

FUCHS, RUTH (East Germany) . . . . 2G; 6 WR; 8 No. 1
    Javelin, 1967-80 . . . . . .12/14/46, 5'6½"/157
    See chapter.

G

GOHR, MARLIES [Oelsner] (East Germany). . . . .
    G, 3 Gr, S; 3 WR; 6 No. 1
    Sprints, 1976- . . . . . . .3/21/58, 5'5"/121
    Gohr was the career-long sprint rival for Ashford—and vice versa. The East German compiled a sparkling career. She set three WRs at 100-meters (10.88 in '77 and '82, 10.81 in '83), ran a close 2nd in the '80 Olympics, won three consecutive European titles ('78, '82, '86) and sped to the '83 World Championship. She also was a member of nine WR-setting 4 x 100 teams, including the 41.37 squad at the '85 World Cup. In the relay, Gohr won Olympic gold medals in '76 and '80, the '83 World title and Euro wins in '82 and '86. She ranked No. 1 in the 100 six times ('77, '78, '80, '82, '83, '85).

A leg on a record-setting 4 x 200 team in 1976 gave Gohr participation in 13 career World Records; added to 8 unofficial indoor bests, she could claim 21 total global records (at the start of 1987). She is one of only three sprinters to run on a pair of Olympic 4 x 100 winners (American Annette Rogers and Gohr's teammate Barbel Wockel are the others). For good luck, Gohr ran in the same national-team jersey since 1981.

GUMMEL, MARGITTA (East Germany) . . . .
    G, S; 4 WR; No. 1; AOY
    Shot Put, 1962-72. . . . . . 6/29/41, 5'10"/198
    A middle-of-the-World-Rankings type of putter in the early 1960s, Gummel ranked 8th in '62, 4th in '63, 5th in '64 (she placed 6th in the Tokyo Olympics) and 6th in '65. But

in 1966, she won the European silver medal and ranked 3rd, and moved to 2nd in '67. She was at her very best in Mexico for the '68 Olympics. She had thrown a WR 61'11"/18.87 before the Games and lengthened that to 62'6¾"/19.07 and 64'4"/19.61 during the Olympic competition. Her records and gold medal gave her Athlete Of The Year honors for 1968. Gummel extended the WR to 65'11½"/20.10 in 1969; she placed 2nd in the Europeans and World Rankings. She rated 3rd in '70 and 2nd in '71 (3rd place in Euros) before closing out her career with a 2nd in the 1972 Olympics (career-best of 66'4¼"/20.22) as well as the World Rankings.

GUSENBAUER, ILONA (Austria) . . . .B; WR; 2 No. 1; AOY
    High Jump, 1967-73. . . . . .9/16/47, 5'11"/148
    The tall Austrian straddler reached her peak in 1970 and '71, seasons she ranked 1st in the world. In '71, she upped the WR to 6'3½"/1.92 and won the European title to secure selection as Athlete Of The Year. Exactly one year after Gusenbauer set her WR (Sept. 4, 1971), Ulrike Meyfarth matched it to win the '72 Olympics, with Gusenbauer 3rd. Ilona's personal high of 6'4"/1.93 also came in '72.

H

HELTEN, INGE (West Germany) . . . . .Sr, B; WR
    Sprints, 1971-76 . . . . . .12/31/50, 5'6½"/126
    Helten was a decent sprinter who had ranked 6th in the world in 1971 and ran a leg on the European title-winning 4 x 100. She didn't rank again until '75 (7th), but burst to record-setting levels with her 11.04 World Record 100 in June of 1976. (The mark lasted only a month, until it was bettered in the Montreal Olympic semis by teammate Annegret Richter.) Helten won the 100 bronze in '76, got her lifetime best of 22.68 in placing 5th in the 200 and won a silver in the 4 x 100. She ranked 3rd in the 100 in '76.

HITOMI, KINUE (Japan) . . . . .S; 5 WR; No. 1*; AOY*
    Jumps/Multi-event, 1926-30 . . . . .1/1/08- / /31
    The first world-class athlete to emerge out of Asia, Hitomi was the first Asian woman to set a World Record and

183

to win an Olympic medal. She made her international debut in 1926 in Goteborg, Sweden, at the second women's World Games. At the age of 18, she won both the running and standing long jumps (the former with a world best of 18'½"/ 5.50), placed 2nd in the discus, 3rd in the 100 and 5th in the 60 meters.

In 1928, with neither of her specialties—the 200 and long jump—on the first Olympic program for women, Hitomi chose an unlikely 100-800 double. She finished 4th in her 100 semi and didn't make the final. Then, despite her inexperience, she ran 2nd in the 800 in 2:17.6 (only 0.8 behind Lina Radke's 2:16.8 WR). Earlier in 1928, Hitomi set an official long jump record of 19'7½"/5.98. In 1929, she had a jump of 19'11"/6.07 which was wind-aided. Also in '29, she sped a straight 200 in 24.7; the previous year, she had become the first woman to run 400-meters under one minute with her 59.0 effort.

In 1930, she set a pentathlon global mark of 3841 points and again starred at the third edition of the World Games, winning the long jump (19'4¼"/5.90) and placing 2nd in the triathlon and 3rd in the 60-meters and discus. She then took part in 20 events in 7 days: seven in a dual meet against Poland, then 6 against Belgium six days later and finally another 7 against France. She was expected to be one of Babe Didrikson's prime challengers in the '32 Los Angeles Olympics, but died of tuberculosis in 1931 at the age of 23.

HOFFMEISTER, GUNHILD (East Germany). .2S, B; 4 No. 1
    800/1500, 1970-76 ...... 7/6/44, 5'7¾"/123
For much of her fine career, Hoffmeister fit the "close but no cigar" description. She finished 2nd in the '71 European 1500; 3rd in the '72 Olympic 800 and 2nd at 1500; then 2nd in the '74 Euro 800. But she finally struck gold by winning the '74 European 1500. It was back to silver in the '76 Olympic 1500. She claimed a pair of No. 1 rankings in both the 800 ('70, '73) and 1500 ('73, '74). Hoffmeister ran on two World Record 4 x 800 teams in her career. Her career bests were 1:58.61 ('76) and 4:01.4 ('76).

HOPKINS, THELMA (Great Britain) . . . . . . =S; WR; No. 1*
High Jump, 1952-56 . . . . . 3/16/36, 5'7"/146

The 4th-placer in the '52 Olympic high jump, Hopkins had her finest season in 1954 when she won the British Commonwealth title (plus a 2nd in the long jump) and the European crown to rank 2nd in the world. In 1956, she set a World Record of 5'8½"/1.74 in May and then tied for 2nd in the Olympics, clearing 5'5¾"/1.67.

HYMAN, DOROTHY (Great Britain) . . . . .S, B; 3 No. 1
Sprints, 1958-69 . . . . 5/9/41, 5'7"/130

Hyman scored a considerable medal haul before her 22nd birthday. At the '58 Commonwealth, she won a gold on England's winning 4 x 110-yard relay team. At the '60 Olympics, she placed 2nd in the 100 and 3rd in the 200. At the 1962 Commonwealth, Hyman won the 100 and 220-yards and ran on the 2nd-place relay team; at the Europeans, she won the 100, placed 2nd at 200 and completed a set of medals on the 3rd-place relay team. She ranked 1st in the world in the 100 in '62 and '63 (the year she twice sped her 11.3 personal best), and the 200 in '63. She didn't qualify for either sprint final at the Tokyo Olympics. Hyman was banned from international competition in 1969 after receiving the proceeds of a book sale. But she returned to compete domestically and won the British 200 title.

I

ITKINA, MARIA (USSR) . . . . 9 WR; 4 No. 1
Sprints, 1954-66 . . . . . . 2/3/32, 5'5¼"/137

Itkina won European titles in 1954 in the 200 and 4 x 100, and set a 220-yard world best of 23.6 in 1956. But it was over one lap where she made her greatest global impact. She set 7 world bests at 400, plus one at 440-yards. She set 3 marks in 1957, two of which were approved and the fastest being 53.6. She matched that time in 1958, but the time never was officially approved. In '59, she got down to 53.4, an en route time during her 53.7 440 record. Itkina matched the 53.4 time in 1962. She paced the world 400 ratings from

Kinue Hitomi

Jarmila Kratochvilova

186

'57 through '59, plus the 200 in 1961.

Fourth place seemed to be Itkina's limit at the Olympics: in '56, she ran 4th in her 200 semi and on the 4th-place 4 x 100. She placed 4th in both dashes in 1960 and the relay again placed 4th. Then in '64, she ran 5th in the 400. Itkina won the '58 and '62 European 400s, however, but retired before the '66 Europeans.

J

JACKSON, MARJORIE (Nelson) (Australia) . . . .
2G; 13 WR; W No. 1*; AOY*
Sprints, 1950-54. . . . . . 9/13/31, 5'7¾"/146

The first of Australia's "golden" sprinters, Jackson won 4 titles at the '50 Commonwealth (100 yards, 220 yards, 2 odd-distance relays). Two years later at the Helsinki Olympics, she succeeded Fanny Blankers-Koen as a double sprint champion, setting World Records of 11.5 in both her semi-final and the final. She tied the WR in her 200 heat (23.6) and then set one in her semi (23.4) as well before taking the final in 23.7. Jackson anchored the Aussie 4 x 100 to a WR 46.1 in the heats, but a fumbled last pass in the final held the squad to 5th place in 46.6. After the Games, she lowered the 100 record to 11.4.

Jackson repeated as double sprint winner at the '54 Commonwealth and also ran on the winning relay. Her 7 gold medals are the most won in Commonwealth Games history. During her career, Jackson set 6 WRs at 100-yards and a pair at 220-yards in addition to her metric bests.

JAHL, EVELIN [Schlaak] (Herberg) (E Germany) . . . .
2G; 2 WR; 4 No. 1
Discus, 1975-81 . . . . . .3/28/56, 5'10½"/198

Jahl had barely turned 20 when she won the '76 Olympic discus with an Olympic Record 226'4"/69.00. In 1978, she won the European title and set a World Record with 232'0"/70.72. She ranked 1st in the world, the first of four consecutive top ratings. In 1980, she retained her Olympic title (Olympic Record of 229'6"/69.96) and upped the WR to 234'7"/71.50.

JOYNER, JACKIE (Kersee) (USA)
See U.S. section.

K

KAZANKINA, TATYANA (USSR) . . . .
3G, B; 6 WR; 4 No. 1; AOY
Middle Distances, 1976- . . . .12/17/51, 5'3¼"/110
See chapter.

KHRISTOVA, IVANKA (Bulgaria). . . . . . G, B; 2 WR; No. 1
Shot Put, 1967-76 . . . . . 11/19/41, 5'7¾"/198
A four-time Olympian, Khristova improved in each of her
Games appearances: 10th '64, 6th '68, 3rd '72, 1st '76. She
set 2 World Records in 1976: 71'9"/21.87 on July 3, and
71'10"/21.89 on July 4. She gained the World Rankings for
10 consecutive years ('67-'76), finally claiming her sole No. 1
for the '76 season.

KLIER, JOHANNA [Schaller] (East Germany) G, S; 2 No. 1
100-meter Hurdles, 1973-80. . . 9/13/52, 5'7¾"/139
Klier won the '76 Olympic 100 hurdles and then the '78
European title. Those were her pair of No. 1-ranked years, although she rated 2nd in '77 and 3rd in '80. She finished 2nd
at the '80 Olympics and clocked her personal best of 12.56
that year. In '78, she led off an East German 4 x 100 relay
which set a World Record of 42.27.

KLOBUKOWSKA, EWA (Poland). . . . . . .Gr, B; WR; 2 No. 1
Sprints, 1964-67 . . . . . . 10/1/46, 5'7"/132
Klobukowska gained her niche in track history not for
her sprinting prowess, but for being the first woman disqualified from a meet after failing a sex test. On the track,
Klobukowska ran 3rd in the '64 Olympic 100 and anchored
Poland's 4 x 100 to a World Record 43.69 triumph with a
powerful effort. The next year, she set a 100-meter World
Record of 11.1 and in 1966, she won the European 100 and
4 x 100 and finished 2nd at 200. She ranked 1st globally in
'65 and '66 for the 100.

Sex testing was introduced in 1966 and Klobukowska was allowed to compete at the European Championships after a visual examination (there are reports she had failed a visual inspection at the Tokyo Olympics but was permitted to compete). Klobukowska's exact problem never was revealed, but chromosome tests indicated she was neither fully female nor male. She had two operations to make her female, but that wasn't enough and she failed to pass the tests in 1967. She was ruled out of the Euro Cup competition, and the IAAF withdrew recognition of her 100-meter WR and Poland's relay. (For more on sex testing, see Introduction.)

KOCH, MARITA (East Germany). . . . .
2G, 2Gr, S, Sr; 11 WR; 12 No. 1; 4 AOY
Sprints, 1975-1986 . . . . . 2/18/57, 5'7¼"/139
See chapter.

KONOPACKA, HALINA (Poland) . . . . .G; 7 WR; No. 1*
Discus, 1925-28 . . . . 11/11/00
The Pole became the first women's champion in Olympic track and field history when she won the discus in Amsterdam on July 31, 1928, with a World Record throw of 130'0"/39.62. That heave was the 7th WR of Konopacka's career, beginning with 102'5"/31.22 in 1925. She had lengthened the record to 128'6"/39.18 in 1927; in the Olympics, she just missed that record with a 39.16 (also 128'6") before her 130'0".

KRATOCHVILOVA, JARMILA (Czechoslovakia) . . . .
2G, S, Sr; 2 WR; 5 No. 1; AOY
Sprints, 1976- . . . . . . .1/26/51, 5'7"/141
Kratochvilova was a national-class sprinter from the mid-'70s, but emerged as a global talent in the 400 with a 2nd in the 1980 Olympics behind Marita Koch. The next year, she beat Koch in the World Cup (missing Koch's WR by 0.01 with 48.61) and ranking 1st worldwide. Koch rebounded at the '82 Europeans with a record 48.16 win ahead of the 48.85 by the Czech.

In 1983, though, the 32-year-old Kratochvilova conquered all. She set an 800 World Record of 1:53.28 in July, despite little experience at the distance. Koch's preparation for the '83 World Championships had been hindered by injury, so she confined herself to the sprints and relays. After what the world saw from Kratochvilova in Helsinki, Koch made the prudent choice.

The Czech's entry in both the 400 and 800 meant a punishing schedule of top-level racing: August 7—2nd 800 heat (2:12.35), 1st 400 heat (52.42); August 8—3rd 400 quarter-final (52.40), 2nd 800 semi (1:59.58); August 9—1st 400 semi (51.08), 1st 800 final (1:54.68); August 10—1st 400 final (World Record 47.99); August 13—3rd 4 x 400 relay heat (3:27.60 with 51.94 anchor); August 14—2nd 4 x 400 final (3:20.32 with 47.75 anchor, fastest leg of the meet).

Of her record 400, Jarmila said, "I only wanted to get close to Koch's 48.16. I wasn't thinking about a sub-48 time at all. Marita's 48.16 also was a great motivator for me during the hard basic training in the autumn and winter. My first real heroine was Irena Szewinska, who proved that being 30 years old doesn't mean an athlete can't set records."

A bullishly-strong runner, Kratochvilova's Helsinki successes brought many snide observations about her well-muscled frame, some critics insinuating she was a product of drug-taking. But no evidence to back up such allegations ever surfaced. Kratochvilova was devoted to massive amounts of weight-lifting. She missed the '84 Olympics due to the Eastern Bloc boycott, but still ranked 1st in the world at 800 in '84 and '85. She was hampered by leg injuries in 1986. Once called "Wonder Woman," Kratochvilova laughed, "The only wonder is that I was able to compete for so long."

KRISTIANSEN, INGRID (Norway) . . . . . . B; 5 WR; 5 No. 1
      Distances, 1977- . . . . . 3/21/56, 5'6½"/128

An Olympic cross-country skiier in 1976, Kristiansen turned more and more to running and by the mid-1980s was a global superstar. She World Ranked in the marathon as early as 1977 (7th), but ran in the shadow of renowned teammate Grete Waitz through 1984. Up to '85, Kristiansen ran 3rd in the first IAAF World Championship at 3000-meters ('80), ran a then global best 5000 in '81 of 15:28.43, placed 3rd in the '82 European marathon and 4th in the '84

World Profiles

Olympics. She missed the '83 season due to maternity—but not before competing in the IAAF Cross Country that March while several months pregnant.

In 1985, Kristiansen set World marks at 10,000 (30:59.42) and the marathon (2:21:06). In '86, she slashed the 5000 and 10,000 WRs dramatically, to 14:37.33 and 30:13.74. She ranked 1st globally at 3000, 5000 and 10,000, and was undefeated over those distances. Ingrid also won the Boston and Chicago marathons to cement her position as the finest all-around distance runner in the world that year.

KRZESINSKA, ELZBIETA [Dunska] (Poland)...........
G, S; 2 WR; No. 1
Long Jump, 1952-1963.... 11/11/34, 5'7"/137
She competed in the '52 Olympics as 17-year-old Miss Dunska, placing 12th. Four years later, Krzesinska won the '56 gold medal with a leap of 20'10"/6.35 to match the World Record she first set several months earlier. She ranked 1st globally that year, the lone No. 1 of her long career (she rated 2nd in '57, '60 and '62). She became the only woman to win two Olympic long jump medals with her 2nd in 1960, and she medaled twice at the European Championships (3rd '54, 2nd '62). Now a coach in the United States, Krzesinska directed '84 Olympians Judi Brown King (2nd 400 hurdles) and Cindy Greiner (4th heptathlon).

L

LATHAN, CHRISTINE [Brehmer] (East Germany)........
Gr, S, Sr, B; WR
400-meters, 1975-80..... 2/28/58, 5'6"/141
East Germany's 400 star between Monika Zehrt and Marita Koch, Lathan clocked history's first automatically-timed sub-50 with her 49.77 World Record in May, 1976. She had won the '75 European Junior title, beating Koch, but was outrun in the Montreal Olympics by Irena Szewinska's WR of 49.29. Lathan anchored her 4 x 400 team to history's first sub-3:20, though, a World Record 3:19.23. She finished 2nd in the '78 European 400 and 3rd in the '80

191

Olympics (the latter in her career-best 49.66). Her highest World Rankings were 2nds in 1976 and '78.

LILLAK, TIINA (Finland) . . . . .G, S; 2 WR; No. 1
Javelin, 1980- . . . . . . 4/15/61, 5'11"/161
From a nation with a long tradition of heroic men's spear throwing, Lillak became the only Finnish woman ever to set a javelin WR with her 237'6"/72.40 in 1982. She upped that mark to 245'3"/74.76 in '83. She gained a degree of athletic immortality among her countrymen at the '83 World Championships when she produced the winning throw on the final effort of the competition. In the absence of the Eastern Bloc throwers from the '84 Olympics, Lillak was considered the favorite. But a severely sprained ankle held her to just one throw, which still placed her 2nd.

M

MANNING, MADELINE (Jackson; Mimms) (USA)
See U.S. section.

MANOLIU, LIA (Romania) . . . . .G, 2B; No. 1
Discus, 1952-72 . . . . . .4/25/32, 5'10½"/187
Although she never set a World Record during her long international career, Manoliu did compile one all-time best: she is the only six-time Olympian in track and field. No man or woman matches her string of 6 consecutive Games; she placed 6th in '52, 9th in '56, won bronze medals in '60 and '64, finally struck gold in '68 and closed out her career with a 9th in '72. Her victory in Mexico made her the oldest winner in discus history (36 years, 176 days). She World Ranked 1st that year, her sole No. 1 in 9 Rankings appearances. She reached her personal best of 203'7"/62.06 in 1972. Manoliu now serves on the IAAF Women's Committee.

MATHEWS, MARLENE (Willard) (Australia) . . . .
2B; 6 WR; 4 No. 1; AOY*
Sprints, 1956-60 . . . . . . 2/14/34, 5'7"/141
Mathews finished 3rd in both Olympic sprints in 1956,

overshadowed by the victories of teammate Betty Cuthbert. The next two seasons belonged to Mathews, however, as she ranked No. 1 worldwide in both sprints in '57 and '58. She set WRs at 400 and 440 in '57 (57.0 in the same 440-yard race), and the next year at 100 yards (10.3) and 220 yards (23.4). She claimed both Commonwealth sprints in '58; at the '60 Olympics, she was eliminated in the 100 semi-finals. She also serves as a member of the IAAF Women's Committee.

MAUERMEYER, GISELA (West Germany)..............
G; 13 WR; No. 1*; AOY*
Throws/Multi, 1933-38.... 11/24/13, 5'7¾"/154

Mauermeyer first appeared on the world stage as a 19-year-old pentathlete who set a WR of 3991 points in 1933. She upped that total to 4155 in '34, and also set a shot record of 47'2¼"/14.38—in her international debut with the implement. The mark lasted as the official WR for more than 14 years. Because neither the shot nor pentathlon were to be included in the women's program at the 1936 Olympics, Mauermeyer took up seriously throwing the discus late in 1934.

In 1935, she lengthened the world's best six times, from 145'6"/44.34 to 154'7"/47.12. In the '36 Olympic season, she had a hot hand on June 14 in Munich, first matching her 154'7" mark and then adding nearly three feet to it with 157'5"/47.98. Later in the season, she got out to 158'5"/48.30. Since the IAAF began ratifying discus records only after the '36 season, just the 158'5" heave ever received official recognition as the WR.

Mauermeyer won the '36 Olympic and '38 European discus gold medals, and finished 2nd in the Euro shot. Also in 1938, she upped her own pentathlon record to 4391 points, a mark which lasted for more than 9 years.

McDANIEL, MILDRED (USA).
See U.S. section.

MEYFARTH, ULRIKE (West Germany)2G, S; 3 WR; 2 No. 1
High Jump, 1972-84..... 5/4/56, 6'1¼"/157

As a 16-year-old high school student, Meyfarth provided

Gisela Mauermeyer

Ulrike Meyfarth

Nadezhda Olizarenko

one of the emotional highs of the '72 Munich Olympics, when she matched the WR of 6'3½"/1.92 to become the youngest individual women's champion in Olympic history (at 16 years, 123 days). If that was a zenith of her career, the nadir must have been four years later in Montreal when she made a paltry 5'10"/1.78 and didn't qualify for the final. She kept jumping, though, and climbed all the way back to No. 1 in the world in 1981 and '82. She won the '82 European title with a WR 6'7½"/2.02 in a scintillating duel with Italy's Sara Simeoni.

At the '83 World Championships, Meyfarth and Soviet Tamara Bykova waged a torrid fight, Bykova finally winning. A week later, though, Meyfarth topped a WR 6'8"/2.03 to win the European Cup. And in '84, Meyfarth came full circle and won the Los Angeles Olympics at an Olympic Record 6'7½". She retired in 1985 to become a highly-paid fashion model.

MICKLER, INGRID (Becker) (West Germany)............
G, Gr; W No. 1
Long Jump/Multi......9/26/42, 5'10"/141
A wide-ranging talent, Mickler competed in 4 Olympics: 9th high jump '60; 4th long jump, 8th pentathlon '64; 1st pentathlon, 6th LJ and 4 x 100 '68; 7th semi 100, did not qualify for LJ final, 1st 4 x 100 '72. The Munich relay gold was won with a World Record 42.81 clocking. At the '71 European Championships, Mickler won the long jump, finished 2nd in the 100 and ran on the sprint relay winner. One of the major upsets of her career came in the 1970 European Cup 100 when she outran East Germany's Renate Stecher, then the WR holder. Mickler's lone No. 1 World Ranking came in the 1971 long jump. She had a personal best of 11.35 in the 100, 22'2¼"/6.76 in the long jump and 5098 points in the pentathlon ('54 tables).

MYELNIK, FAINA (USSR)......G; 11 WR; 7 No. 1; AOY
Discus, 1970-81.......6/9/45, 5'8½"/194
The most prolific World Record setter in discus history, Myelnik set 11 marks from 210'8"/64.22 in 1971 to 231'3"/70.50 in 1976. She won the '72 Olympic title and was un-

defeated during the '73, '74 and '75 seasons. She was voted Athlete Of The Year in '75. A two-time European champion ('71, '74), she won her second title despite being stung by a bee on her right (throwing) arm the day of the final. Myelnik placed 4th in the '76 discus; her concentration was shaken when an official ruled a warmup swing began her throwing motion and when she then did not complete the throw, it was ruled foul. She did not qualify for the '80 Olympic final. Myelnik's shot best was 65'8¾"/20.03, and she once threw the men's discus 170'7"/52.00.

N

NEUBERT, RAMONA (East Germany) . . . G, 3 WR; 3 No. 1
      Long Jump/Multi, 1978-84 . . . 7/26/58, 5'8½"/141

Neubert placed 4th in the 1980 Olympic pentathlon, the last 5-eventer contested in history. With the advent of the heptathlon at the start of '81, Neubert exerted a 3-year dominance over the 7-eventers. She was undefeated in '81, '82 and '83 and set a World Record each year (6788, 6845, 6935 respectively). She won the '82 European and '83 World titles and won her first 9 competitions before suffering her first loss in her lone heptathlon of 1984. In the long jump, she spanned her career best of 22'7¾"/6.90 in 1981 (as well as a wind-aided 22'11¾"/7.00), and World Ranked 2nd in '81 and 3rd in '82. Neubert missed the '85 season due to an injury and then retired.

O

OLIZARENKO, NADEZHDA [Mushta] (USSR) . . . .
                                G, B; 2 WR; No. 1
      800/1500, 1977- . . . . . . 11/28/53, 5'5"/126

Combining good speed with endurance, Olizarenko emerged in 1978 with a 2nd in the European 800 plus a leg on the runner-up 4 x 400 team. She was never faster than in 1980, when she first matched the 800 WR with 1:54.85, then shattered the mark while running away from the Moscow

Olympic field with 1:53.43. She also won the 1500 bronze medal; earlier in the season, she ran her personal best of 3:56.8. She closed out her fine '80 season by leading off a WR 4 x 800 team which ran 7:50.17.

After ranking 1st in the world at 800 in 1980, Olizarenko missed the next three seasons due to injury and maternity. She was back in stride by '84, ranking 3rd globally. In 1986, she returned all the way, winning the European 800.

OSTERMEYER, MICHELLINE (France) . . . . . 2G, B; No. 1*
Shot/Discus, 1946-50 . . . . 12/23/22, 5'10"/143

Possessor of a wide span of abilities, Ostermeyer scored in championship meets over an unusual range of events. At the '46 Europeans, she placed 2nd in the shot and 5th in the high jump. Two years later, she first graduated from the Paris Conservatory of Music in classical piano, then won the shot and discus gold medals at the London Olympics. For good measure, she added a bronze in the high jump.

Ostermeyer won the Olympic throws with her career-best marks of 45'1½"/13.75 and 137'6"/41.92. Only Soviet Aleksandra Chudina ever has matched Ostermeyer's feat of winning medals in three different Olympic field events. At the 1950 Europeans, Ostermeyer placed 3rd in the shot and 4th in the discus—as well as claiming the bronze medal in the 80-meter hurdles. She then went on to a career as a concert pianist.

OTKALENKO, NINA (USSR) . . . . 9 WR; No. 1
800-meters, 1951-60 . . . . 5/23/28

Otkalenko set the most World Records in the 800, five accepted marks and two unofficial bests. She pared the record down from 2:12.0 in '51 to 2:05.0 in '55. She also set a pair of 880-yard marks, the fastest of 2:06.6 in 1956. She won the '54 European title, but was past her prime by the time the 800 was added back to the Olympic program in 1960. Otkalenko led the world at 400 in 1956. She ran her 55.0 PR in 1955.

OZOLINA, ELVIRA (Lusis) (USSR) . . . . . G; 4 WR; 3 No. 1
Javelin, 1957-73 . . . . . . 10/8/39, 5'9¼"/148

Ozolina set two WRs in 1960 (190'0"/57.92 and 195'4"/

198

59.54) and won the Rome Olympics. She ranked 1st globally in '60-'62, and won the '62 Euro crown. In '63, she upped her WR to 196'1"/59.78. But in '64, her throw of 201'4"/61.38—history's first beyond 200 feet—was never okayed as a WR and Ozolina slipped to 5th at the Olympics. She kept throwing for almost another decade, and threw well enough in 1973 to rank 7th worldwide. Although she used her maiden name in sport, her husband is javelin great Janis Lusis.

P

PACKER, ANN (Brightwell) (Great Britain) . . . . . . G, S; WR 400/800, 1960-64. . . . . . 3/8/42, 5'6½"/134

After placing 6th and last in the '62 European Championships 200, Packer moved up to the 400 the next season and ran well enough to rank 4th in the world. She recorded a personal best of 53.4. For the Olympic year of 1964, she added the 800 to her repertoire. She went to Tokyo with only five races worth of 800-meter experience and her prime goal was to win the 400. She ran a European Record 52.2 but finished 2nd behind Betty Cuthbert. Three days later, though, Packer ran an inspired 800 final to win in a World Record 2:01.1. She then retired and married Robbie Brightwell, captain of the British men's team in Tokyo. Packer ranked 2nd globally in the 800 for '64 and 3rd at 400.

PETERS, MARY (Great Britain). . . . . G; WR; No. 1 Multi-event, 1955-74. . . . . . 7/6/39, 5'8"/157

When the '72 Olympic pentathlon began, Peters was the veteran's veteran: she had been competing in the 5-eventer for 17 years, although overshadowed by the successes of Mary Rand. Still, Peters placed 4th in the '64 Olympics, but a twisted ankle held her to 9th in '68. She took off the '69 season, returned in '70 to win the Commonwealth shot and pentathlon, then took off '71 to prepare for Munich. In a tough contest with Heide Rosendahl, the 33-year-old Peters won by 10 points with a World Record 4801 points. She ranked No. 1 in '72 and, after winning the '74 Commonwealth pentathlon, Peters retired.

Track's Greatest Women

POLLAK, BURGLINDE (East Germany) . 2B; 3 WR; 3 No. 1
Multi-event, 1969-80. . . . . 6/10/51, 5'11¼"/172
Pollak was a pentathlete who could set World Records,
but wasn't ever able to win the big meet. She set a WR of
4775 points in 1970 and ranked 1st in the world, then placed
2nd in the '71 Europeans. She claimed the '72 Olympic
bronze medal behind Peters and Rosendahl, then returned to
the top in '73 with a pair of records (4831, 4932) and a No.
1 ranking. In '74, it was another European silver medal. In
'75, she was undefeated and ranked 1st. In '76, she was 3rd
behind two teammates in Montreal. In '78, a third European
silver. And in 1980, she placed 6th in Moscow before retiring.

PONOMARYEVA, NINA [Romashkova] (USSR) . . . .
2G, B; WR; 5 No. 1
Discus, 1952-1963 . . . . . . 4/27/29, 5'8"/176
Ponomaryeva was the first woman to regain an Olympic
title in the same event. She won the '52 discus, slipped to 3rd
in '56 and returned to the winner's platform in '60 thanks to
her career-best throw of 180'9"/55.10. She also won the '54
European title, and ranked 1st in the world five straight years
('56-'60). She set a World Record in 1952 of 175'10"/53.60.
Ponomaryeva gained historical notoriety when the 1956
USSR-Great Britain match was cancelled after she was caught
shoplifting hats in a London store. The Soviet team went
home and Nina never appeared in court.

PRESS, IRINA (USSR). . . . . 2G, B; 14 WR; 10 No. 1; AOY*
Hurdles/Multi-event, 1958-66. . . .3/10/39, 5'6"/165
The younger of the talented Press sisters, Irina made a
global impact in the hurdles and shot, as well as the pentathlon. She set the most World Records in the various formats of
the 5-eventer, producing 8 bests between 1959 and '64. Her
highest pentathlon total, 5246 points, gave her the '64
Olympic gold medal.
Irina also ran the most approved records over the 80-
meter hurdles with five (and she had one non-approved
record equaler). She won the '60 Olympic title, placed 3rd in
'64 and ran her fastest clocking of 10.3 in 1965. She led the
global pentathlon rankings in '59-'62 and '64-'66 and the

200

Faina Myelnik

Tamara Press (left) and sister Irina.

Sara Simeoni

hurdles in '60, '61 and '65.

In 1965, Press twice tied the hurdles WR of 10.4 before lowering the mark to that 10.3. She also led the pentathlon at 5208, second highest score all-time only to her Tokyo WR. During her career, Press also threw the shot well enough to place 6th in Tokyo at 54'10"/16.71. A reported knee injury kept her out of the '66 Europeans and she returned to domestic competition only briefly in 1967 before retiring.

PRESS, TAMARA (USSR) .3G, S; 12 WR; 10 No. 1; 3 AOY*
Shot/Discus, 1956-66 . . . . . 5/10/37, 5'11"/225

Tamara won the 1960 Olympic shot on September 2, one day after Irina won the hurdles. Thus, they became—and still are—the only sisters ever to win Olympic track and field titles. Tamara already had set 3 shot WRs, so after Irina matched the global record in her hurdles semi, they also became the only sisters ever to both win Olympic gold medals and set World Records.

Tamara began her ascendance to the top of the world in the shot and discus in '58 when she ranked 2nd in the disc. Her first shot WR, 56'7¼"/17.25, came in '59; by the end of her career, she had put the mark out to 61'0"/18.59 in 1965. She ranked No. 1 each year between 1959 and 1966, save '61 when she rated 2nd.

Her six discus records ranged from 187'5"/57.14 in '60 to 195'10"/59.70 in 1965. She finished 2nd in the '60 Olympic discus, but claimed both titles in 1964. Also in '64, Tamara produced 8 of the 10-longest shot throws ever and 3 of the top 6 in the discus. Press also scored a double victory at the '62 Europeans. She ranked 1st in the discus in '61, '62 and '64.

PROKOP, LIESE (Austria) . . . . S; WR; No. 1
Multi-event, 1962-75 . . . . . 3/27/41, 5'10"/159

Prokop won the '68 Olympic silver medal in the pentathlon. One year later, she upped the World Record to 5352 points for the event format then contested, won the European gold medal and ranked No. 1 in the world.

R

RAND, MARY [Bignal] (Toomey) (Great Britain). . . . .
G, S, Br; WR; 4 No. 1; AOY*
Long Jump/Multi, 1957-67. . . . 2/10/40, 5'8"/134

Rand first emerged in 1957 by ranking 9th worldwide in the high jump at age 17. A year later, she placed 2nd in the Commonwealth long jump. She ranked 1st globally in '59, but at the '60 Olympics, she placed only 9th. In Rome, Rand also ran 4th in the 80-meter hurdles and on the 4 x 100 relay team which didn't finish. Her overall long jump season in 1960, though, was good enough to earn her a second No. 1 ranking.

After having a daughter in 1961—but still competing well enough after maternity to rank 9th globally—Rand placed 3rd in the '62 Euro long jump. In '63, she was back in the top LJ slot, and also rated 2nd in the pentathlon (she also ranked No. 2 there in '59).

The '64 Olympic season saw Rand in grand form: she started off in Tokyo on October 14 with a World Record leap of 22'2¼"/6.76 to claim the long jump gold from Irena Szewinska. Two days later, Rand finished 2nd to Irina Press in the pentathlon. And three days after that, she completed a set of Olympic medals by running on Britain's 3rd place 4 x 100.

She retired after the '67 season and served as a broadcaster at the Mexico Olympics. At the Games, she met American Bill Toomey, who won the decathlon. They were married late in 1969, the day after Toomey had raised the 10-event World Record to 8417 points. They had personalized California license plates which read BIL2ME and MAR2ME.

RICHTER, ANNEGRET [Irrang] (West Germany). . . . .
G, Gr, S, Sr; WR; No. 1
Sprints, 1971-79. . . . . . .10/13/50, 5'6"/115

Richter ran on the West German team which won the '71 European 4 x 100 title. At the '72 Olympics, she finished 5th in the 100 and then won a gold medal in the short relay when the West Germans equaled the WR of 42.8. At the '74 Europeans, Richter duplicated her 5th in the 100, but the relay team finished 2nd to East Germany this time. Richter reached her best form ever in 1976. In the 100 semi-finals in Montreal, she sped 11.01 to cut 0.03 off the World Record set 6 weeks earlier by teammate Inge Helten. Richter then clocked 11.08 to take the gold medal. She ran her career-best 200 of 22.39 to place 2nd, but rather than have her anchor the 4 x 100, West Germany's coaches put her on the 3rd leg. The team finished second to East Germany. Richter ran on a pair of Europe Select 4 x 100 teams which upset East Germany in the '77 and '79 World Cups.

ROBINSON, BETTY (USA)
    See U.S. section.

ROSENDAHL, HEIDE (West Germany).................
                        G, Gr, S; WR; 4 No. 1; AOY
    Long Jump/Multi, 1966-73 . . . 2/14/47, 5'8½"/146
    Rosendahl placed 2nd in the '66 European pentathlon at the age of 19 and went to the '68 Olympics a strong favorite. But she was injured warming up and had to withdraw. In 1970, however, she extended the long jump World Record to 22'5¼"/6.84. The next year, she won the European pentathlon and finished 3rd in the long jump. She went into the Munich Olympics as an even-heavier favorite than four years earlier. Heide was the host nation's darling, appearing on endless magazine covers and in countless newspaper stories.
    Heide remained unruffled, however, as she first won the long jump at 22'3"/6.78. It was a very close win, though, as Bulgarian Diana Yorgova jumped 22'2½"/6.77 on her final leap to place 2nd. Then Heide locked horns with Mary Peters and Burglinde Pollak in the pentathlon three days later. Rosendahl's strong second day with the long jump and 200 was expected to offset the high jump/shot supremacy of the other two. Rosendahl handled Pollak, but fell just 10 points short of Peters (4801-4791). Keen-eyed statisticians point out that Heide held the pentathlon World Record for 1.12 seconds—the difference between her 22.96 200 and the 24.08 of Peters. Rosendahl never received official recognition for her brief claim to the record, however.
    Probably Rosendahl's finest effort in Munich, though,

came in the 4 x 100 relay when she held off the hard charge of double sprint winner Renate Stecher of East Germany to give the West Germans both the gold medal and a share of 42.8 World Record. Heide was voted Athlete Of The Year for '72 by *Women's Track & Field World*. Rosendahl ranked 1st globally twice in both the long jump ('70, '72) and pentathlon ('68, '71).

RUDOLPH, WILMA (USA)
See U.S. section.

RYAN, PAM [Kilborn] (Australia). . . . . S, B; 9 WR; 3 No. 1
Hurdles, 1961-72 . . . . . . 8/12/39, 5'2"/115

One of only three hurdlers ever to make three consecutive Olympic finals, Ryan finished 3rd in Tokyo (10.5) and 2nd in Mexico (10.4) over the 80-meter barriers, and 4th in Munich (12.98) in the 100-meter hurdles. She also ran the 100 in '68 and '72, making it to the semi-finals both times. Ryan set two WRs in the 80-meter hurdles (10.5, 10.4; both '64), one accepted mark in the 100 hurdles (12.5 '72) and four over the 200-meter barriers (her fastest of 25.7 in '71 was the last WR accepted in the event before it was phased out). She won three consecutive Commonwealth short hurdles titles ('62-'66-'70), plus two relay golds and even the '62 long jump. Ryan ranked 1st globally in the hurdles in '63, '66 and '67 and 2nd in '62, '65, '68 and '69.

S

SCHMIDT, KATE (USA)
See U.S. section.

SHCHELKANOVA, TATYANA (USSR) . . B; 4 WR; 3 No. 1
Long Jump, 1961-66 . . . . . 4/18/37, 5'6"/128

Shchelkanova set a long jump World Record of 21'3¼"/ 6.48 and rated 1st in the world in 1961. She upped her record to 21'5¼"/6.53 in '62, won the European Championships and repeated her No. 1 ranking. She also spanned 21'8¾"/6.62 in '62, but the mark never was applied for record recognition. In 1964, Shchelkanova leaped a WR 21'11¾"/6.70, but later placed only 3rd in the Tokyo Olympics. Great Britain's Mary Rand won the gold by leaping her own WR of 22'2¼"/6.76. Shchelkanova regained her No. 1 ranking in 1965 and in 1966 produced her all-time best with an indoor 22'1"/6.73, as well as a wind-aided 22'10"/ 6.96 outdoors at the Soviet championships.

SHEVTSOVA, LYUDMILA (USSR)......G; 2 WR; 3 No. 1
    800-meters, 1956-63.....11/26/34, 5'4½"/117
    Shevtsova ran 3rd in the 1954 European 800, and later ranked 1st globally in '56 and '59. In 1960, she set a World Record of 2:04.3. Then at the Rome Olympics, she matched that mark to win the gold medal. The 800 had been run first in the '28 Games, but stodgy Olympic officials were so disturbed by the exhausted appearance of the runners, they cancelled the distance from the Olympic program until 1960. Shevtsova ranked 1st in the world in '60 and 2nd in '61.

SIMEONI, SARA (Italy)...........G, 2S; 2 WR; 2 No. 1
    High Jump, 1971-86.....4/19/53, 5'9¼"/132
    The Italian was one of the world's premier high jumpers through the 1970s and much of the '80s. She grew up in the Romeo-and-Juliet city of Verona and dreamed of a career as a ballet dancer. But as she grew, her dance teachers told Sara her long legs and large feet would only work against her as a dancer. She turned to sport and first tried the high jump at age 13; she cleared a national age record of 4'5"/1.35 that first year.
    By the time she was 19, Simeoni had placed 6th in the Munich Olympics, a competition won by an even younger teenager, Ulrike Meyfarth. One place behind Simeoni came East Germany's Rosemarie Ackermann; this formidable trio would be career-long friends and rivals. Sara placed 3rd at the '74 Europeans and 2nd in the '76 Olympics, both titles going to Ackermann who had ascended to the top of the women's high jump world. But in '78, Simeoni became the event's prima ballerina as she set a World Record of 6'7"/2.01 before the Europeans. Then in Prague, she waged a taut duel with Ackermann, finally matching her fresh WR to beat her rival.

"I never felt pressure," Simeoni commented. "If it was there, it only made me want to jump higher."

Although she never jumped higher, she scored her biggest victory at the 1980 Moscow Olympics when she won with an Olympic Record clearance of 6'5½"/1.97 (Ackermann finished 4th and retired shortly after). Sara ranked 1st in the world in those glorious years of '78 and '80, and tallied 2nd places in '76, '77, '79 and '81. She placed 3rd in the '82 Europeans, but suffered an ankle injury during the qualifying round of the '83 World Championships and had to be carried out of the stadium on a stretcher.

It was an ecstatic Simeoni, then, who returned in 1984 to place 2nd at the Los Angeles Olympics, behind Meyfarth. She competed sparingly the next two seasons and at the '86 Europeans, Simeoni did not qualify for the final. A few weeks later, she announced her retirement from high jumping, having enjoyed a career even longer than either Ackermann or Meyfarth.

SLANEY, MARY [Decker] (USA)
See U.S. section.

STANCIU, ANISOARA [Cusmir] (Romania)....G, S; 4 WR
Long Jump, 1980- .....6/28/62, 5'7¾"/139

Stanciu was the first long jumper to better the 24-foot barrier. She spanned 24'4½"/7.43 in 1983, her third WR that year. She had hit the highest global level the previous season, when Stanciu and rival teammate Valy Ionescu waged a scintillating duel at the Romanian national championships on August 1. Stanciu first reached a WR 23'5½"/7.15, only to have Ionescu reply minutes later with 23'7½"/7.20. Ionescu later won the European Championships, with Stanciu 2nd.

In '83, Stanciu opened hot by hitting 23'8"/7.21 in May. Then on June 4, she reached 23'10¼"/7.27 and followed moments later with 24'4½"/7.43. But she couldn't win the big meet as she placed 2nd in the World Championships to 18-year-old East German Heike Daute (later Drechsler). But in 1984, Stanciu didn't set any World Records; still, she defeated Ionescu for the Olympic gold medal in Los Angeles.

STECHER, RENATE [Meissner] (East Germany) . . . .
2G, Gr, S, Sr, B; 13 WR; 8 No. 1; AOY
Sprints, 1969-76. . . . . . 5/12/50, 5'7¼"/154
See chapter.

STEPHENS, HELEN (USA)
See U.S. section.

SZEWINSKA, IRENA [Kirzenstein] (Poland) . . . .
2G, Gr, 2S, 2B; 9 WR; 16 No. 1; 2 AOY
Sprints/Long jump, 1964-80. . . 5/24/46, 5'9¼"/132
See chapter.

T

TKACHENKO, NADEZHDA (USSR). . . . . G; 2 WR; 4 No. 1
Multi-event, 1972-80 . . . . . 9/19/48, 5'5"/163
After placing 9th in the '72 Olympic pentathlon, Tkachenko moved to 1st in the World Rankings for 1974 following her victory in the European Championship 5-eventer. She placed 5th in the Montreal Olympics, but regained the top slot in '77 thanks to a World Record total of 4839 points. In 1978, she defended her European title, but produced a positive doping test and was suspended from international competition for 18 months. (A positive test for banned drugs supposedly drew a "lifetime" ban, but sentences usually were commuted to 18 months following an appeal by the athlete's national federation.)

Tkachenko regained her eligibility early in 1980 and proceeded to up her WR to 4880 points. That mark never received recognition as the WR, however, because Tkachenko obliterated it in the Moscow Olympic pentathlon, the final 5-eventer staged in track history. The 7-event heptathlon became the standard women's multi-event after 1980. In Moscow, Tkachenko showed a remarkable range of abilities, covering the 100-meter hurdles in 13.29, putting the shot 55'3"/16.84, high jumping 6'½"/1.84, long jumping 22'1"/6.73 and closing with a 2:05.2 800, phenomenal two-lap running for an athlete of her size. She scored a WR 5083.

In an ironic twist, the USSR's Olga Kuragina won the 800 with 2:03.6 and totaled 4875 to up the accepted WR by 36 points. Teammate Olga Rukavishnikova finished 1.2 seconds later with 2:04.8 to up the record to 4937. Just 0.4 later, Tkachenko finished her 800 to put the record over 5000 points. Rukavishnikova thus earned the dubious distinction of holding a World Record for the shortest span of time in history.

TYLER, DOROTHY [Odam] (Great Britain). . 2S; WR; No. 1*
High Jump, 1935-66 . . . . . 3/14/20, 5'6"/115
Tyler first cleared five feet as a 15-year-old in 1935—and she still was clearing that height three decades later. She won the '38 and '50 Commonwealth. She also set a World Record of 5'5¼"/1.66 in 1939. However, Tyler probably is best known for how she didn't win the biggest prize: at both the '36 and '48 Olympics Tyler cleared the same height as the eventual champion. Under the rules then in force to break ties, Tyler placed 2nd each time, but under current rules, she would have won both gold medals. Tyler got her lifetime best of 5'6"/1.68 in placing 2nd to Alice Coachman in London; the Briton cleared that height again nine years later in 1957. Tyler tied for 7th in '52 and 12th in '56.

TYUS, WYOMIA (USA)
See U.S. section.

U

ULMASOVA, SVETLANA (USSR) . . . . WR; 3 No. 1
Distances, 1975-83 . . . . . . 2/4/53, 5'3¼"/117
Each year that Ulmasova won a major 3000-meter title, she also ranked 1st in the world: '78—won European Championships in a meet record 8:33.16; '79—won World Cup, beating Norwegian star Grete Waitz; '82—defended her European title and lowered the meet best to 8:30.28. Also in '82, Ulmasova cut the World Record for 3000 down to 8:26.78, as well as clocking her personal best 1500 of 3:58.76. She finished 4th in the '83 World Championships 3000 in 8:35.55.

World Profiles

V

VISCOPOLEANU, VIORICA (Romania) . . . . . G; WR; No. 1
Long Jump, 1964-73 . . . . . 8/8/39, 5'5¾"/121

Viscopoleau is the only woman to gain the long jump World Rankings 10 times. She ranked 1st in the world only once, but it was for her finest year ever: in 1968, she leaped a World Record 22'4½"/6.82 in the rarefied atmosphere of Mexico City to claim the Olympic title. She had placed 5th four years earlier in Tokyo. Viscopoleanu finished 2nd in the '69 European Championships, and ranked 2nd globally in 1970. She placed 7th in the '72 Olympics.

VOIGT, ANGELA (East Germany) . . . . G; WR; 2 No. 1
Long Jump, 1973-79 . . . . . 5/18/51, 5'8"/137

After winning the 1973 European Cup long jump, Voigt was ranked 1st in the world. But then she placed 4th in the '74 European title meet and only 5th in the '75 Euro Cup, so her competitive elan was a bit of a question mark heading into 1976. She set a World Record of 22'8½"/6.92 early in the season. Then at the Montreal Olympics, Voigt's opener of 22'¾"/6.72 held up to win the gold medal and she ranked 1st again. In '78, Voigt finished 2nd in the European Championships (behind Soviet Vilma Bardauskiene, who set a WR of 23'3¼"/7.09 in the qualifying round) and World Rankings.

W

WAITZ, GRETE [Andersen] (Norway) . . G, S; 3 WR; 10 No. 1
Distances, 1971- . . . . . 10/1/53, 5'6½"/110

If one athlete could be considered to have put the marathon for women squarely on the map of world track, it would be Waitz. She debuted over the 26-mile distance at the New York Marathon in October of 1978 and proceeded to run a world's best time for women of 2:32:30. Her next two marathons—the '79 and '80 New York races—also produced women's bests (2:27:33, 2:25:42). Even if the course eventually turned up slightly short of the full distance of 26.2-miles, Waitz easily was the best woman marathoner of

Grete Waitz (left) and Svetlana Ulmasova.

her time. And she won those New York races on nationally-televised contests which spread her name and fame, as well as demonstrating to the world that women could run the marathon and run it well.

But Waitz was no latecomer to running. She began competing as a high jumper, clearing 5'3¼"/1.61 in 1971. That same year, she set a European Junior Record in the 1500 with 4:17.0 and competed in the European Championships in the 800 and 1500. The next year, Grete ran the 1500 in the Munich Olympics. At the '74 Europeans, she won the bronze medal in the 1500—beating into 4th place no less than future Olympic 800/1500 champ Tatyana Kazankina.

Waitz ranked No. 1 in the world at 1500 and 3000 in 1975; she set a 3000 WR of 8:46.6. At the '76 Olympics, she placed 8th in her 1500 semi-final (the 1500 was the longest distance on the Olympic women's program at the time). She also cut her 3000 WR to 8:45.4. In 1977, she won the 3000 at the inaugural World Cup and ranked 1st worldwide (and 3rd at 1500). In March of 1978, Waitz won her first of four consecutive (and five overall) IAAF Cross Country titles. In August, she placed 3rd in the European Championships 3000 and 5th in the 1500 (in her career best of 4:00.55). Then came New York, and women's marathoning never would be the same again.

"I never really wanted to run the marathon. My longest run, even in training, had been only 12 miles," Waitz recalled. "But my husband Jack urged me to try it, just to see how it would go. I stayed with the women's leaders until 16 miles and then I was all alone." Grete still was reluctant to admit it, but she had found her distance.

Waitz rated 1st globally five times, 1978-'80 and '82-'83. By the end of the 1986 season, she had run 14 career marathons, won 11, finished 2nd once and failed to finish twice. By 1982, Waitz knew the marathon was her race, so she contested her last major track contest and set a European Record for 5000 with 15:08.80 in Oslo's Bislett Stadium. Her clocking missed the World Record by just 0.54 of a second.

In April of 1983, Waitz won the accurately-measured London Marathon in 2:25:29 to match the World Record. Later that summer, she won the first World Championships

26-miler in 2:28:09, three minutes ahead of American Marianne Dickerson. Waitz and teammate Ingrid Kristiansen were expected to duel with American Joan Benoit at the '84 Los Angeles Olympics.

But when Benoit broke away from the Olympic field after only three miles, Waitz let her go. Grete was being cautious, considering the rising temperatures at the time—and the fact there were 23 miles left to run. By the time Grete realized Benoit was running away with the race, it was too late. But Waitz held strongly to 2nd place, finishing in 2:26:18 to Benoit's 2:24:52.

Waitz ranked 2nd in the world for '84, then 5th in '85 (she ran only New York, but scored her 7th win in 8 tries). One reason for Waitz's slight tail-off in marathoning was that she had become an international running celebrity. She ran road races in many different countries, conducted clinics and made personal appearances. Always a quiet, self-effacing person, Grete nonetheless adapted to being famous. In 1986, both a biography on her life was published and her own fitness videotape was released.

The running world saw in 1986, though, that Waitz was not content just to jog off into the sunset of her career. She won the two marathons she ran that year, a personal-best 2:24:54 in London and her 8th New York (2:28:06). She garnered her 6th No. 1 ranking, besting Kristiansen (who had set a WR of 2:21:06 in 1985). Waitz was far from running her last race.

Her fame in Norway is such that a statue of Waitz in running stride now stands outside Bislett Stadium in Oslo. Waitz's track bests included: 2:03.1 800 ('75), 4:00.55 1500 ('78), 8:31.75 3000 ('79) and 15:08.80 5000 ('82).

WAJSOWNA, JADWIGA (Marcinkiewicz) (Poland) . . . .
S, B; 8 WR; No. 1*
Shot/Discus, 1932-48 . . . . . 1/30/12, 5'5¼"/159
Wajsowna followed Halina Konopacka as Poland's discus great. She set 8 World Records between 1932 and '34. Her longest record measured 144'11"/44.18. Her longest throw ever came in 1936 at 152'8"/46.54; it never was accepted as a Polish record since the required number of officials were

not present. Wajsowna also set four shot NRs during her career, the longest measuring 40'2"/12.24 in 1938.

She finished 3rd in the 1932 Olympic discus and moved up a notch in '36 to 2nd. After World War II, Wajsowna returned to place 3rd in the '46 European discus and 4th in the '48 London Olympics.

WALSH, STELLA [Stanislawa Walasiewicz] (Poland) . . . . . .
G, S; 24 WR; No. 1*; AOY*
Sprints/Long Jump, 1930-38 . 4/11/11-12/4/80, 5'4"/120

One of the most versatile athletes in history, Walsh was born in Poland but went to the United States at age 11 and spent her life there. She became a U.S. citizen in 1947. But it was while representing the nation of her birth that Walsh amassed her considerable championship honors: 1st '32 Olympic 100 (11.9), 6th discus (110'3"/33.60); 2nd '36 Olympic 100 (11.7); 1st '38 European 100 and 200, 2nd long jump and 4 x 100; 1st '30 Women's World Games 60-meters, 100, 200; 1st at '34 Games in 60-meters, 2nd 100 and 200.

Walsh set five IAAF-approved World Records: 2 at 100-meters (11.6 in '37 the fastest), one at 200-meters (23.6, a mark which lasted nearly 17 years), one at 60-meters (7.3), and one at 220-yards (24.3). The 60-meter mark, which Walsh set on September 24, 1933, lasted for more than 26 years, the longest duration ever for a women's World Record.

However, during her long career, Walsh produced at least 24 world-best marks: 4 at 60m, 2 at 100y, 13 at 100m, 3 at 200m, 1 at 220y and 1 long jump. She won a total of 49 outdoor national titles during her prime career, 33 in the U.S. and 16 in Poland. Of the U.S. wins, she won 4 at 100-meters, 11 at both the 200 and long jump, 2 discus and 5 pentathlon.

Many of Walsh's performances were the stuff of legends, such as the 11.2 100-meter time she ran in 1945. The official World Record at the time was her own 11.6 from 1937. The time never was submitted for record acceptance. Walsh observed, "The officials thought it was impossible for a woman to run that fast. The years have just shown I was merely ahead of my time."

Walsh was married and lived for years in Cleveland, Ohio. On the night of December 4, 1980, she was shot dead in a robbery attempt in a grocery store parking lot. An autopsy revealed that Walsh had internal male sex organs, but no female sex organs.

WESTERMANN, LIESEL (West Germany)...............
S; 4 WR; 2 No. 1; AOY
Discus, 1966-74...... 11/2/44, 5'7¾"/181
Westermann became the first discus thrower to exceed 60-meters (196'10") when she threw a World Record 201'0"/ 61.26 in 1967. She ranked 1st globally and was named Athlete Of The Year by *Women's Track & Field World.* She upped her record to 205'2"/62.54 in '68 and finished 2nd in the Mexico Olympics. In '69, Westermann regained the No. 1 rating after twice throwing world marks (205'8"/62.70 and 209'10"/63.96). She was 2nd in the '66 and '71 Euros, 5th in the '72 Olympics and ranked 2nd globally in '66, '68 and '71.

WILLIAMS, YVETTE (New Zealand)....... G; WR; No. 1*
Long Jump, 1950-54........ 4/25/29
The versatile Kiwi scored her major international successes in the long jump, winning the '52 Olympics, the '50 and '54 Commonwealth titles and setting a World Record in 1954 with 20'7¼"/6.28. But she also was a talented thrower, placing 2nd in the '50 Commonwealth javelin, 6th in the '52 Olympic shot and 10th in the discus and winning both the shot and disc at the '54 Commonwealth. She is one of only two women in Commonwealth history to win three individual titles in one Games (the other is Australia's Decima Norman, winner of the 100-yards, 220-yards and long jump in 1938).

WOCKEL, BARBEL [Eckert] (East Germany)...........
2G, 2Gr; 2 No. 1
Sprints, 1974-84...... 3/21/55, 5'8½"/137
Three women have won four gold medals in Olympic history: Fanny Blankers-Koen, 4 in '48; Betty Cuthbert, 3 in '56, 1 in '64; and, Wockel, 2 in both '76 and '80. A hurdler-sprinter early in her career, Wockel concentrated on the 200 for the '76 Olympics and won in an Olympic Record 22.37. She later anchored the 4 x 100 to victory at 42.55. Wockel surprised herself with her 200, as well as the track world. "I

felt Renate Stecher was the favorite, even though I ran well in the semi-finals. I felt like I was riding the crest of a wave, but even so, I still couldn't believe for several seconds that I had won."

Wockel missed the '78 and '79 seasons for maternity, but returned in 1980 and won again in Moscow, thus becoming the only double winner in the history of the Olympic 200. She set an Olympic Record of 22.03 from lane 1, outrunning Soviet teenager Natalya Bochina, who set a World Junior Record of 22.19. Wockel then sprinted the second leg on the 4 x 100 team which won in a World Record 41.60. It was the sixth WR 4 x 100 unit on which Wockel had run (although she never set an individual global record).

Barbel ranked 1st in the world in 1980, and again in 1982 after she won the European Championship. She also ran 2nd in the 100 and won another 4 x 100 gold medal. She clocked career-best times in '82 of 10.95 in the 100 and 49.56 in an infrequent effort over 400-meters (a time which handed Marita Koch a rare defeat). Wockel's best-ever 200 of 21.85 came in 1984.

Z

ZATOPKOVA, DANA (Czechoslovakia)...G, S; WR; 2 No. 1
Javelin, 1948-61......9/19/22, 5'5¼"/148
On July 24, 1952, Zatopkova hurled the spear an Olympic Record 165'7"/50.46 to win the gold medal in Helsinki. Several hours later, her husband—renowned distance runner Emil Zatopek—won the 5000, the second of the three victories he scored that year. Naturally, reporters dubbed the Zatopek family double, "Czech and Double Czech." Coincidentally, the pair shared the same birthday, although Emil was born about six hours earlier than Dana.

Zatopkova was the world's leading javelinist in the mid-1950s, winning the '54 and '58 European titles, ranking 1st in the world in '57 and '58 and setting a World Record of 182'10"/55.72 in '58. She competed in 4 Olympics, placing 7th in '48, 4th in '56 and winning the silver medal in 1960. Her 1958 world mark was bettered a month after she set it,

Barbel Wockel

Dana Zatopkova and husband Emil Zatopek.

but Dana produced her career-best throw later that season, 185'11"/56.66.

Her 1958 World Record was produced at the age of 35 years, 255 days, and made her the oldest woman WR setter ever until Soviet Marina Stepanova ran the 400 hurdles in 52.84 in 1986 more than four months past her 36th birthday.

ZEHRT, MONIKA (East Germany).......G, Gr; WR; 2 No. 1
400-meters, 1970-73..... 9/29/52, 5'6"/123
Zehrt equaled the 51.0 World Record (51.08 automatic timing) before the '72 Olympics. Then in Munich, she ran 51.08 again to claim the gold medal a month before her 20th birthday. She won her second gold medal by anchoring East Germany to a 4 x 400 WR of 3:22.95. It was the fourth relay WR of her career. Zehrt ranked No. 1 globally in '72 and repeated in '73 after winning the European Cup title.

ZYBINA, GALINA (USSR)....G, S, B; 15 WR; No. 1*; AOY*
Shot/Discus, 1950-66......1/22/31, 5'6"/176
The greatest number of improvements in the shot World Record is the 15 authored by Zybina between 1952 and 1956. Eight of the marks received official IAAF approval, the longest of 55'0"/16.76 coming in '56. Zybina won the '52 Olympic shot (plus 4th in the javelin), and then competed in three more Games: 2nd '56, 7th '60, 3rd '64. She won the '54 European shot (3rd discus), placed 3rd in '62 and 4th in '66.

Despite her record setting, Zybina never ranked 1st in the world, principally because the Rankings were established in 1956. She certainly would have led from 1952-55. She did rate 2nd in '56-'58 and 3rd in '61-'62 and '64-'65. She was suspended from the Soviet national team in 1958 for "egotistical, uncomradely behavior" after she refused to accept her 2nd-place medal at the USSR championships. Soviet officials soon realized Zybina's importance to the team, she was reinstated, and went on to compete for nearly another decade.

PROFILES OF OTHER WOMEN'S GREATS: U.S.

KEY TO THE SYMBOLS

As with the World section, athletes are listed alphabetically, with a parenthetical name signifying a married name and a bracketed name the maiden name.

The line of major honors won follows as with the World section, and may also include:

AR = An outdoor American Record, as approved by the Amateur Athletic Union (AAU) prior to 1980 and The Athletics Congress (TAC) after 1980, or recognized by *T&FN*.

U.S. = No. 1 ranking in U.S., as selected by *Women's Track & Field World* ('67-'74) or *Track & Field News* ('76-'86). The same asterisk designation applies as with the World section. (An asterisk following "No. 1" or "AOY" indicates that, in the opinion of the author and *T&FN* Women's Editor Howard Willman, the athlete would have ranked No. 1 in an event, or been named Athlete Of The Year, one or more times [undetermined unless preceded by a number] prior to the first Jan Popper World Rankings in 1956.)

TAC = United States open national championship(s) won (under the auspices of the AAU until 1980, and TAC after 1980). Listed as "TAC" for easiest notation.

USAOY = U.S. Athlete Of The Year named by *Track & Field News* (since 1976). Any American named world AOY automatically is U.S. AOY and the latter designation is omitted in such cases.

A

ASHFORD, EVELYN. . . . . ,. G, Gr; 2 WR; 9 AR; 10 TAC; 5 W No. 1 (14 U.S.); 2 AOY; USAOY Sprints, 1976- . . . . . . .4/15/57, 5'5"/115
See chapter.

B

BENOIT, JOAN (Samuelson) . . . .
G; WR; 7 AR; 1 TAC; 2 W No. 1 (6 U.S.)
Distances, 1976- . . . . . . 5/16/57, 5'3"/105
See chapter.

BRISCO-HOOKS, VALERIE . . . .
2G, Gr; 3 AR; 1 TAC; 5 U.S. No. 1
Sprints, 1979- . . . . . . 7/6/60, 5'6½"/130
A decent sprinter (2nd TAC 200 and 10th in World
Rankings in '79) Brisco-Hooks missed the '82 season due to
the birth of her son. She emerged in 1984 as a superstar when
she won Olympic gold medals in the 200 (21.81), 400
(48.83) and 4 x 400 relay (3:18.29), all American Records.
She ranked among the world's 10 leading performers at all
three sprint distances in 1984, '85 and '86.

BROWN, DORIS (Heritage) . . .14 AR; 5 TAC; 3 U.S. No. 1*
Distances, 1960-76 . . . . . . 9/17/42, 5'4"/110
The first American woman distance runner of note,
Brown won the International Cross Country the first five
times it was staged ('67-'71). Lack of competitive opportunities at longer distances in major championships confined her
to the 800, but she placed 2nd in the '67 and '71 Pan-Am
Games and 5th in the '68 Olympics. She set American
Records in the 800 (2), 1500 (5), mile (5) and 3000 (2)
during her career. She served as an assistant coach on the
1984 Olympic and '87 World Championships teams.

BROWN, EARLENE. . . B; 7 AR; 11 TAC; W No. 1 (9 U.S.*)
Shot/Discus, 1956-64 . . . . . 7/11/35, 5'8"/220
The leading American thrower of the '50s and '60s,
Brown finished 6th in the '56 Olympic shot and 4th in the
discus. She returned in 1960 to claim the shot bronze, the
only American ever to win an Olympic shot medal. An
American Record toss of 53'10½"/16.42 gave her that placing and she later upped the AR to 54'9¼"/16.69. Those were
the longest of Brown's four shot ARs. She ranked 1st in the
world in '58. Brown also set 3 discus ARs, the longest

176'10"/53.90 in 1960. Because of her size, she was known in track as "Big Mama." After leaving track, Brown competed on the professional rollerderby circuit—where she was known as "747."

C

CHEESEBOROUGH, CHANDRA . . . . S, 2Gr; 3 AR; TAC
Sprints, 1975- . . . . . . .1/10/59, 5'5"/132

A precocious sprint talent, Cheeseborough emerged in '75 at age 16 when she won the Pan-American Games 200 in a World Junior Record 22.77(A). She won the '76 TAC 100 in a WJR 11.13 and then placed 6th in the Olympic dash. She also ran the 200 and 4 x 100 in Montreal. She qualified for the ill-fated '80 Olympic team in both sprints, but 1984 saw a "new" Cheeseborough emerge in the 400. She set 2 ARs before the Olympics, then placed 2nd in Los Angeles in a career-best 49.05 to earn the silver medal behind Brisco-Hooks. Cheeseborough made Olympic history by first running a leg on the champion 4 x 100 team and then returning minutes later to anchor the 4 x 400 quartet to victory. No other runner ever has been on both relay winners in the same Games.

COACHMAN, ALICE . . . . G; AR; 18 TAC; W No. 1* (U.S.*)
High Jump, 1939-48. . . . . 11/9/23, 5'6¼"/148

Coachman's career was restricted by World War II, but she wasn't prevented from winning 10 consecutive TAC outdoor high jump titles (plus three at 100-meters and five at the discontinued 50-meters). She won the 1948 Olympic high jump title with an American Record leap of 5'6¼"/1.68, an AR which survived for more than six years.

CONNOLLY, OLGA [Fikotova] .G; 4 AR; 5 TAC; 5 U.S. 1*
Discus, 1956-72 . . . . . .11/13/32, 5'11"/176

Connolly won the 1956 Olympic discus title while competing for her native Czechsolovakia. She also won the heart of men's hammer champion Harold Connolly. After their marriage, Olga went on to represent the U.S. in the Olympics of 1960 (7th), '64 (12th), '68 (6th) and '72 (did not qualify for the finals). She lengthened the American Record four times officially during her career, the longest throw measuring 189'0"/57.60 in 1972.

CONNOLLY, PAT [Daniels] (Winslow; Bank) . . . .
15 AR; 11 TAC; 8 U.S. No. 1*
Multi-event, 1960-70 . . . . . 9/1/43, 5'11"/160

Pat (she married Harold Connolly after his divorce from Olga Connolly) made her first national impact as a 17-year-old high schooler in 1960 when she made the U.S. Olympic team—in the 800. She set 4 American Records at 800 that year, plus one at 400. She fell in her qualifying heat in Rome and failed to finish. In 1961, she set her 5th AR at 800, 2:13.1.

That same '61 season, Connolly won her first TAC pentathlon, the first of 7 in a row and 8 overall. She finished 7th in the '64 Olympics and 6th four years later in Mexico. The highest of her nine AR scores in various formats of the pentathlon was 4877 in '68. She World Ranked 3rd in '67, the year she won the Pan-American Games title. Injury forced her to retire from competition after 1970, but she turned to coaching several years later. Her most successful pupil was 1984 100-meter Olympic champion and World Record holder Evelyn Ashford.

COPELAND, LILLIAN. . . . .
G, S; 6 WR*; 12 AR*; 9 TAC; W No. 1* (U.S.*)
Throws, 1923-32 . . . . . . 11/25/04-2/7/64

The first all-around thrower from the U.S., Copeland won the 1932 Olympic discus after placing 2nd four years earlier. She won 4 consecutive national shot titles ('25-'28), plus another in 1931. She also won a pair of U.S. championships in both the discus ('26-'27) and javelin ('26, '31). Her 12 career American Records included 4 in the shot, 5 in the discus and 3 in the javelin.

She set three global bests in the shot (40'4¼"/12.30 in 1926, which she matched in '28 and upped a week later to 43'1½"/13.14) and javelin (112'5"/34.28 and 116'7"/35.54 in '26, and 125'8"/38.30 in '27). And her medal-winning efforts in the Olympic discus (121'8"/37.08 in '28; 133'2"/

40.58 in '32) were the longest throws ever by an American at the time.

D

DIDRIKSON, MILDRED "Babe" (Zaharias)..............
2G, S; 4 WR; 11 AR; 10 TAC; W No. 1* (U.S.*); AOY*
Hurdles/Jumps/Throws, 1930-32. 6/26/11-9/27/56, 5'6½"/126
See chapter.

F

FAGGS, MAE.........Gr, Br; 3 AR; 3 TAC; 5 U.S. No. 1*
Sprints, 1948-56.......4/10/32, 5'2/110
The first national-class sprinter to come out of the Ed Temple-coached Tennessee State program, Faggs made U.S. Olympic teams in 1948, '52 and '56. She ran the 200 in all three Olympics, reaching the '56 semi-finals. She placed 6th in the '52 100, and then led off the U.S. 4 x 100 team which won the gold medal in a World Record 45.9. She returned four years later to start the bronze-winning U.S. team in Melbourne.

Besides being a member of U.S. 4 x 100 teams which set four American Records in Olympic competition, Faggs also set a pair of 100 ARs in 1952, her fastest of 12.0 coming in the Olympic quarter-finals.

FERRELL, BARBARA..............................
Gr, S; 2 WR; 4 AR; 3 TAC; 3 U.S. No. 1*
Sprints, 1966-1972 ..... 7/28/47, 5'2½"/108
Although overshadowed by Wyoma Tyus, who successfully defended her 100 title, Ferrell also was of World Record caliber speed at the '68 Olympics. She sped 11.1 in her semi-final to match the WR she had first equaled the season before. Ferrell won the silver medal at 11.1, took 4th in the 200 (22.9) and won a gold medal on the WR-setting 4 x 100. In the 200, she set ARs in her heat (22.9) and semi (22.8). She returned four years later to place 7th in both Munich sprints.

Valerie Brisco

FREDERICK, JANE. . . . .
12 AR; 10 TAC; W No. 1; 10 U.S. No. 1; USAOY
Multi-events, 1972- . . . . 4/7/52, , 5'11½"/160

The American multi-event performer of unparalleled
longevity, Frederick ranked No. 1 in the U.S. in the pentath-
lon/heptathlon in 1975-'79 and 1981-'85. She also paced the
'85 World Rankings, the first American multi-eventer ever to
rank 1st globally. She is the only American who can claim 10
World Rankings appearances in *any* event. In the multis, she
is the world's best in that category.

Frederick placed 7th in the '76 Olympic pentathlon, after
a 21st in '72. During her career, she set 7 ARs in the pentathlon and 5 in the heptathlon. She set 2 of the heptathlon
marks in 1984, the highest score tallying 6803 points. But
she didn't clear a height in the high jump at the Olympic
Trials, so missed the Olympic team.

As an indication of her all-around talent, Frederick won
the TAC 100 hurdles in 1975 and '76 and placed 2nd in the
'77 shot and '79 long jump.

G

GINDELE, NAN. . . . . . WR; AR; 1 TAC; W No. 1* (U.S.*)
Javelin, 1932-33 . . . . 8/5/10

On June 18, 1932, Gindele hurled the javelin a World
Record 153'4"/46.74, a mark which lasted as the WR until
July of 1938—and survived as the American Record until
March of 1955. It also was the first IAAF-ratified World
Record set by an American in any event. Gindele placed only
5th in the '32 Olympics (124'6"/37.94) in the competition
won by celebrated teammate Babe Didrikson. Chicagoan
Gindele won the 1933 TAC javelin title.

H

HAMMOND, KATHY. . . . .Sr, B; 5 AR; 1 TAC; 3 U.S. No. 1
400-meters, 1967-72 . . . . . 11/2/51, 5'7"/121

World-ranked 5th in 1967 at the age of 16, Hammond
was expected to be a contender at the '68 Olympics, but a leg
muscle injury ended her chances early in the '68 outdoor
season. She returned in '69 to win the one TAC title of her

career and set two American Records (52.3, 52.1). She ranked 2nd in the world, and 3rd in '70. The Sacramento, California, native had her year of years in 1972, setting 3 ARs with her fastest of 51.64 gaining her the Olympic bronze medal. She then won a silver on the 4 x 400 team which set an AR 3:25.15, the fastest of the 5 relay ARs she ran on during her career. Hammond again ranked 3rd in the world in 1972.

J

JONES, BARBARA ....2Gr; AR; 3 TAC; U.S. No. 1*
        Sprints, 1952-60...... 3/26/37, 5'7¼"/132
As a member of the '52 Olympic champions in the 4 x 100 relay, Jones became the youngest track and field gold medalist in Games history, man or woman. She was 15 years, 4 months and 1 day old when her relay team won in Helsinki. Another Tennessee State-bred sprinter, Jones won TAC 100s in '53, '54 and '57, two Pan-Am Games golds in '55 (100 in an AR-equaling 11.5; 4 x 100) and another in '59 (4 x 100). She didn't make the '56 Olympic team, but returned in 1960 to compete in the 100 (4th in her semi) and then win a second gold medal in the 4 x 100. Both teams Jones ran on in the Olympics set World Records (45.9 '52, 44.4 '60). Her highest World Rankings were 3rds in '58 and '59 in the 100.

JOYNER, JACKIE (Kersee) ....
        S; 2 WR; 5 AR; 1 TAC; W No. 1 (4 U.S.); AOY
Long Jump/Multi-events, 1979- . . 3/3/62, 5'10"/155
A talent of wide-ranging abilities, Joyner placed 2nd (by 5 points) in the '84 Olympic heptathlon and 5th in the long jump. She compiled a brilliant 1986 season in the 7-eventer, twice breaking the World Record (7148, then 7158 less than a month later) to earn Athlete Of The Year honors. Her four heptathlons during '86 averaged better than 7000 points, a mark no other woman in history had exceeded even once. Joyner ranked among the U.S. Top 10 in the long jump since '79 (she set an AR of 23'9"/7.24 in 1985) and heptathlon since '81, and also performed at world-class levels in both hurdles.

Madeline Manning

L

LARRIEU, FRANCIE (Smith) . . 16 AR; 9 TAC; 11 U.S. No. 1
Distances, 1969- . . . . . .11/23/52, 5'4"/105
Larrieu made her first national impact in 1969 at age 16
by matching the 1500 AR (with a World Junior Record of
4:16.8) and ranking 9th in the world. She gained World
and/or U.S. Ranking at distances from the 800 though the
marathon every year from '69-'86. She set ARs at 1500 (7),
the mile (5) and 3000 (4) and won 7 TAC titles at 1500/mile,
plus one each at 3000 and 10,000. She ran the 1500 at the
'72 and '76 Olympics, advancing to the semi-finals each time.
Larrieu ran in the '77 World Cup (2nd 1500) as well as '79
(3rd 3000, 4th 1500). Her older brother Ron was a member
of the 1964 Olympic team at 10,000.

M

MANNING, MADELINE (Jackson; Mimms). . . . .
G, Sr; 7 AR; 6 TAC; 3 W No. 1 (5 U.S.*)
800-meters, 1965-1981. . . . 1/11/48, 5'9"/132
Manning ran 7 American Record clockings at 800
between 1967 and '76. Her 2:00.92 in Mexico's altitude gave
her the '68 Olympic title. She made 3 more U.S. Olympic
teams: 5th 800 semi, 2nd 4 x 400 '72; 8th 800 semi '76; won
the '80 U.S. Olympic Trials 800. She became the first American under 2 minutes with her 1:59.81 and 1:57.9 efforts in
'76. She led the World Rankings 3 years in a row ('67-'69).
She ran on four teams which set American Records in the 4 x
400 relay, the fastest being the 3:25.15 in the '72 Olympics
which won the silver medal. Manning is an accomplished
gospel singer with several recordings to her credit.

McDANIEL, MILDRED . . . .
G; WR; 3 AR; 3 TAC; 1 W No. 1 (U.S.*)
High Jump, 1953-56 . . . . . 11/4/33, 5'9"/120
She jumped two American Records in 1955, the highest
5'6¼"/1.69. Earlier she had matched the AR of 5'6"/1.68 to
win the Pan-American Games. In 1956, nobody jumped
higher than McDaniel: five weeks before the Olympics, she
cleared 5'9½"/1.765, 1½" above the official WR but unac-

Edith McGuire at the 1964 Olympics.

ceptable for record consideration since it came in an exhibition. At the Olympics, McDaniel was only ¼" shy of that mark as she cleared 5'9¼"/1.76 for the gold medal.

McGUIRE, EDITH G, S, Sr; 4 AR; 4 TAC; 1 W No. 1 (U.S.*)
Sprints, 1963-66.......6/3/44, 5'8"/126
McGuire gave Tennessee State an incredible one-two punch in the mid-1960s as she combined with Wyomia Tyus. McGuire was undefeated in the 200 in 1964, including claiming the Tokyo Olympic title in an American Record 23.0 (23.05). She finished 2nd in the 100 to Tyus and ran on the silver-winning 4 x 100 team. She earned World Record credit when the U.S.'s time of 43.9 (43.92) was elevated to WR status following the sex-test disqualification of Poland's Ewa Klobukowska in 1967. McGuire led the 200 World Rankings in '64 and rated 2nd in the 100; she rated 3rd in the 200 in both '65 and '66.

R

ROBINSON, ELIZABETH ("Betty")....................
G, Gr, Sr; 4 WR* (4 AR*); 1 TAC; No. 1*; AOY*
Sprints, 1927-36.........8/23/11
Robinson was a 16-year-old Illinois high schooler when she became the first women's track champion in Olympic history. She won the 1928 100-meters on July 31, only a short time after Poland's Halina Konopacka had won the discus in Amsterdam to become the inaugural women's victor in Olympic track *and* field.

Betty had begun sprinting the year before after she ran to catch a train which took her to school. A teacher/coach on the train saw her speed and suggested that she should develop her talent. "Up to then, I didn't even know there were races for women," Robinson recalled.

She was a quick learner, matching the world's best of 12.2 in 1927, the 100-yard best of 11.0 in '28 and then setting a 100-meter mark of 12.0 before the Olympics. Robinson was in a plane crash in 1931 which broke a leg in several places and put her in rehabilitation for nearly a year.

Betty Robinson

World Record-setting javelinist Kate Schmidt.

But she came back to make the '36 Olympic team as a relayist (her leg could not bend fully at the knee, so she couldn't crouch down in the sprint starting position, but she could take the running start of a relay runner). She ran the third leg on the winning U.S. team in Berlin. During her competitive days, she was known as "Babe." Robinson also set WR at 200m/220y in the same race (25.1 in '31).

ROGERS, ANNETTE . . . . 2Gr; 2 TAC; U.S. No. 1*
Sprints, 1932-36. . . . . . .10/22/13, 5'4"/110

Rogers combined speed and jumping ability. She finished 6th in the '32 Olympic high jump and tied for 6th in '36. She also placed 5th in the Berlin 100. But Rogers gained her greatest renown by running on gold-medal winning 4 x 100 teams in both '32 and '36; she is the only American woman to run on back-to-back relay victors and one of only three women to do so (East Germany's Marlies Gohr and Barbel Wockel are the others). The '32 U.S. team ran a WR 47.0.

RUDOLPH, WILMA . . . .
2G, Gr, Br; 4 WR; 9 AR; 3 No. 1; 5 TAC; AOY*
Sprints, 1956-62. . . . . . .6/23/40, 5'11"/130
See chapter.

S

SCHMIDT, KATE . . . .
2B; WR; 9 AR; 7 TAC; 7 U.S. No. 1; USAOY
Javelin, 1968-84. . . . . . .12/29/53, 6'1"/165

Schmidt's name was synonymous with top-level javelin throwing for more than a decade. She was the top-ranked American from 1972 through '77 and also in '79. She set her first of 9 American Records in 1972; her heave of 200'6"/ 61.12 made her the first American to throw beyond 200-feet. She won the '75 and '76 TAC titles with AR throws, but her greatest toss ever came on September 11, 1977, in Furth, West Germany. The lanky Californian threw a World Record 227'5"/69.32 to wrest the global best away from two-time Olympic champion Ruth Fuchs of East Germany (Schmidt herself had finished 3rd in the Munich and Montreal Olympic competitions won by Fuchs).

Known as "Kate The Great," Schmidt compiled a brilliant lists of placings in the TAC Championships: she placed 4th in '68 and won in '69 before missing the '70 and '71 meets due to injury. But from '72 through '84, she placed in the top 3 every year save in '82 when 4th. Besides winning the '72 and '76 Olympic Trials, she placed 2nd in '80 and just missed her 4th team in '84 when she placed 4th.

SEIDLER, MAREN............. 8 AR; 11 TAC; 11 No. 1
Shot Put, 1967-80 ......6/11/51, 6'2"/215
The Brooklyn-born Seidler dominated U.S. shot putting like no other thrower. She won her first TAC crown in '67 and followed up with the win in '68. Then from 1972 through '80, Seidler won 9 straight titles. She made four consecutive Olympic teams, finishing 11th in Mexico and 12th in Montreal. She didn't get her first American Record until 1974 when she threw 54'10½"/16.72. But then she hit two more records in '74, produced three in '78 (including a 60'3"/18.36 to become the first American over 60-feet) and reached 62'7¾"/19.09 to win the '79 TAC title. That mark lasted as the AR until 1985. Seidler finished 4th in the '77 and '79 World Cups and won the '79 Pan-American Games silver medal.

SHILEY, JEAN........G; WR; 3 AR; 4 TAC; U.S. No. 1*
High Jump, 1928-32........11/20/11
Shiley placed 4th in the 1928 Olympics while still a high school student from Haverford, Pennsylvania. She won TAC titles in '29, '30 and '31 and tied for the '32 crown with the renowned Babe Didrikson. At the '32 Los Angeles Olympics, Shiley and Didrikson matched each other jump for jump. Each cleared a World Record 5'5"/1.65 and then each made 5'5¾"/1.67 in a jumpoff. But the judges ruled Didrikson dove headfirst over the bar, which was illegal at the time, so Shiley was declared the winner.

SLANEY, MARY [Decker] ....
2G; 6 WR; 21 AR; 6 W No. 1 (16 U.S.); 4 USAOY
Distances, 1972- ......8/4/58, 5'6"/112
A precocious running talent, Slaney always was a favorite

Mary Decker Slaney

of fans, with her long pigtails, braces on her teeth and a fearlessness against older, more experienced runners. In 1972, at the age of 13, she ran a 4:55.0 mile indoors, fastest ever for that age. But she couldn't compete in the U.S. Olympic Trials; rules prohibit athletes younger than age 14 from competing. She turned 14 a month after the Trials.

In 1973, Slaney compiled a season good enough to rank her 1st in the 800 in the U.S. However, her career was dogged by injury. She missed the '75, '76 and '77 campaigns with leg miseries, but returned to run well in 1978 and '79. In 1980, she emerged as a world-class talent. She set a mile World Record of 4:21.68, won the Olympic Trials 1500 and ranked 1st among Americans at 1500 and 3000. She cut the 1500 AR four times, becoming the first American under 4:00 with her 3:59.43 in Zurich to finish 2nd behind Tatyana Kazankina's stunning WR of 3:52.47. More leg problems struck in 1981, however, and Mary missed the entire season.

Slaney roared back with a vengeance in 1982, showing her stuff over longer distances as well as her usual prowess at the 1500 and mile. She set a 5000 WR of 15:08.26 early in June, a mile WR of 4:21.46 late in the month, and then a 3000 AR of 8:29.71 and a mile WR improvement to 4:18.08 within 3 days in early July. She returned home to Eugene, Oregon, at the middle of the month; deciding to run in an all-comer's meet just for a workout, she entered a 10,000—and ran a global record of 31:35.3.

Even though she was a veteran of the European invitational circuit in the summers, Slaney was untested in international championship-level competition—that is, until 1983. In that year, she silenced any doubters of her competitive ability by first outkicking the field in the World Championships 3000-meters, and then by outrunning a trio of aggressive Soviets to take the 1500. She set American Records that year at 800 (1:57.60) and 1500 (3:57.12) as well.

Slaney won the 3000 at the U.S. Olympic Trials, but was upset in the 1500 by Ruth Wysocki. Mary opted for only the longer race in the Games. She was one of the U.S.'s biggest hopes, but midway in the race, she collided with Britain's Zola Budd and fell to the infield, injuring her hip.

Out of the ashes of Los Angeles rose a fiery phoenix of

a Slaney in 1985. She lowered her 5000 AR to 15:06.53 in her first outdoor race on June 1, and then during the summer set U.S. records in the 800 (1:56.90), 1000-meters (2:34.8), mile (4:16.71, also a World Record) and a pair at 3000 (8:29.69, 8:25.83). At the end of the summer, she discovered she was pregnant; it would be the first child for Mary and her husband, British discus thrower Richard Slaney.

Daughter Ashley was born May 30, 1986; Mary was back to training almost immediately and competed in a road mile in New York and a track race in Brazil before minor leg pains forced her to curtail competing. A planned indoor campaign during the winter of 1987 never occurred because of Achilles tendon problems.

Slaney always maintained, "There is no reason why a runner should not be able to compete well into her 30s. Some top Soviet runners have done it. I'm not ruling out competing in even the 1992 Olympics—if I'm in one piece."

STEPHENS, HELEN.............................
G, Gr, 5 WR; 13 AR; 5 TAC; No. 1*; AOY*
Sprints, 1935-36.......2/3/18, 6'0"/130

Like '28 Olympic 100 champion Betty Robinson, Stephens and her sprinting talent were discovered by accident. She was a high school sophomore in Fulton, Missouri, in 1933 and in fitness tests during physical education class, she sprinted 50-yards in 5.8 seconds. That was equal to the world's best time and coach Burt Moore knew he had a world-beater on his hands.

Stephens didn't get her first taste of national-level competition until 1935, but after she beat reigning Olympic 100 champ Stella Walsh in the TAC 100, Stephens became famous overnight. Twice in 1935 she dashed 100-meters in 11.6, although neither time ever was officially accepted by the IAAF. That September, Stephens blazed 10.4 for 100-yards in a handicap race in Toronto. The official WR at the time was only 11.0.

In her brief career, Stephens never lost a race, and the Olympic season of 1936 was no exception. She defended her TAC 100-meter title and showed her versatility by winning the shot and discus crowns, too. In May, she sped 11.5

in the metric century, another effort that never received official record acceptance. In the Berlin Olympics, Stephens reigned supreme, winning her heat with a wind-aided 11.4 and then claiming the gold medal with an 11.5, also wind-aided.

Stephens collected her second gold medal in the 4 x 100 relay. The German foursome had lowered the World Record twice before the Games and boasted three of the six finalists in the 100. Stephens expected to have to race all out to win. Sure enough, Germany held a lead of several meters as third runner Maria Dollinger handed the stick to anchor Ilse Dorrfeldt. Stephens got the stick from Robinson in a clear 2nd place.

But suddenly the German runners were clasping their hands to their heads in anguish as their baton fell to the track. Stephens powered home with her long, loping strides as the Germans could only dissolve into tears. Stephens later was taken to the private box of German chancellor Adolf Hitler to receive his personal congratulations. Some accounts of their meeting claim Hitler tried to become chummy with Stephens. Helen herself once was quoted, "Heck, I just gave him a good ol' Missouri handshake."

Stephens didn't win her third event in Berlin—she placed 9th in the discus with 112'7"/34.32. Shortly after the Games, at a meet in Dresden, she again ran 11.5 for 100-meters. But for the fourth time in her career, paperwork problems prevented the mark from receiving official record acceptance. Stephens retired from track the next year, but played professional basketball well into the 1950s.

T

TYUS, WYOMIA. . . . .
2G, Gr, Sr; 6 WR; 9 AR; 5 TAC; 2 W No. 1 (U.S.*)
Sprints, 1964-68 . . . . . . 8/29/45, 5'7"/134
See chapter.

V

VON BREMEN, WILHELMINA . . . .
Gr, B; AR; 1 TAC; U.S. No. 1*
Sprints, 1932 . . . . . 8/13/09-7/23/76, 5'6"/115
San Franciscan von Bremen won the 1932 TAC 100-
meters, and finished 3rd in the Los Angeles Olympics, matching the American Record of 12.0. She then anchored the U.S.
4 x 100 relay team to the gold medal and a World Record
clocking of 47.0.

W

WHITE, WILLYE . . . . . . S, Sr; 6 AR; 10 TAC; 9 U.S. No. 1*
Long Jump, 1956-76 . . . . . 12/31/39, 5'4¼"/123
White is the only American-born track athlete, man or
woman, to compete in five Olympics. Her best place came in
her first appearance, 2nd in 1956 at the age of 17. She placed
16th in '60, 12th in '64 and 11th in both '68 and '72. In
1964, she ran a leg on the U.S. 4 x 100 team which won the
silver medal. The squad's clocking of 43.9 (43.92) later
received recognition as a World Record after Poland's winning 43.6 (43.69) was disallowed following the disqualification of Ewa Klobukowska from competing in the women's
ranks. She placed 6th in the 1976 Olympic Trials long jump.

White set a half-dozen American Records during her
career, from the 19'11¾"/6.09 which won her the '56 silver,
to 21'6"/6.55 in 1964. She won the Pan-American Games
long jump in 1963 and ran on the champion sprint relay and
finished 3rd in the long jump in both 1959 and 1967. She
once described herself as the "grand old lady of American
track and field."

WILLIAMS, LUCINDA . . . . . . Gr; 4 AR; 1 TAC; U.S. No. 1*
Sprints, 1956-60 . . . . . . 8/10/37, 5'5¼"/112
Another sprint product from Tennessee State, Williams
competed in both dashes at the '56 Olympics, reaching the
semi-finals in the 200. In 1958, she won her lone TAC title,
the 220-yards with an AR 24.3. Later that summer, she set a
200-meter U.S. best of 23.9. In 1959, she won three gold

medals at the Pan-American Games in Chicago in the two sprints and 4 x 100 relay. She ran her career bests of 11.7 and 23.8 in 1960, but made only the relay ream for the Rome Olympics. That was good enough, though, as the team won the gold medal and set a WR of 44.5 (44.72).

RELAY WORLD RECORD SETTERS

Below are listed Americans who have been members of World Record-setting relay teams. None are profiled in the U.S. section.

4 x 100-meters
Catherine Hardy '52
Janet Moreau '52
Martha Hudson '60
Vivianne Brown '61
Ernestine Pollards '61
Marilyn White '64
Margaret Bailes '68
Mildrette Netter '68

4 x 110-yards
Iris Davis '71
Diane Hughes '71
Debra Wedgeworth '71

4 x 220-yards
Dolores Dwyer '52

4 x 440-yards
Linda Iddings '69
Janene Jaton '69
Debbie Newing '69
Joan Pirie '69
Gale Fitzgerald '70
Shelly Marshall '70
Michele McMillan '70
Cheryl Toussaint '70
Linda Reynolds '71
Debra Edwards '72
Mable Fergerson '72

4 x 880-yards
Julie Stibbe '75
Debbie Vetter '75
Diane Vetter '75
Janis Vetter '75

ATHLETES OF THE YEAR

Athlete Of The Year polls were conducted by *Women's Track & Field World* from 1967-74, and by *Track & Field News* from 1974 through the present. Selections from 1947-66 were made by the author and *T&FN* Women's Editor Howard Willman. All other selections by the author.

1928	Betty Robinson (US) Sprints
1929	Kinue Hitomi (Japan) Sprints/Jumps
1930	Hitomi
1931	Grete Haublein (Germany) Shot
1932	Mildred "Babe" Didrikson (US) Hurdles/Jumps/Throws
1933	Stella Walsh (Poland) Sprints/Long Jump
1934	Kathe Krauss (Germany) Sprints
1935	Gisela Mauermeyer (Germany) Shot/Discus
1936	Helen Stephens (US) Sprints
1937	—
1938	Walsh
1939	Claudia Testoni (Italy) Hurdles
1947	Herma Bauma (Austria) Javelin
1948	Fanny Blankers-Koen (Holland) Sprints/Hurdles
1949	Aleksandra Chudina (USSR) Pentathlon
1950	Blankers-Koen
1951	Blankers-Koen
1952	Marjorie Jackson (Australia) Sprints
1953	Galina Zybina (USSR) Shot/Discus
1954	Zybina
1955	Shirley Strickland de la Hunty (Australia) Sprints/Hurdles
1956	Betty Cuthbert (Australia) Sprints
1957	Marlene Mathews (Australia) Sprints
1958	Galina Bystrova (USSR) Hurdles/Pentathlon
1959	Tamara Press (USSR) Shot/Discus
1960	Wilma Rudolph (US) Sprints
1961	Iolanda Balas (Romania) High Jump
1962	T. Press
1963	Mary Rand (Great Britain) Long Jump/Pentathlon
1964	T. Press
1965	Irina Press (USSR) Hurdles/Pentathlon
1966	Irena Szewinska (Poland) Sprints/Long Jump
1967	Liesel Westermann (West Germany) Discus
1968	Margitta Gummel (East Germany) Shot
1969	Chi Cheng (Taiwan) Sprints/Hurdles
1970	Chi
1971	Ilona Gusenbauer (Austria) High Jump
1972	Heide Rosendahl (West Germany) Long Jump/Pentathlon
1973	Renate Stecher (East Germany) Sprints
1974	*WTFW:* Szewinska
	T&FN: Szewinska
1975	*WTFW:* Faina Myelnik (USSR) Discus
	T&FN: Myelnik

Athletes Of The Year

1976	Tatyana Kazankina (USSR) 800/1500
1977	Rosemarie Ackermann (East Germany) High Jump
1978	Marita Koch (East Germany) Sprints
1979	Koch
1980	Ilona Briesenick (East Germany) Shot
1981	Evelyn Ashford (US) Sprints
1982	Koch
1983	Jarmila Kratochvilova (Czechoslovakia) 400/800
1984	Ashford
1985	Koch
1986	Jackie Joyner-Kersee (US) Long Jump/Heptathlon

Illustrations

Illustrations

BOOKS

FROM TRACK & FIELD NEWS

THE LITTLE GOLD BOOK. *T&FN's* popular track fan's companion. Metric conversion tables, decathlon/heptathlon tables, equipment & facilities specs, historic firsts in t&f, pacing charts, etc. and much other essential info. $7.50

TALKING TRACK. The best interviews from the pages of *T&FN*, 38 in all, including Bayi, Walker, Wilkins, Juantorena, Oerter, Rodgers, Jenner, 62 photos. Great reading. Edited by Jon Hendershott. $3.00

HOW WOMEN RUNNERS TRAIN, ed. by Vern Gambetta. Training profiles of Joan Benoit, Leann Warren, Maggie Keyes, Deby LaPlante, Grete Waitz, Wendy Knudson, Linda Goen, 30 others. Lots of good suggestions and training data. 128pp. 1980. Illus. $4.50

IN QUEST OF GOLD: The Jim Ryun Story. Excellent biography tells it all: the astonishing high school exploits, the great years, the dreams unfulfilled—to the present. Good reading. 222pp. Hard cover. 1984. Many photos. $12.95

WINNING TRACK & FIELD DRILLS FOR WOMEN, Coach Terry Crawford, U. of Texas, and Bob Bertucci. Dozens of training drills for all events, well presented and illustrated. A terrific idea source for every coach, athlete. 128pp. 1985. $11.95

TRACK'S GREATEST CHAMPIONS, Cordner Nelson. Chapters on 21 of history's greatest, Nurmi and Zatopek to Moses and Coe. With short profiles and statistics on 257 other top trackmen past and present. Great reading, great reference. 385pp. 1985. Many excellent photos. $15.00

THE MILERS: A History of the Mile/1500m., Cordner Nelson and R.L. Quercetani. All the great mile/1500 races and stars from the 1800s thru the 1984 season. More than 100 photos. Great reading and a great reference source. 554pp. Hard cover. $16.50

OLYMPIC TRACK & FIELD, Vols. I and II, by the Editors of Track & Field News. NEW 2nd Volume, 1987, brings OTF up to date through the 1984 Games. Vol. I, published 1979, has all Olympic track results and event accounts 1896-1976. Vol. II covers 1980 and '84 Games, plus '83 World Championships, and has a wealth of current Oly stats and esoterica: medals won, records, rankings, etc. Vol. II is $7.00, both volumes. $9.50

Book prices subject to change.

Order from **Track & Field News, Box 296, Los Altos, CA 94023.** Add $1.50 postage/handling. Calif. residents add 6% sales tax.